Direct Democracy
in Europe

T3-BQR-948

Direct Democracy in Europe

A Comprehensive Reference Guide to the Initiative
and Referendum Process in Europe

Part of the Citizen Lawmaker Series of Educational Tools

Sponsored by

IRI Europe
Initiative & Referendum Institute Europe

and

IRI
Initiative & Referendum Institute

Edited by

Bruno Kaufmann and M. Dane Waters

CAROLINA ACADEMIC PRESS
Durham, North Carolina

ISBN 0-89089-262-8
LCCN

Carolina Academic Press
700 Kent Street
Durham, NC 27701
Telephone (919) 489-7486
Fax (919) 493-5668
www.cap-press.com

Printed in the United States of America

Contents

What Is the Initiative & Referendum Institute Europe?

The Initiative & Referendum Institute Europe (IRI Europe) was founded in 2001 to become the premier research and educational institute on I&R in Europe. Our mission is to develop insight into the theory and practice of I&R among politicians, the media, NGOs, academics and the public throughout Europe. IRI Europe is an independent, non-partisan and non profit-making organization. We are advocates of the I&R process and we are dedicated to offering facts, promoting research, providing services to the public and bringing together key actors in the field of democracy.

The first working years were dedicated to developing new information channels, networks and educational tools. In the context of the european integration process and the debate on the European Constitution IRI Europe initiated, coordinated and evaluated major efforts to bring more participation by the citizens into the political processes on all levels—concentrating in the first hand on promoting new I&R tools and securing the quality of existing ones.

These were the main achievements of the 2001–03 period:

- IRI established a paneuropean network of I&R experts in politics, academia, media and civil society, providing meeting places, interactive communication (www.iri-europe.org) tools and an improved understanding about the potentials of direct democracy.
- With major publications as the first IRI Europe "Index on Citizenlawmaking" (featuring a ranking of I&R tools in 32 states), the "European Referendum Monitoring Report" (assessing the EU accession referendums 2003), the "IRI Europe Handbook—Transnational Democracy in the Making" (following up the EU-dimensions of the I&R process) and *Direct Democracy in Europe* (the most comprehensive reference book on European I&R) we delivered the basics for a further educated and well-informed development.
- IRI also established expert and working groups around government and parliament structures in the EU and many countries. As initiator and coordinator of the EU Convention working group on "direct democratic tools in the European Constitution" the institute was contributing to the establishment of the "European Citizen Initiative" in the Draft Constitution. In many member states IRI advised official- and non-official bodies in setting up the necessary tools for a referendum on the European constitution.

In the next three-year period (2004–06) IRI Europe will work with the following priorities:

- IRI will increase it's basic commitment to offer the basics for stronger european democracy/ies by offering new tools of information and education as the multimedia, multilingual " CHDD Pocket Guide to Swiss Direct Democracy" (which will be the first comprehensive and reader-friendly insight into the most experienced I&R country in the world), the "ABC of Direct Democracy" (a new I&R learning structure) as well as improved and enlarged services on the Internet at www.iri-europe.org
- By following up the networking work inside the European Convention, where more than half of all members from 25 european states joined the call for more I&R, IRI will establish competence-centres in many countries, offering a platform for the specific needs around I&R in these countries.
- On the European level, IRI Europe will initiate a state-of-the-art expert work around the new "European Citizen Initiative" in close cooperation with the EU. Furthermore the effort to develop and establish a list of Basic Criteria for Free and Fair Referendums in Europe will contribute to quality checks of most future referendums. Finally, IRI Europe will advise and assist the development and establishment of further I&R tools in the European Constitution by the European Parliament and future Conventions.

What Is the Initiative & Referendum Institute?

In 1998, in recognition of the influence of the initiative and referendum process on America, the Initiative & Referendum Institute was founded. The Institute, a 501(c)(3) non-profit, non-partisan research and educational organization, is dedicated to educating citizens about how the initiative and referendum process has been utilized and providing information to citizens so they understand and know how to utilize the process. No other organization does what we do.

Edwin Meese, III, former U.S. Attorney General under President Ronald Reagan, had this to say about the Institute: "[T]he Initiative & Referendum Institute performs a valuable service to the nation by providing research and educational programs to protect and expand the democratic process of initiative and referendum by the people in the several states. Having this electoral ability is a critical 'safety valve' for effective citizenship."

The Initiative & Referendum Institute extensively studies the initiative and referendum process and publishes papers and monographs addressing its effect on public policy, citizen participation, and its reflection of trends in American thought and culture. We also research and produce a state-by-state guide to the initiative and referendum process, and we work to educate and update the public on how the process is being utilized across the country. We analyze the relationship between voters and their elected lawmakers and when and why the people turn to initiative and referendum to enact changes in state and local law. The Initiative & Referendum Institute has garnered significant media attention. We have been interviewed or cited by almost every major media outlet in the nation as well as by dozens of other publications, newspapers and radio stations around the world.

The Institute is uniquely qualified to undertake this mission. Comprising the Institute's Board of Directors, Advisory Board and Legal Advisory Board are some of the world's leading authorities on the initiative and referendum process, including prominent scholars; experienced activists—who know the nuts and bolts of the process and its use; skilled attorneys; and political leaders who have seen firsthand the necessity of having a mechanism process through which citizens can directly reform their government.

Wayne Pacelle, Senior Vice President of the Humane Society of the United States, stated that "the Initiative & Referendum Institute is the only independent voice for preserving and expanding the right of citizens to make laws directly through the initiative and referendum process. This vital tool of democracy is under siege by special interests, and the Initiative & Referendum Institute is a powerful and persuasive voice for the right of I&R." For additional information, please visit our informative website at www.iandrinstitute.org.

Acknowledgments

This is the first comprehensive overview of I&R in Europe that has ever been done and is designed to complement the *Initiative and Referendum Almanac* that was produced to provide information on I&R in the United States. This Reference Guide includes European-wide analyses, reports on many countries, and an extensive amount of data about I&R in Europe and the rest of the world. The collection and preparation of this data could not have happened without the cooperation of numerous individuals who have invested many days of work on this unique project.

As front-line support we should list by name such individuals as *Andreas Gross, Heidi Hautala, Hans-Urs Wili, Rolf Büchi and Frank Remeth*, who contributed directly and indirectly to this book with their wide-ranging knowledge, experience, and data.

But there are many, many others without whom this almanac would never have been possible. *Paul Carline* put a lot of hard work into translating and checking this English-language publication and *Arjen Nijeboer* at the IRI office was an important backup for the editors in many ways. We would also like to thank *Shirley Starke* who spent countless hours editing the Almanac so that American readers could better comprehend the European perspective on direct democracy.

The same is true for our other friends on the IRI Europe Board: *Adrian Schmid, Niesco Dubbelboer, Heiko Dittmer and Thomas Rupp*. The following contributed to other IRI project groups involved in preparing this almanac: *Fredi Krebs (Herznach), Gerhard Schuster (Vienna), Jürgen Zinnel (Marburg), Diana Wallis (York), Alain Lamassoure (Biarritz), Jürgen Meyer (Freiburg), Giuliano Amato (Rome), Bruno Frey (Zürich), Gebhard Kirchgässner (St.Gallen), Roger de Weck (Berlin), Otmar Jung (Berlin) Lars Feld (Marburg)*, and *Michael Efler (Berlin)*.

In a continent as varied and complex as Europe, it is of decisive importance to have experts in the different cultural regions. The following IRI correspondents provided us with the necessary information: *Christian Schaller (Vienna), Jos Verhulst (Antwerp), Paul Carline (Edinburgh), Nelly Sirakova (Sofia), Milan Valach (Prague), Steffen Kjærulff-Schmidt (Copenhagen), Jüri Ruus (Tartu), Dag Anckar (Turku), Carsten Berg (Paris), Ralph Kampwirth (Bremen), Georges Kokkas (Athens), Pal Reti (Budapest), Anna Olofsdottir Björnsson (Reykjavik), Dolores Taaffe (Limerick), Roland Erne (Florence), Gita Feldhune (Riga), Algis Krupavicius (Kaunas), Arjen Nijeboer (Amsterdam), Tord Björklund (Oslo), Andrzej Kaczmarczyk (Warsaw), Elisabete Cidre (Lisbon), Horia Terpe (Bucarest), Igor Luksic (Lubljana), Guillem Rico (Madrid), Matthias Goldmann (Stockholm), Paul Ruppen (Brig), Sigward Wohlwend (Vaduz)*, and *Alfred Groff (Luxembourg)*.

We must also give thanks to our publisher, Carolina Academic Press whose support of our projects has made this series of Almanacs possible.

Last but not least, we both must express our gratitude to our wives and children. The Waters family—Catherine, Mason and Conrad have shown their support for my work as I have striven to make the Institute the best it can be and for that I owe them my eternal love and devotion.

The Kaufmann family—*Elisabeth Erlandsson* and our two daughters *Wanja Louise* and *Nina Sophie*, followed the extensive work on this book in many different places with a healthy mixture of criticism and support. Their joie de vivre gave me the decisive measure of energy necessary to complete this almanac, which hopefully will serve the citizens of Europe in their struggle for better and more direct democratic rights.

About the Editors

Bruno Kaufmann: Born in 1965, Bruno studied Political Sciences, Eastern European History and Peace and Development Research at the Universities of Zurich, Uppsala, Gothenburg, Cambridge and Hawaii. He is editor of "Demokratins Utmaningar" (1996) and co-editor of "Frieden mit Europa" (1989) and "Transnationale Demokratie" (1995). He was a member of Die ZEIT-Reformwerkstatt, Hamburg (1998–2000) and currently covers Northern European Affairs for the Swiss Broadcasting Company DRS and the biggest Swiss daily newspaper "Tages-Anzeiger" in Zurich. Kaufmann is the columnist of the German bi-monthly "Nordis" and writes regularly for "Open Democracy" and "EU Observer." He has worked as an I&R expert for the Constitutional committee of the German Parliament and is a founding member of eurotopia, the pan-European citizen network for a european constitution with direct democratic rights and the "Permanent Study Group for European Constitution." He resides in Falun/Sweden. Bruno is Co-Founder and President of IRI Europe.

M. Dane Waters: Dane is the founder, President and Co-Chairman of the Institute. He also is the co-founder and board member of the Initiative & Referendum Institute Europe, a non-profit and non-partisan educational organization that studies the initiative and referendum process in Europe. Dane has lectured all over the world on governmental and electoral issues. He has provided strategic advice to individuals all around the world as well as to various foreign governments on the initiative and referendum process. Dane has authored and edited numerous articles and books on the importance of the initiative and referendum process. He has provided commentary on initiative and referendum to newspapers, radio talk shows and television stations around the world. Dane also writes a regular column on the initiative process for *Campaigns & Elections Magazine*.

About the Authors

Adamiak, Aimée Lind (1974). Diploma in Political Science (University of Oslo). Coordinator of a public project towards better reporting of local referendums in Norway. aimee@innboks.com

Anckar, Dag. PhD. Professor of Political Science at the Åbo Akademi. University, Finland. He is a former President of the Nordic and Finnish Political Scientist Associations. danckar@abo.fi

Berg, Carsten (1975). Diploma in Political Science (University of Potsdam). PhD candidate at Institut de Science Political Science Politique Associations Lille. cberg@rz.uni-potsdam.de

Büchi, Rolf, PhD is social scientist in Helsinki and works as Educational Secretary with the Initiative & Referendum Institute Europe. Buchi@iri-europe.org.

Carline, Paul is a Scottish musician, teacher and democracy activists. He is working as an Editor at the Initiative & Referendum Institute Europe. Carline@iri-europe.org.

Cidre, Elisabete Maria Pires (1969). PhD Candidate in Planning Studies at the Bartlett School of Planning in London. Architect and urban designer in Porto and London. emcidre@hotmail.com

Cuesta, Victor. PhD in Constitutional Law. Teacher at Las Palmas University. victor_cuesta@hotmail.com.

Erne, Roland (1968). PhD in Political Science (European University Institute in Florence). Lecturer for „transnational working relations" at University College in Dublin. roland.erne@dcol.ie.

Feldhune, Gita. PhD in Juridical Science (Central European University in Budapest). Director of the Human Rights Institute of the Faculty of Law, University of Latvia and Editor of the Latvian Human Rights Quarterly. gitulens@hotmail.com

Goldmann, Mattias is working for Stockholm-based Public Relation Company and is project leader for the Initiative & Referendum Institute Sweden. Mattias.goldmann@iri-sverige.org.

Gross, Andreas (1952). Phil Lic in Political Science (University of Lausanne). Director of Atelier for Direct Democracy in St.Ursanne, MP Swiss Parliament, Vice-President of European Council and IRI Europe Research Director. info@andigross.ch

Ivanova Sirakova, Nelly (1977). MA in Political Science (University of Sofia). Secretary General of the Foundation "EKIP 5—Center to research of ethnics, culture, economy and politics". ekip_5@abv.bg

Jung, Otmar, PhD, is Lecturer at the Otto-Suhr Institute (Freien Universität Berlin). jungotma@zedat.fu-berlin.de.

Kaczmarczyk, Andrzej (1934). PhD in Information Technology (University of Warszawa). Director of the Institute of Mathematical Machines in Warsaw. akamar@imm.org.pl

Kampwirth, Ralph (1968). Diploma in Political Science (University of Bremen). Journalist and Press spokesperson of the German NGO „Mehr Demokratie. " presse@mehr-demokratie.de

Kaufmann, Bruno (1965), MA in Peace- and Conflict Studies is a journalist leaving in Falun/Sweden and works as President of the Initiative & Referendum Institute Europe. Kaufmann@iri-europe.org.

Kjærulff-Schmidt, Steffen. Attorney at law and legal consultant in Christiansborg Castle, the Danish Parliament. Steffen.Kjaerulff-Schmidt@ft.dk

Krupavicius, Algis. PhD in Political Science. Director at the Policy and Public Administration Institute in Kaunas and Professor at Department of Public Administration at Kaunas University of Technology. a84601@pikuolis.omnitel.net

Luksic, Igor (1961). PhD in Political Science (University of Ljubljana). Professor aof Political Sciences at the Faculty of Social Sciences at the University of Ljubljana. Editor of "Teorija in praksa". Igor.Luksic@Uni-Lj.si

Malheiros, Manuel Luís Macaísta (1940). Judge of the Administrative and Fiscal Courts in Portugal and honorary Director of the EU Justice Court. mmalheiros@tribconstitucional.pt

Nijeboer, Arjen (1974). Diploma in Journalism (Windesheim College in Zwolle). Coordinator of the Dutch Referendum Platform and Secretary General of IRI Europe. Nijeboer@iri-europe.org

Réti, Pál. PhD in Economics (University of Budapest). Editor of HVG, Hungary s leading newsmagazine. p.reti@hvg.hu

Ruppen, Paul. PhD in Sociology and Political Science (University of Bern). He is the Editor of "Europa-Magazin" and President of the "Forum für Direkte Demokratie" in Zürich. forum@europa-magazin.ch

Ruus, Jüri (1957). PhD in Modern History (University of Tartu). Professor of Political Science at Tartu University. J.Ruus@ec.ut.ee

Schaller, Christian, PhD in Social Sciences is Director of the Sozialwissenschaftliche Studiengesellschaft in Vienna. swsrs@aon.at

Terpe, Horia Paul. Student in Political Science at the National School of Political Studies and Public Administration in Bucharest. NGO's program coordinator. horiaterpe@hotmail.com

Hans-Urs Wili is Director at the Department of Political Rights of the Swiss Federal Chancellery in Bern. Hans-Urs.Wili@bk.admin.ch.

Valach, Milan (1956). PhD in Philosophy (Masaryk University Brno). Professor in Philosophy and Ethics, spokesperson of the Czech Movement for Direct Democracy. Valach@iol.cz

Verhulst, Jos, PhD is an independent writer and teacher in Antwerp. He is author on many books on direct democracy. Verhulst-Dekegel@pi.be.

Introduction

The right of *initiative* is the right of citizens to put an issue onto the political agenda of a polity. The *referendum* is a ballot vote on a political issue. In both cases citizens are involved, by registering or signing an initiative and by taking part in the final decision-making in a referendum. Wherever direct democracy exists through I&R, it has not replaced representative democracy but has complemented the work of parliamentarians and political parties. Thus, direct democracy doesn't diminish the present representative democracy, but adds direct-democratic channels to that predominantly representative democracy. I&R makes a difference. I&R restores the power of the people in some measure and thus makes democracy stronger. I&R offers more and new opportunities for real citizens' participation and contributes to the restoration of democracy at the transnational level.

Almost 400 years of direct-democratic practice through I&R show that the design of the process is of crucial importance. Good I&R means a limited entry quorum for approving an initiative and no participation quorum at all for referendums. Furthermore, the outcomes of votes must be binding in order for them to be useful tools for citizens. I&R has to be clearly distinguished from plebiscites. These are votes on issues implemented from above by a government, without the support or influence of the citizens. Plebiscites have nothing to do with I&R; on the contrary, they are often used by governments which want to secure special legitimacy for their policies by bypassing existing laws and constitutional rules.

Never before in the history of Europe and the world has the legitimacy of democracy been so highly and broadly recognized, or the citizens so well prepared and competent to be involved in political decision-making—but neither has democracy ever been as greatly challenged as it is today. These challenges are both structural and conceptual. Structurally, globalization and transnational markets are undermining national democracies; conceptually, democracy is too often reduced to choices in elections between political parties which no longer offer a real choice.

It is no coincidence that since the end of the Cold War, almost 30 countries have given themselves new constitutions and only three of them did not include elements of I&R. So over the last ten years, hundreds of millions of citizens have become acquainted with direct democracy.

Old democracies, too, have begun to incorporate I&R into their constitutions: Portugal began this reform in 2000; the Netherlands have been struggling with it for many years; the Belgian parliament has just started to discuss reforms. In spite of the growing basic openness to the idea of I&R, knowledge of how to design the I&R process in the interest of the majority of the citizens is rather limited, as is insight into the political culture, the philosophy and the history of direct democracy.

The first constitutional referendum took place in North America in 1639, when a few thousands citizens accepted the *Fundamental Orders of Connecticut*. Later, the people of Massachusetts and New Hampshire were also able to decide directly on their constitutions. The concept of this new form of democracy had been established by the famous Mayflower Treaty in 1620, which outlined the foundations of American democracy.

In Europe, Geneva citizen Jean Jacques Rousseau wrote *The Social Contract*, in which he described popular sovereignty as a counter-weight to the absolute power of kings and emperors. This inspired the French revolutionaries of 1793 to introduce a new constitution with—for the very first time in history—comprehensive I&R, including an initiative right for the citizens and an obligatory referendum on constitutional matters.

From revolutionary and centralistic France, where the old undemocratic order was soon re-established by Napoleon Bonaparte, the idea of I&R moved to nearby Switzerland. Here the first nationwide referendum took place in 1803. In the new Constitution of 1848, an obligatory constitutional referendum was introduced; the right to facultative Referendum was added in 1874, and finally, in 1891, the right of popular initiative was included. The establishment of a strong I&R process was only possible step-by-step, through the pressure of strong citizens' movements.

By the end of the 19th century, the successful establishment of I&R in Switzerland inspired many center-right and center-left progressive movements to fight for the reform of representative democracy. Between 1898 and 1912, more than 22 state-level constitutions in the United States were modified in a direct-democratic direction. In Australia and New Zealand, too, the citizens obtained the empowering instruments of I&R. At the beginning of the 20th century many social-democratic and liberal politicians welcomed I&R as additional democratic instruments. However, communists on the far left and fascists on the far right were opposed, and they tried instead to kidnap the process by using plebiscites, as Hitler did several times in Nazi Germany.

The World Wars and the Cold War slowed down, if they did not stop, democratization all over the world and especially in Europe. Later, however, the European integration process in the Western part and the fall of the Berlin Wall in the Eastern part provoked a new wave of democratization with more than 30 new nationwide constitutions in this part of the world. I&R even entered into centralistic polities such as Sweden and Finland and is now seen by the World Bank as "one of the most important political developments" in the world.

Between 1990 and 2003, referendums took place in 91 sovereign states of the world, including 30 in Europe. Before making their decisions on the new EU Treaty establishing the very first European constitution, many member states, including Portugal, Spain, Luxembourg, Denmark and Ireland, held referendums. An even more dynamic development has recently taken place at local and regional polity levels: from being an almost unknown instrument, I&R has become an important issue and tool, e.g. in France, Germany, Britain, Sweden, and the Baltic States. Germany, with its population of over 80 million, is on the way to becoming the largest I&R polity so far.

Most national constitutions of today have some basic I&R provisions, but far too often these instruments are designed in such a way that they literally cannot be used by the citizens. In 60 nation states, I&R elements exist in the constitutions but have never been used.

The purpose of this Almanac is not to persuade people to support the initiative and referendum process, but to discuss the misinformation about it and give the reader a factual and historical base from which to work when debating or discussing I&R. The data contained here has been collected from numerous sources over several years. In most cases, the information is a compilation of studies, tables, books and articles: a compilation that did not exist before in any country. Though this Almanac may not contain the answer to every question you may have regarding the initiative and referendum process, it is—in our humble opinion—one of the most comprehensive sources of information currently available on this important law-making process.

Direct Democracy
in Europe

Chapter One

A Comparative Evaluation of Initiative & Referendum in 32 European States

by Bruno Kaufmann

Jean Jacques Rousseau's idea was extremely simple: people need laws to govern their social behavior, and if everyone is involved in formulating these laws, then ultimately everyone has to obey only one person—himself—and no one rules over anyone else. Current opinion says this is beautifully simple, but quite impractical. Current opinion notwithstanding, in an ever-increasing number of communities, regions and countries, more and more people are having a say when it comes to creating new laws, determining public expenditure, and enacting constitutions.

Direct democracy, as a complement to indirect democracy, is by no means an idealistic pipe-dream belonging to the past or a hobby-horse of out-of-touch fanatics. On the contrary, it is proving to be an extremely practical tool.

In 2003, almost 10,000 local referendums were recorded in the United States alone, and in the German state of Bavaria more than 700 local referendums have been held since the introduction of citizens' decision-making in 1995. There is no shortage either of issues or of committed activists in Bavaria: on the contrary, local politics have been invigorated, as the Munich Landtag representative Klaus Hahnzog noted in the publication entitled "Mehr direkte Demokratie wagen" ("Be brave: try more direct democracy").[1] Citizens want to get involved, particularly on issues of traffic, planning, and waste management.

The forward march of direct democracy is not restricted to the lower floors of the state edifice. Between 1993 and 2003, the number of national referendums was more than double that of the previous decade.[2] Between 1981 and 1990 there were only 200, of which 76 were in Switzerland. Between 1991 and 2003, 497 recorded countrywide referendums took place: 83 in the Americas, 54 in Africa, 30 in Asia, and 30 in Oceania. The vast majority took place in Europe: 301, of which 135 were in Switzerland alone.

I. Democratic Revolution and European Integration

There are two main reasons for this clear trend toward more referendums: first, the democratic revolutions in Eastern Europe led to no less than 27 new constitutions, the majority of which were approved by popular referendum; and second, the accelerated integration process within the European Union has launched a direct-democratic wave with transnational consequences.

Practically all the new constitutions of Central and Eastern Europe include elements of direct democracy. Among the Eastern countries, the Lithuanians have made most extensive use of the possibilities of a co-determination unthinkable in Soviet times: between 1991 and 1996 they voted nationally on 10 issues, including independence, the withdrawal of Russian troops, and their new constitution. In Western Europe, referendums on accession to the EG/EU, or on greater integration, have become the norm. When, in September 2003, the Latvians went to the polls to vote on the accession to the European Union, this was the 40th countrywide referendum on the question of European integration since 1972. No other set of issues internationally has resulted in so many referendums as European integration.

What can we learn from these facts—and what not? They clearly point to the fact that more and more citizens—especially in Europe—are not only voting to elect their representatives, but are increasingly voting on issues. However, the figures tell us relatively little about the real quality and effectiveness of direct-democratic institutions and decisions, i.e. how good they are in practice. For that we need a qualitative evaluation of existing I&R procedures and practical experience.

---

1. Hermann K. Heussner, Otmar Jung (Hg.), Mehr direkte Demokratie wagen, Volksbegehren und Volksentscheid: Geschichte—Praxis—Vorschläge. Olzog-Verlag 1999.

2. Plebiscites were included in the figures for national referendums. Plebiscites are distinguished by being initiated, managed and in part also controlled and manipulated from above; they may sometimes work counter-productively for direct democracy.

II. What Exists? And in What Form?

Our analysis concentrates on the countries represented in the European Convention (15 EU member states and 13 candidate states) and the four EFTA member states (Iceland, Norway, Liechtenstein and Switzerland).

We chose to approach the task of compiling the following comparative evaluation of 32 European countries by asking a number of preliminary questions:

1. Do I&R institutions and practices exist at the national level?

2. Are there I&R institutions which can be launched by the citizens themselves, such as the popular initiative and the facultative referendum?

3. Are there provisions for obligatory referendums, such as are used in Denmark and Ireland for European questions?

In only two instances, (Liechtenstein and Switzerland) was it possible to answer all three questions in the affirmative. There were three countries (Italy, Slovenia, and Latvia) in which citizens can initiate national referendums independently of parliament or the government, as well as four countries which have obligatory referendums (Ireland, Denmark, Lithuania, and Slovakia). In all the other countries examined, parliament and/or the government/the president have powers which can prevent popular referendums.

III. Six Qualitative Sets

Using these rough criteria as the basis for determining the quality of direct-democratic procedures, we were able to divide the 32 countries into the following six sets:

Set 1 — The Avantgarde. Citizens have access to a broad spectrum of direct democratic procedures. As well as the binding popular initiative, these include the right of facultative referendum and of obligatory referendums for alterations to the Constitution and for state treaties.

Set 2 — The Democrats. In the countries in this set, citizens have at least in part the possibility of initiating national referendums without the express permission of the organs of the state (parliament, government, president); alternatively, there are procedures for obligatory referendums.

Set 3 — The Cautious. In the countries in this set, the electorate does have practical experience of popular initiatives and/or national referendums. But these procedures are essentially plebiscitary in nature: they are not protected or controlled by the citizens themselves or by the law, but are controlled "from above" by parliament (political parties) or by the executive.

Set 4 — The Fearful. The political elites in the countries of this set appear to be afraid of popular participation in political decision-making, whether out of a fear of having to share power or because of certain historical experiences. Even here, however, there are still some traces of statutory I&R procedures which may form the basis for future improvement.

Set 5 — The Hopeless. Almost entirely lacking institutional procedures and practical experience, the countries of this set make it very hard for themselves to complement indirect democracy. In addition, the political and cultural circumstances scarcely provide a stimulus for the introduction or the strengthening of elements of popular decision-making. But the issue is occasionally debated.

Set 6 — The Tail Enders. In the countries belonging to this set, there is at present no basis at all for the development of direct democracy.

We have consciously dispensed with statistical methods of analysis for the IRI Europe Country Index 2004 of citizen lawmaking: such methods are yet to be developed for the relatively new research area of direct democracy.

In order to refine the qualitative comparison somewhat, we have divided the six sets into two classes: "A" and "B." This subdivision has been made not on absolute, but on relative considerations. The result shows, for example, that even in the top set (#1) there is still need for reform; or that in set 4 (the "Fearful"), some countries do have practical experience of referendums (subset 4A), while others currently do not (subset 4B).

Finally, the potential developments and prospects in some countries are an important element of IRI Europe's Country Index on Citizen Lawmaking. For example, we took into account whether or not there was an active public debate on direct democratic reforms in a country (indicated by a (*) after the name of the country). In addition, we tried to determine whether the trend in an individual country could be said to be "rising" (indicated by a (+), or "falling" (-)). What follows is, first, a summary of the Country Index, and then a short individual commentary on each country.

IV. Summary 2004

1A: None in this category
1B: Switzerland (+)
2A: Liechtenstein (-), Italy (-), Slovenia, Latvia
2B: Ireland, Denmark, Lithuania (*)
3A: Slovakia (*), the Netherlands (*), France (*), Spain, Austria (*), Portugal
3B: Sweden (*), Norway (*), Hungary (-), Poland (-), Luxembourg (+)
4A: Great Britain (+), Finland, Estonia, Belgium
4B: Iceland, Germany (+), Greece (*), Czech Republic (+)
5A: Romania (-),
5B: Bulgaria, Malta (*)
6A: Cyprus
6B: Turkey

V. Country by Country Commentary

Switzerland: This federal state in the heart of Europe has the widest, most varied, and most comprehensive experience of citizen lawmaking anywhere in the world. In addition, there is vigorous debate on how the procedures should be shaped and reformed. The latest package, with the introduction of a non-binding legislative initiative, has clear weaknesses, and in addition, such conditions as transparency and fairness continue to be undervalued by the majority and are therefore inadequately protected and institutionalized.

Liechtenstein: This small principality between Austria and Switzerland knows and practices the three basic procedures of direct democracy (popular initiative, facultative referendum, obligatory referendum) on a regular basis and with sensible parameters. However, the prince of the only direct-democratic hereditary monarchy in the world retains a right of veto and won a constitutional referendum in March 2003 after threatening to leave the country. For this reason, the Council of Europe is considering a monitoring process on the micro-state.

Italy: After Switzerland and Liechtenstein, it is the Italians who have the greatest practical experience of initiative and referendum. Over the last 30 years, the population of 50 million has put legal issues to the vote in 53 so-called "abrogative" referendums, which are similar to popular initiatives. However, the counter-productive role of the 50% turnout quorum, as well as the undemocratic monopoly of television and political power, has consistently weakened the potential of Italian direct democracy. 18 referendums were invalidated.

Slovenia: The republic of Slovenia is one of the "new" I&R countries in Europe. Although citizens have only a non-binding initiative right, in practice they can subject all laws passed by Parliament to popular approval by means of facultative referendums. Direct democracy appears to have considerable potential. In 2003 alone, four countrywide referendums took place, including membership in EU and NATO. Negative aspects are the 50% participation quorum, the right of parliament to make a counterproposal, and the restriction of popular rights solely to legislation.

Latvia: Although Latvia has been an independent state only since 1991, its fairly comprehensive I&R procedures actually date from the country's first period of independence between the two world wars. These procedures allow for 10% of the electorate to initiate a change to the Constitution or a new law; a decision of parliament can also be subjected to referendum. However, there are extremely restrictive rules excluding certain issues and a participation quorum. In September 2003 a majority voted in favor of EU membership, paving the way for another EU referendum on the constitution.

Ireland: Ireland is the prototype of a country with obligatory constitutional referendums. Irish citizens have the last word not only on questions of European integration, but also on moral and institutional questions. However, the electorate itself cannot initiate referendums. Neither is there any serious debate on reform of the system. Nonetheless, the role of the courts (in favor of the obligatory referendum), the current debate about the parameters (keywords: Referendum Commission; payment of expenses), and the absence of participation and approval quorums are positive features.

Denmark: Although in domestic politics the obligatory referendum functions only in relation to European issues, its significance has extended far beyond the country's borders. Danish referendums on the EU were responsible for bringing the questions of the I&R process and of European integration itself into the European public domain. In autumn 2003, when the government wanted to radically change environmental laws, the right of initiative of a parliamentary minority became important. At the local level, there have been an increasing number of consultative referendums. However, the initiative element is almost totally lacking, and the 40% approval quorum for national referendums remains a problem.

Lithuania: This Baltic republic has the popular initiative, the obligatory constitutional referendum, and the facultative referendum. During a brief period between 1991 and 1996 there were no less than 10 national referendums. However, this practical experience revealed some clear procedural weaknesses: after 1996, seven referendums failed to meet the 50% participation quorum. This caused citizens to lose interest in participatory politics. However, the successful EU membership referendum in 2003 has empowered the people again and has led to a more citizen-friendly design of the I&R process, including reduced thresholds.

Slovakia: Over the last three years this young country has made enormous steps forward, despite many traumatic experiences. It has a binding popular initiative right, which among other things led in 2000 to a referendum on holding new elections. However, as in many other countries of Central and Eastern Europe, the prospects for more democracy are extremely modest; in addition, the 50% participation quorum threatens to invalidate almost every referendum. The country also has a 50% approval quorum. Furthermore, the referendum on EU accession in spring 2003 received a lot of criticism for its unfair conduct.

The Netherlands: On the one hand, the Netherlands is one of the very few countries in Europe and even in the world which have never held a national referendum; on the other hand, it is also one of the very few countries in which the issue of the introduction of direct democratic elements brought about a government crisis. This happened in 1999 and led to the creation of a provisional referendum law, under which the question will be examined nationally and some conclusion reached by 2005. Unfortunately, because of the excessively high quorums and the restriction to a non-binding facultative referendum, the prospects do not appear very favorable. A first referendum could be held on the EU constitution.

France: Although France was a co-discoverer of direct democracy in the form of initiative and referendum during its revolution at the end of the 18th century, in practice only the Presidential plebiscite has remained. The "referendum" is therefore understood primarily as an instrument of the elite and not as a tool of the ordinary citizen. Nonetheless, there is a tradition of presenting important constitutional changes to the people, whose decision is binding. Before his re-election in 2002, President Chirac announced that he would promote the introduction of the popular initiative in his second term of office. A rather weak local referendum process was introduced by law in 2003. In the island province of Corsica a referendum on autonomy was defeated.

Spain: The last time the Spanish were able to vote on a substantive issue was in 1986, in the referendum on accession to NATO. There have been a few popular initiatives in some regions, Catalonia for example, but at the national level only petitions are allowed. On the other hand, Spain refunds the expenses of initiative committees and has no participation quorums. Popular referendums are not seen as complementing the parliamentary process, but as threatening it, because parliament would be forced to resign if a referendum went against it. As a new trend, the government and the parliament have announced the first referendum on the European Union, dealing with the new constitution.

Austria: The only direct-democratic elements in Austrian politics were included in the constitution (in 1958 and 1963) against the will of the two main political parties. Of two national referendums which have been held so far, the result of the first (a referendum in 1978 on the commissioning of the Zwentendorf nuclear power station) also went against the will of the ruling elite. In other words, the Austrian people have shown a clear desire for a share of political power along with parliament and government, evidenced in the high level of participation in the recent campaigns against the Czech nuclear power station at Temelin and for the preservation of the welfare state. The political institutions are lagging far behind the social reality.

Portugal: In 1998 a very badly prepared and executed attempt was made to hold referendums on the questions of abortion and European integration. The first was rushed through within a matter of a few weeks; the second (on Europe) was deleted from the referendum calendar by the constitutional court. What was especially bad is that leading politicians were attempting to discredit popular rights on grounds for which they themselves were responsible. Fortunately, the outlook is brighter: the government has promised a citizen decision on the EU constitution.

Sweden: Like France, Sweden's experience of referendums is primarily one of plebiscites. However, unlike France, where the President has total control, it is the ruling Social Democratic Parties which exercise this role. Referendums, which are binding only under quite specific circumstances, are (mis)used as instruments of power. Citizens effectively have no rights, even at the communal level, where a right of petition which has been called an "initiative right" has produced a great deal of frustration. One positive aspect is the fact that real referendums were held in 1994 on EU membership and in 2003 on Euro membership: these were real because both the government and the parliament announced their respect for the outcome BEFORE the results were known. Another positive aspect is the courage of some communities to use their very limited scope for autonomy to introduce greater direct democracy.

Norway: Norway, whose constitution dates from 1814, has no *de jure* direct democratic procedures at all. Yet, thanks to its actual practice, Norway can be placed within the center-ground of this league table, for its citizens have for decades been asked to give their approval on questions of EU membership. In addition, there exists a relatively comprehensive level of direct involvement in decision-making at the communal level, where there have been more than 500 local referendums between 1972 and 2002. However, almost all control of these procedures is in the hands of parliament and the political parties, which have shown no great willingness to share their power with the people.

Hungary: Under the constitution, 200,000 signatures collected within four months give the people the right to hold a referendum. But in practice, a wide-ranging list of exemptions undermines the democratic potential of this provision; in addition, the courts, if they so wish, are able to curtail or dismantle the direct-democratic procedures and decisions. In 1997 the participation quorum was cut from 50% to 25% for the NATO referendum: a ruling which will help the government to achieve its desired EU accession.

Poland: Political parties have not yet succeeded in exploiting the democratic potential which certainly exists in this huge new EU country. In 1996, when 600,000 citizens signed petitions to demand a referendum on the privatization of state property (only 500,000 were needed to satisfy the constitutional requirement), the government used its constitutional veto to deny the citizens' request. Even at the local level, the high participation quorums mean that referendums are often declared invalid, which naturally tends to weaken people's motivation to take part in political life. But the EU accession referendum in 2003 was a positive experience which furthered the idea of increased I&R.

Luxemburg: The Grand Duchy owes its independence to a quasi direct-democratic movement: the "Petition Movement" of the 1860s. But in contrast to the principality of Liechtenstein, for example, the appetite for greater civilian rights remained weak. Since 1996 it has been legally possible to hold a referendum, and in summer 2003, the government surprisingly announced a referendum on the EU constitution.

Britain: Not only does the United Kingdom have no written constitution, having instead a motley collection of written and unwritten laws and traditions: sovereignty is not even invested in the people, but rather in Parliament. Its wholly indirect democratic system has been called an "elective dictatorship." Despite this, there have been some significant changes in the last few years, in particular the devolution arrangements for Scotland, Wales and Northern Ireland, which were chosen by referendum. In addition, there have been a number of local referendums, some of which resulted from initiatives. In 2004 three regional assembly referendums will be held in the North of England.

Finland: The Finns have been able to vote only twice in their history on a substantive issue, and at the communal level there have been only about 20 referendums in all. This rather limited experience shows that the country has a long way to go on the question of popular participation in decision-making. Proposals for relevant reforms were rejected when the new constitution was being decided in 2000: a lost opportunity for modernization. Nonetheless, the EU referendum of 1994 was a positive experience and awakened an appetite in many people for more democracy. The current Prime Minister, Matti Vanhanen, has once announced that the citizens shall have a say on the new EU constitution — later, he started to hesitate on this commitment.

Estonia: Unlike its southern neighbor Latvia, Estonia did not take up the direct democratic traditions in the inter-war period after the country regained its independence in 1991, but rather began to orient itself towards its politically centralized northern neighbors. The result is that ordinary Estonians have no rights of initiative or referendum: these are the exclusive right of a majority in parliament. However, the obligatory constitutional referendum does exist and was invoked for the first time when the Estonians voted on EU membership in autumn 2003.

Belgium: In common with the other Benelux countries and with Germany, Belgium appears to have a difficult relationship with national referendums. Since the Second World War, only two plebiscites have been held. Binding national referendums are still not allowed, which may lead to problems with the European integration process. The current Prime Minister, Guy Verhofstadt, is believed to support more direct democracy, but he is hindered in his ambitions at the national level by Walloon socialists. At the regional level, however, Flanders is on the point of agreeing to a reform which, among other things, would provide for the right of popular initiative.

Iceland: This island state in the North Atlantic has not had a referendum since gaining its independence in June 1944. However, there seems to be some potential, even though this is dependent on the will of the President of the country, who can submit a parliamentary decision to the people. This provision, which has existed since 1994, will prove to be important especially in questions of European integration: Iceland is currently debating whether to enter into negotiations to join the EU. Between 1908 and 1944 the Icelandic people voted on six occasions on questions of independence and the use of alcohol.

Germany: In 2002 the necessary two-thirds majority was not reached for the incorporation of the popular initiative, the popular demand, and the referendum into the constitution. Germany remains for the time being a country with no direct democratic procedures at the national level. However, in a country of more than 80 million people, the federal states (Länder) and the communes play a very important role, and here popular rights have increased enormously over the past 10 years. In most places these still require reform in order to make them more people-friendly, i.e. the existing quorums should be lowered or removed and the numerous difficulties in collecting signatures should be eased.

Greece: The democratic constitution of 1975 provided the basis for three different kinds of popular vote: initiative, referendum and constitutional referendum. However, all three forms are dependent on the willingness of the country's president to present issues to the people, and so far this has been absent. Nonetheless, for some years now strong forces within Greek society have been pressing for popular votes on such issues as European integration and secularization. The Orthodox Church collected several million signatures on the issue of removing the declaration of religious affiliation from Greek identity cards.

Czech Republic: Neither in the case of the restoration of democracy, nor in separating from Slovakia, nor in the question of accession to NATO did the Czech Parliament give the people the opportunity to vote. Until 2003 the Czech Republic was one of the very few countries in the world which had never held a referendum. But with the EU accession this has changed, bringing the people into the decision-making process for the first time. There is a good chance that Czech citizens will also vote on the new EU constitution. There are strong forces within the political parties arguing for increased decision-making rights for citizens in general.

Romania: Romania is a young democracy which is still suffering considerably from its totalitarian heritage. This includes the experience of the dictator's plebiscite of 1986, when Nikolai Ceausescu arranged a referendum on an issue involving the army and officially achieved a 100% "yes" vote on a turnout of 99.99%! Despite this, there is another, older, tradition: that of the constitutional referendums which took place after 1864. In addition, there is a right of petition which could force a parliamentary debate although, if a referendum did result, it would be burdened by a 50% turnout threshold. In October 2003 only "unfair" interventions by governing bodies secured a higher turnout in a constitutional referendum.

Bulgaria: During the last ten years of democratic reconstruction, Bulgaria's citizens have not been able to vote on a single substantive issue. In addition, constitutional change is specifically excluded as a subject of a popular referendum, which can be launched by a majority in parliament. There is no experience of direct democracy at the local level either. The only legally-based provision for I&R is in the case of boundary changes affecting local communities. However, in the end of 2003 the government has proposed the introduction of a popular initiative right as well as an optional referendum.

Malta: According to the EU Commission, this small Mediterranean island state fulfills "all the standards of democracy and human rights" and has a few instruments of direct participation. But the combination of a very small country with very strong political parties has not promoted I&R. Furthermore, the Labour party, which was against EU membership, tried to delegitimize a referendum decision in spring 2003.

Cyprus: Cyprus is the odd man out in terms of European integration, as it has been effectively divided in two since the Turkish invasion of 1974. In this country whose geopolitical exposure has made it the target of foreign forces for millennia, there have been no signs of movement towards direct democracy except two presidential plebiscites in the Turkish-occupied northern half of the country. Apart from a possible accession to the EU, which would necessitate the first referendum in Cyprus, there is nothing to indicate any likely moves in the direction of more democracy.

Turkey: Although officially an EU candidate country that was represented in the European Convention, Turkey still fails to meet even the minimum standards in Europe for democracy and human rights. The Turkish constitution refers to the possibility of holding referendums, but the basis for these is neither developed nor defined.

Chapter Two

Survey 2004 on the New Challenge of Initiative & Referendum in Europe

By Bruno Kaufmann

In this chapter, the Initiative & Referendum Institute Europe offers an overview of the most important facts about the growing importance of direct-democratic tools and trends in Europe.

We start with a global outlook of democracy, then assess the 41 national referendums on Europe which took place between 1972 and 2003 and present a first list of criteria for "free" and "fair" European referendum standards. The survey concludes with a look at the prospects for a Europe-wide constitutional referendum until 2006, as well as for the implementation and further development of the new "European Citizens' Initiative" until the end of this decade.

I. Introduction

It was an impressive crowd which gathered outside strategic buildings in central Vilnius, the Lithuanian capital, in January 1991. They were trying to defend with their own bodies the newly declared Lithuanian independence from the Soviet Union. But the feared OMON militia (special units of the Soviet Ministry of the Interior) attacked and killed 13 women and men.

Twelve years later, another big crowd gathered in Europe's geographical heart:[1] thousands of Lithuanians were celebrating the overwhelming "yes" vote in the referendum on EU accession. Two thirds of the electorate had turned out; nine out of ten voters had approved membership. "This referendum delivered a common identity to a divided people," says Algis Krupavicius, Professor of Political Science at Kaunas University.[2]

"If you want a crowd, start a fight,"[3] said the famous 19th century American showman Phineas Taylor Barnum, founder of the Grand Travelling Circus. We still need them today—both the crowds and the fights. But with the help of (direct) democracy, they have become far less violent. The two Lithuanian fights of 1991 (to leave the Soviet Union) and 2003 (to join the European Union) impressively demonstrate this qualitative change in the culture of fighting.

Initiative and referendum has become a key concept in the European integration process. According to Dan O'Brien and Daniel Keohane, referendums "inject a dose of human drama into the technocratic machinery and arid theory of EU integration" and "generate understanding and encourage participation by focusing attention on the EU and its workings." "This should be welcomed," conclude the two London-based political analysts, as "referendums specifically on the EU are the only way of putting the Union and what it does at political centre-stage."

Europe's citizens are pioneers in taking direct part in crucial decisions on their continent's behalf. Since 1972, no fewer than 47 national referendums in 23 countries have been held on European integration. No other issue worldwide has been the subject of such wide and direct participation by the citizens. But this is still by far not enough, as EU integration is still seen by most people as a remote, elitist and rather undemocratic matter.

But changes are on the way, as many more Europeans will get the opportunity to have a say on the new EU constitution—the constitution which was adopted in June 2003 by a constitutional convention and which in spring 2004 was under evaluation by an intergovernmental conference. The EU Convention has also introduced the very first direct-democratic tool at the transnational level, the so-called "European Citizens' Initiative." Finally, both the European Union with its 25 old and new member states and many European NGOs are now trying to learn from the Europe-wide experience with initiative and referendum in developing common criteria for "European Initiative and Referendum Standards."

---

1. The geographical center of Europe (between the Ural and the Atlantic) is situated on 25'19/54'54. This is 25 kilometers north of the Lithuanian capital Vilnius.

2. Algis Krupavicius made this statement at the IRI Europe Referendum Monitoring conference in Sväty Jur (Slovak Republic) on June 21, 2003. Professor Krupavicius' assessment of the Lithuanian EU accession referendum will be part of the forthcoming IRI Europe Referendum Monitoring Reports, Amsterdam, 2004.

3. Quoted by Dan O'Brien & Daniel Keohane, "Why Europe needs referendums" in "Transnational Democracy in the Making," IRI Europe, Amsterdam, 2003.

a. Civil participation moves to centre-stage

A recent assessment by the United Nations Development Program (UNDP)[4] reached two main conclusions:

- *The democratisation of societies is one of the most important positive trends of our time.*
- *The democratisation of democracy is one of the greatest challenges of the near future.*

Indeed, as recently as 1980, only a minority (46%) of the world's population lived in countries—54 in number—which enjoyed fundamental democratic rights such as free multi-party elections.

By the beginning of this millennium, the "democratic" minority had become a clear majority: 68% of the more than 7 billion people in the world now lived in 129 nominally democratic countries.[5] During the last two decades of the 20th century, 81 countries went through a process of democratisation, 21 of those in Europe—where "Freedom House" now characterizes only Belarus as "undemocratic."[6]

However, the United Nations World Development Report states: "True democratisation means more than elections. People's dignity requires that they be free—and able—to participate in the formation and stewardship of the rules and institutions that govern them."[7]

This was the first time that the United Nations has placed civil participation in making laws—in the form of initiatives and referendums (I&R)—at the centre of a global democratic challenge for the 21st century. European integration plays a central role in this, for in no other transnational political process does the question of democracy enjoy such a high priority as in the European Union.

b. Strengthening representative democracy by I&R

Since the French Revolution, democratic procedures for dealing with substantive issues have been developed in the shadow, as it were, of procedures for electing parliaments and assemblies. Along with the various possibilities within indirect democracy for the active and passive election of political representatives and/or political parties, we can add the right of citizens to launch initiatives, to vote on substantive issues, or to decide—in a popular referendum initiated "from below"—on the recall of a politician before the end of his/her mandated period of office: all these latter belong to the portfolio of direct democracy.[8] With good design[9] and working in a way in which each complements the other, the procedures of both direct and indirect democracy have the potential to strengthen representative democracy. They are also the precondition for improvements in the quality of life within and between political communities.

In federal countries such as the USA and Switzerland, I&R procedures have played a very important role in legislation for more than a hundred years.[10] But it was only with the ending of the Cold War that elements of direct democracy could be incorporated into the constitutions and political practice of many other states. Europe has played a pioneering role in this: almost all of the 27 new constitutions in the countries of Eastern and Central Europe have been adopted by their citizens in referendums. Most of these constitutions contain some direct-democratic elements. In Western and Northern Europe, the European integration process has brought about numerous national referendums. No other single issue in the world has resulted in so many referendums and individual acts of voting: since 1972, more than 250 million Europeans in 23 countries have been able to participate in the European integration process on a total of 41 separate occasions.

This is only the beginning of a process of development: the proposal for referendums on the EU constitution has gained broad support. The governments of countries such as Portugal, Spain, France, Luxembourg, Ireland, Denmark and the Czech Republic have already announced citizens' decisions. In other member states such as Austria and Belgium, the governments have announced their willingness to take part in a Europe-wide constitutional referendum in the near future. In the shadow of this dynamic development, which must be exciting to both promoters and skeptics of the referendum tool,

---

4. Ibid.

5. The UNDP figures are taken from: Marshall, Monty G. and Jaggers, Keith, Polity IV Project: Dataset Users Manual. April 2002. Web link: www.bsos.umd.edu/cidcm/inscr/polity

6. Countries such as the Russian Federation, Ukraine, Moldavia and Albania are labeled "partly democratic" in the yearly index of democracy published since 1972 by Freedom House. Web link: www.freedomhouse.org/ratings/index.htm

7. UNDP Report 2002, p. 14.

8. For a detailed description of the instrument of recall used especially in the USA, see. "The Recall Device" in "Direct Democracy: the politics of initiative, referendum and recall," by Thomas E. Cronin, 1989, p. 125 ff.

9. Cf. the article: "The design of direct democracy—basic principles for evaluating sub-optimal procedures of citizen lawmaking," in Gross, Andreas and Kaufmann, Bruno, "IRI Europe Country Index of Citizen lawmaking," Amsterdam, 2002.

10. In the USA, however, I&R rights are still limited to state and municipal levels.

many countries are about to strengthen the institutional foundations of participatory democracy through initiative and referendum. The most recent example is the introduction of a municipal referendum in France.[11]

II. 41 Referendums on Europe in 23 countries

The founding fathers of the European Union did not like the idea of including citizens directly in decision-making processes at the transnational political level. This was due less to the experience of the Second World War than to the growing threat of the Cold War, which initially spoiled the ideas for a democratic European Federation which were developed in the 1940s. This resulted in the integration process of the 1950s being dominated by economic and bureaucratic considerations: Jean Monnet's system did not provide for direct civilian participation in decision-making.

It was another great Frenchman, President Charles de Gaulle, who first formulated the challenge of a Europe-wide referendum at the beginning of the '60s:

"Europe will be born on the day on which the different peoples fundamentally decide to join. It will not suffice for members of parliaments to vote for ratification. It will require popular referendums, preferably held on the same day in all the countries concerned."[12]

It was to be another 10 years before de Gaulle's successor, Georges Pompidou, finally dared to make a start and made the citizens of his country the first Europeans to take part in a referendum on Europe: on March 23, 1972, a two-thirds majority voted in favour of extending the then European Community northwards to include Denmark, Great Britain, Ireland and Norway. In retrospect, this decision opened the door not only to the north, but also to more direct democracy in Europe. On May 10 of the same year, voters in both the Irish Republic and Denmark decided in favour of joining the EC. That was not the end of the matter thirty years ago: there were European referendums in both Norway and Switzerland. On September 26, 1972, the Norwegians voted narrowly against accession, while on December 3, the Swiss voted massively in favour of a Free Trade Treaty with the EEC (European Economic Community), with 72.5% voting "yes."

This first Europe-wide referendum year revealed the great disparity between referendum procedures in the different countries: whereas the French referendum was called by the French president and the result was merely advisory, the Irish popular decision on accession was prescribed in the constitution and was binding on the political leadership of that country. In Denmark, transfers of sovereignty to international organizations have to be put to referendum only when there is no 5/6 majority in the national parliament.[13] In Norway and Switzerland, it was parliament (in the former case) and the government (in the latter case) which voluntarily decided to submit the issue of accession to the EC (Norway) and to the EEC Free Trade Treaty (Switzerland) to referendum.[14]

---

11. The new law provides the option for binding referendums at the level of neighbourhoods, municipalities and regions. There is still a debate between the Senate and the National Assembly on the introduction of turnout quorums.

12. Quoted by Peyrefitte Alain, C'etait de Gaulle, Fayard, Paris, 1994 in Hug, Simon. "Voices of Europe: Citizens, Referendums, and European Integration," Rowman & Littlefield Publishers, Oxford, 2002.

13. svensson, Palle, "The Danish Perspectives—six referendums on Europe" in Kaufmann, Lamassoure, Meyer (Eds) "Transnational Democracy in the Making," IRI Europe, Amsterdam, 2003. Extract: "The 1915 constitution introduced the obligatory referendum in Danish politics as a part of the procedure for constitutional amendments. According to the 1915 constitution an amendment proposal—when passed by Parliament and afterwards by the newly elected Parliament—should be submitted to the voters for approval or rejection. An approval demanded a majority from the participating voters and at least 45 per cent of the whole electorate to cast their vote in favour of the Parliament's decision on a new constitution. In principle, the same procedure for constitutional amendments holds today (Article 88 of the constitution). However, the percentage required for approving a constitutional amendment has in the 1953 constitution been lowered to 40. The 1953 constitution introduced the facultative referendum in Denmark. Article 42 in the 1953 constitution describes the facultative law referendum, which states that one third of the members of the Folketing can demand a passed bill to be submitted to the voters for either approval or rejection. A rejection of the bill requires a negative majority that comprises at least 30 per cent of the electorate."

14. In Switzerland there was also the option of questioning accession by means of a facultative referendum. The government took the offensive and were rewarded with a very clear majority.

Table 1: Gives an overview of all 41 national referendums on Europe since 1972, with results and basic information on procedures[15]

	Country	Final voting day	Subject	Proportion of "Yes" votes	Turnout	Requirements & Quorums	Type: who triggers? Binding?	Basis in the Constitution
1	France	4/23/1972	EEC expansion	68.28%	60.27%	No	President/ No	Art. 11 & 89
2	Ireland	5/10/1972	EC accession	83.1%	70.88%	No	Obligatory referendum/Yes	Art. 46.2
3	Norway	9/26/1972	EC accession	46.5%	79.2%	No	Parliament/ No	None
4	Denmark	10/2/1972	EC accession	63.29%	90.4%	Non-approval requirement 30%	Obligatory referendum/ Yes	Art. 20
5	Switzerland	12/3/1972	Free Trade Treaty with EEC	72.5%	52%	Double majority (cantons, people)	Obligatory referendum/ Yes	None
6	Britain	6/5/1975	EC member-ship	67.23%	64.03%	No	Government / No	None
7	Greenland	2/23/1982	EC member-ship	45.96%	74.91%	No	Parliament / No	None
8	Denmark	2/27/1986	Common market	56.24%	75.39%	Non-approval requirement 30%	Parliament/ Yes	Art. 42
9	Ireland	5/26/1987	Common market	69.92%	44.09%	No	Obligatory referendum/Yes	Art. 46.2
10	Italy	6/18/1989	European constitution process	88.06%	85.4%	No	Citizens' initiative / No	Art. 71
11	Denmark	6/2/1992	Maastricht Treaty	47.93%	83.1%	Non-approval requirement 30%	Obligatory referendum/ Yes	Art.20
12	Ireland	6/18/1992	Maastricht Treaty	68.7%	57.31%	No	Obligatory referendum/Yes	Art. 46.2
13	France	9/20/1992	Maastricht Treaty	51.05%	69.69%	No	President/ Yes	Art. 11
14	Switzerland	12/6/1992	EEA accession	49.7%	78%	Double majority (cantons, people)	Obligatory referendum/ Yes	(Art. 89.5 and Art.123)
15	Liechtenstein	12/12/1992	EEA accession	55.81%	87%	No	Parliament/ Yes	Art.66
16	Denmark	5/18/1993	Maastricht Treaty	56.77%	85.5%	Non-approval requirement 30%	Parliament/ Yes	Art. 42.
17	Austria	6/12/1994	EU accession	66.58%	82.35%	No	Obligatory referendum/Yes	Art.44
18	Finland	10/16/1994	EU accession	56.88%	70.4%	No	Parliament/ No	Art. 22
19	Sweden	11/13/1994	EU accession	52.74%	83.32%	No	Parliament/ No	Chap. 8 § 4
20	Åland-Islands	11/20/1994	EU accession	73.64%	49.1%	No	Parliament/ No	None
21	Norway	11/28/1994	EU accession	47.8%	89%	No	Parliament/ No	None
22	Liechtenstein	4/9/1995	EEC	55.88%	82.05%	No	Obligatory referendum/ Yes	Art.66 bis
23	Switzerland	6/8/1997	EU accession procedures. Blocking.	25.9%	35%	Double majority (cantons, people)	Citizens' initiative / Yes	Art. 121
24	Ireland	5/22/1998	Treaty of Amsterdam	61.74%	56.26%	No	Obligatory referendum/ Yes	Art. 46.2
25	Denmark	5/281998	Treaty of Amsterdam	55.1%	76.24%	Non-approval requirement 30%	Obligatory referendum/Yes	Art.20
26	Switzerland	5/21/2000	Bilateral treaties with the EU	67.2%	48%	No	Facultative referendum/Yes	Art. 141

15. *Table notes

Country: EU = "old" and "new" member states; EFTA = European Free Trade Association, members Switzerland, Liechtenstein, Norway; Autonomous regions = Greenland, Åland Islands

Final voting day: in many countries the time for voting is expanded to two days or even several weeks.

Subject: Accession = to European Community, European Union, European Economic Area, Euro

Proportion of "yes" votes = results somewhat misleading due to specific Swiss Initiatives such as forbidding accession negotiations and Greenland's withdrawal proposal.

Turnout = 1994–2003: "old" member states 69%, "new" member states 61%.

Requirements & Quorums: Non-approval quorum in Denmark = 30% of the total electorate must vote "no" in order to veto a decision; double majority in Switzerland = individual votes are counted twice: 1) on a national basis, and 2) on a cantonal basis: overall approval needs a "yes" in both counts.

Type: top-down = plebiscite triggered by president, parliament or government; bottom-up = citizens decision referendum triggered by citizens or constitution.

	Country	Final voting day	Subject	Proportion of "Yes" votes	Turnout	Requirements & Quorums	Type: who triggers? Binding?	Basis in the Constitution
27	Denmark	9/28/2000	Euro accession	46.87%	87.2%	Non-approval requirement 30%	Obligatory referendum/Yes	Art. 20
28	Switzerland	3/4/2001	EU accession procedures. Start.	23.2%	55%	Double majority (cantons, people)	Citizens' initiative /Yes	Art. 139
29	Ireland	6/7/2001	Treaty of Nice	46.13%	34.79%	No	Obligatory referendum/ Yes	Art. 46.2
30	Ireland	10/19/2002	Treaty of Nice	62.89%	48.45%	No	Obligatory referendum/ Yes	Art. 46.2
31	Malta	3/8/2003	EU accession	53.6%	91.0%	No	Parliament/No	None
32	Slovenia	3/23/2003	EU accession	89.6%	60.3%	Turnout 50%	Parliament/ Yes	Art. 169
33	Hungary	4/12/2003	EU accession	83.8%	45.6%	Approval 25%	Parliament/Yes	Art. 19 et 28
34	Lithuania	5/11/2003	EU accession	91.1%	63.4%	Turnout 50% Approval 33%	Parliament/ Yes	Art. 147
35	Slovakia	5/17/2003	EU accession	92.5%	52.2%	Turnout 50%	Parliament/ Yes	Art. 93.2
36	Poland	6/8/2003	EU accession	77.5%	58.9%	Turnout 50%	Parliament/ Yes	Art. 125
37	Czech Republic	6/14/2003	EU accession	77.3%	55.2%	No	Parliament/ Yes	Ad-hoc law
38	Estonia	9/14/2003	EU accession	66.8%	64%	No	Parliament/ Yes	Art. 105
39	Sweden	9/14/2003	Euro accession	42%	82.6%	No	Parliament/ No	Art. 4
40	Latvia	9/20/2003	EU accession	67%	72.5%	50% of turnout at last election	Parliament/ Yes	Art. 79
41	Romania	10/19/2003	EU preparation	89.7%	55.7%	Turnout 50%	Obligatory Referendum/Yes	Art. 147
*	23 countries: 18 EU 3 EFTA 2 autonomous-regions	41 votes –1983: 7 84–93: 9 94–03: 25	28 accession 10 reform 1 constitution 1 enlargement 1 withdrawal	Average 62% Yes 9 x No 32 x Yes	Average 67% –83: 70.2 –93: 73.9 –03: 63.3	17 countries with specific majority requirements	Top-down: 22 Bottom-up: 19	7 votes without constitutional basis

An analysis of this overview shows that:

- In a clear majority of the 25 "old" (8) and "new" (9) member states, citizens have been able to express their opinion directly on European integration.[16]
- More than a third of all the referendums have taken place in only three countries: Ireland and Denmark (six times each) and Switzerland (five).[17]
- On the average, more than two thirds of the electorate (67%) took part in the European referendums. This compares with an average 55.75% turnout in elections to the European Parliament since 1979.[18] Europe's citizens are clearly more interested in taking part in referendums on Europe than in elections to the European Parliament.
- Two issues dominate the list of referendums: membership accession to European institutions (27) and the reform of European treaties (10).
- Europe's citizens are being asked to vote more and more frequently. Nearly three quarters of all the referendums on Europe have been held since 1994.

Attention must be given to the design of referendums. The design of direct-democratic procedures and ballots and the manner of their incorporation into parliamentary decision-making processes are decisive for the quality of I&R procedures.[19] An analysis of the 47 referendums which have taken place so far reveals important divisions between:

---

16. To be added are: the separate referendum on EU accession in the Åland Islands, which belong to Finland, but which have autonomous status; the decision of the likewise autonomous Greenland to pull out of the EU; and the referendums on Europe in the non-member states of Norway, Switzerland and Liechtenstein.

17. The citizens of France, Norway and Liechtenstein have all voted twice. To date, the following have all had a single referendum: Great Britain, Italy, Austria, Finland, Sweden, the Åland Islands and Greenland.

18. 15 For a review cf. Turnout and electoral participation, by Richard Corbett (www.corbett-euro.demon.co.uk/turnout.htm). Since the introduction of direct elections to the European Parliament, participation has slipped by 13% from 62% to 49%. However, the geographical bases of the two average turnouts are only partly identical.

19. cf. "IRI Country Index on Citizen Lawmaking 2002," Andreas Gross and Bruno Kaufmann.

- Referendums which can be called by the majorities in power (plebiscites) — and those which can be initiated by a minority in society (popular initiative) or by parliament. Linked to this second category are the obligatory constitutional referendums, which are known in many countries.
- Referendums which are purely consultative (whose result those in power can accept or reject) — and those which are binding on the authorities (citizens' decisions).

Table 2: A survey of the existing/chosen procedures:[20]

	Non-Binding	Binding
Plebiscites	FR 1972 NO 1972, 1994 GB 1975 GL 1982 FI 1994 SE 1994 ÅL 1994 MT 2003 SE 2003	FR 1992 IRL 2002 DK 1986, 1993 SL 2003 HU 2003 LT 2003 SK 2003 PL 2003 CZ 2003 EE 2003 LV 2003
Initiative & Referendums	ITA 1989	CH 1997, 2000, 2001
Obligatory Referendums		IRL 1972, 1987, 1992, 1998, 2001 DK 1972, 1992, 1998, 2000 CH 1972, 1992 Liechtenstein 1992, 1995 Austria 1994 Romania 2003

From this table, we can see that:

- Two categories of referendum on Europe dominate: the obligatory constitutional referendum (15), which is always binding, and the consultation exercises initiated by government or parliament (22). To these we can add four citizen-initiated referendums.
- A clear majority of the votes on Europe were binding in nature (30), with the rest being consultative (11).

Over the period in question, the proportion of obligatory and binding referendums has steadily increased:

- 1972–1981: only two out of six cases were binding on government.
- 1982–1991: just 25% of all decisions were *de jure* binding on the executive.
- Since 1992: the proportion of binding referendum decisions has risen to 80% (16 out of 20).
- Since 1995: all the referendums on European integration, with the exception of Malta and Sweden, have been binding.

Conclusions:

- More and more people in more and more countries are able to participate in European politics in increasingly binding ways.
- The body of experience of direct democracy in relation to European issues is growing and confirms the general trend towards more direct participation at all political levels.[21]
- It has become a European norm to have a referendum on accession to the European Union.

---

20. Hug, Simon (2002), p. 44.
21. Between 1990 and 2000 the number of national referendums almost doubled compared to the number for the previous decade. Of the 405 documented national referendums worldwide, 78 were in the Americas, 37 in Africa, 26 in Asia and 16 in Oceania. The vast majority were in Europe: 248. cf. "IRI Country Index on Citizen Lawmaking 2002."

III. On the Building Site for a European Referendum Standard

A qualitative analysis of the 41 European referendums presents more difficulties than a merely quantitative one. Both as an institutional package and as a dynamic process, initiative and referendum can restrict the power of existing institutions, and as a result and for very simple reasons—as UN general secretary Kofi Annan observed in a recent UNDP report[22]—those in power frequently resist such a democratisation of democracy.

It therefore becomes necessary to make very clear the advantages which accrue to a modern representative democracy from a combination of indirect and direct institutions, compared to the traditional and dominant model of a purely parliamentarian democracy. Complementing indirect democracy by adding direct forms of co-determination can be considered "social innovation with beneficial economic consequences."[23] The benefits of this social innovation include: reduced alienation from politics, greater legitimacy and transparency, a greater identification of citizens with the policies introduced, and an increased capacity for learning in civil society. I&R is actually linked to an increase in per capita income and the efficiency of tax regimes (lower taxes and less tax avoidance).

In short, direct democracy can raise the quality of life of a society—provided that well-designed procedures have been chosen. For example, obligatory referendums and those resulting from citizen-initiated referendums produce more added social value than non-binding consultations.[24]

In relation to Europe and its integration process, Andreas Gross,[25] vice-president of the parliamentary assembly of the Council of Europe, listed the following among the advantages of direct democracy:

- It makes possible a new relationship between politicians and citizens: this includes a higher level of awareness and perception and an improved dialogue between the two groups.
- It strengthens the citizens' role in politics: as a result of confronting substantive issues on a regular basis, citizens become more competent, more highly motivated, and more ready to learn.
- It contributes to a strengthened force for integration. In relation to the EU, it can become a more efficient political counterbalance to the global economy.

Academics such as Simon Hug, Matthias Benz and Alois Stutzer have also tried to demonstrate a quantitative effect of the qualitative aspects of referendums. Hug[26] found that:

- In countries with obligatory referendums or referendums resulting from initiatives, European policies are in greater harmony with the wishes of the citizens than in countries using only plebiscites or in those with no instruments of direct co-determination at all.
- Referendums about Europe contribute over the longer term to increased support for the integration process.
- Governments of countries which have had referendums on Europe are in a better position to determine the agenda of treaty negotiations than countries which have never had referendums on Europe.

Benz and Stutzer[27] show that:

- Citizens are politically better informed when they have greater political participation rights. This is especially true for the European Union, where national governments act as European lawmakers and therefore occupy a dual position of power—and where, as a result, such core concepts of democracy as accountability, transparency and participation cannot be met in a satisfying manner.

But in order to achieve these positive effects, I&R processes must meet basic requirements of "freedom" and "fairness." "Free and fair" has become the catchphrase of UN officials, journalists, politicians and political scientists alike. But as Elklit and Svensson[28] ask, what actually constitutes a "free and fair" referendum? Since the Togoland independence referendum in 1956, hundreds of elections and referendums have been observed worldwide, intensifying the demand for

---

22. "Obstacles to democracy have little to do with culture or religion, and much more to do with the desire of those in power to maintain their positions at any cost. This is neither a new phenomenon nor one confined to any particular part of the world. People of all cultures value their freedom of choice and feel the need to have a say in decisions affecting their lives." UNDP Report 2002, Human Development Report 2002, Deepening democracy in a fragmented world, Oxford University Press, p.14.
23. cf. Direct democracies for transition economies, Bruno Frey, 2002. Collegium Budapest, Institute for Advanced Study project on "Honesty and Trust."
24. For a survey of the arguments and benefits cf. The process of democracy and state-building, Rolf Buchi, University of Helsinki (working paper), 2002.
25. "What Direct Democracy has to offer to the European integration process." Statement by Andreas Gross, Vice-president of the Council of Europe at the IRI conference in Berlin. cf. www.iri-europe.org.
26. "Voices of Europe: Citizens, Referendums and European Integration," Simon Hug, Rowman and Littlefield Publishers Inc., 2002.
27. Benz, Matthias and Stutzer, Alois, "Are Voters Better Informed When They Have a Larger Say in Politics?", Journal of Public Choice, December 2002.
28. Elklit, Jörgen and Svensson, Palle, "What makes elections free and fair?" in Larry Diamond & Marc F. latter, The Global Divergence of Democracies, The Johns Hopkins University Press, 2001, pp. 200–214.

standardized assessment criteria. However, the development of "checklists" has been hindered by disagreement over what should be included.[29]

There is a common understanding that referendum monitoring must include the whole process, not merely to the events of the actual election day or days. The preconditions for democratic referendums must not be ignored, leading Elklit and Svensson[30] to the following definitions:

- Freedom contrasts with coercion. It deals primarily with the "rules of the game," such as the legal/constitutional basis and the timing.
- Fairness means impartiality and includes consistency (the unbiased application of rules) and reasonableness (the not-too-unequal distribution of relevant resources among competitors).

In practice, these definitions lead us to more concrete monitoring parameters.

Freedom:
a) The ability to initiate a referendum process. Broad access to the process—not restricted to governing majorities—increases freedom.
b) The binding/consultative effect of a decision. Non-binding votes create the potential for manipulative actions by those in power.
c) The risk of invalidation of a vote by turnout and approval thresholds. High turnout requirements of up to 50% have undemocratic effects, as non- and "no"-voters are counted together. Such turnout requirements do not encourage voter participation, they discourage it.

Fairness:
a) The disclosure of donations and spending in a referendum campaign. This is the first step; a second is to apply spending limits; a third step is to introduce "affirmative action."[31]
b) Access to public media (broadcasters) before a referendum. There should be voluntarily agreed standards of fairness in the print media as well as free air hours/minutes to designated campaign organisations in a referendum process.[32]
c) The role of government and civil servants in a referendum debate. This has been a major concern in recent EU accession referendums, where EU Commission members regularly played a role in the debates.

The growing importance of initiative and referendum to the European integration process has led to an increased interest in monitoring referendums in Europe and to developing "European Referendum Standards." Think tanks such as the Robert Schumann Foundation in Paris,[33] as well as activist organizations such as "Democracy International" and the "European alliance of EU-critical movements: TEAM,"[34] have developed projects and criteria for assessing referendums. Official bodies such as the EU Commission[35] and the Council of Europe[36] have begun to discuss the creation of internal European observation missions as well as proper referendum standards. Other international monitoring agents, which until now have concentrated on electoral processes, are the International Institute for Democracy and Electoral Assistance (IDEA) in Stockholm, the United Nations Electoral Assistance Division, and the Democracy Agency ODHIR of the Organization for Security and Cooperation in Europe (OSCE).

For the Initiative & Referendum Institute Europe (IRI Europe), assessing the current EU accession referendums and developing European standards has become a top priority, which is now being implemented through the "IRI European Referendum Monitoring Program." Key elements of this program are conferences,[37] reports, and an IRI Europe Referendum Monitoring Team.[38]

---

29. Ibid, p.201.

30. Ibid, p.203.

31. In Sweden, the No-side in the September referendum on Euro accession will receive some extra tax money for their campaign from the pro-Euro government. The Swedish Foreign Ministry has published a booklet on the design of useful elements around an accession referendum, such as financial aid to both sides and non-partisan information (http://www.utrikes.regeringen.se/fragor/eu/pdf/publicawareness.pdf).

32. In this respect the Referendum Unit of the UK Electoral Commission has developed a comprehensive system of rules of conduct. Cf. electoralcommission.org.uk.

33. The Robert Schuman Foundation does have a designated European Elections & Referendum Monitoring Website with well-updated reports and articles: www.robert-schuman.org/anglais/oee/.

34. The Robert Schuman Foundation has a designated European Elections & Referendum Monitoring Website with well-updated reports and articles: www.robert-schuman.org/anglais/oee/.

35. DG Justice and Home Affairs, JAI.A.5, Citizenship, Charter of Fundamental Rights, Racism and Xenophobia, Programme DAPHNE

36. The Council of Europe (CoE) is running a democracy project whose main aim is to "to consolidate common European standards." http://www.coe.int/t/e/integrated_projects/democracy/. Also, the Coe Venice Commission is preparing a list of criteria for free and fair referendums.

37. A first conference was held in Sväty Jur (Slovakia) on June 20/21; a second took place in Tartu (Estonia) in September (25–27). For updates and reports check www.iri-europe.org.

38. Members of the this team were Karin Gilland, Ludo de Schutter, Thomas Rupp, Douglas Stewart, Palle Svensson, Jüri Ruus, Algis Krupavicius, Paul Carline, Andreas Gross and Bruno Kaufmann.

Table 3: A first assessment of the EU and Euro accession referendums held in 2003, in both their positive and negative aspects[39]

Country	Date/Result: yes	Main positive aspects	Main negative aspects
Malta	March 8; 53.6%	– Issue well known and debated for many years – 'Yes' and 'no' sides have access to media – Intense debate and public communication – Acceptance of result after confirmation at elections	– No legal rules of the game – Non-binding outcome – Almost non-existent I&R culture, but very strong two-party-system – Both sides try to interpret result in their own way – Confirmation of referendum outcome only – through elections
Slovenia	March 23; 89.6%	– Relatively well established initiative & referendum traditions (including citizen-initiated referendums) – Parliament confirmed de facto binding character before voting day	– EU accession did not fit into any legal form of referendum – Parliament, not legal framework, controls the process – Unequal access to media – 50% turnout quorum
Hungary	April 12; 83.8%	– Consultation process with electorate before the referendum (letter to all households) – Website in 15 languages on all relevant documents	– Very poor quality of debate by both 'yes' and 'no' sides – Disappointing turnout below 50% (estimate was 60–70%) – Prosecution of no-side by police units (for use of swastika)
Lithuania	May 11; 91.1%	– Relatively well established initiative & referendum traditions (including citizen-initiated referendums) – Fairness commission secures equal access to media (7 hrs. free air time for yes and no) – Almost no division in voting between urban areas and countryside	– Due to very little opposition to EU membership, critical aspects of EU membership are almost unknown, which could increase risk of public disillusion – Private companies try to influence turnout by offering cheaper goods to voters – 50% turnout quorum
Slovakia	May 17; 92.5%	– First valid referendum in modern Slovak history – Self-critical assessment by responsible officials after the referendum on conduct; new commission to improve I&R tools.	– High mutual distrust between electorate and political elite – Breach of laws on propaganda on referendum day – Government not ready to accept de jure binding character of poll before the referendum No-side promoted referendum boycott
Poland	June 8; 77.5%	–Constitutional changes to extend voting time (to 2 days) and to make EU referendums possible in future agreed before the vote – Lively and varied debate – No referendum boycotts – Demands to abolish 50% turnout quorum after the referendum	– Not clear what would have happened if 50% turnout quorum had not been met – Pope (is he still a Polish citizen?) used church institutions for yes-propaganda
Czech Republic	June 14; 77.3%	– First referendum experience in Czech history – Binding character of the vote without any turnout requirements President did not support one side	– Almost non-existent I&R culture, no tradition of participating even in parliamentary elections – High mutual distrust between electorate and political elite ("do not talk to communists" campaign)

---

39. This is a preliminary analysis and does not represent final assessment by IRI Europe. Every comment is most welcome: info@iri-europe.org. For a comprehensive documentation of the EU accession referendums, cf. IRI Europe Referendum Monitoring Reports, forthcoming, Amsterdam, 2003/2004.

Country	Date/Result: yes	Main positive aspects	Main negative aspects
Estonia	September 14;	– Broad debate as biggest party in parliament was against accession – Indirect financial contribution to no-side by the government – International assistance to both sides in campaign	– One-sided media coverage in favour of pro-camp – Unequal access to financial resources
Sweden	September 14	– High turnout in spite of consultative status – Intense and well balanced debate and campaign – 63% of voters felt the referendum was „fair" – non-citizens with resident permits could participate	– full respect by all parties only after the murder of foreign minister Anna Lindh – undisclosed campaign financing – referendum under full control of political majority – Prime minister indicated that he does not like having the people a say on the issue
Latvia	September 20	– Very high turnout in spite of internal political problems – Low-key propaganda in campaign	– Large part of population not able to vote due to huge population of non-citizens – Unequal access to campaign funding
Romania	October 19	– Mandatory referendum for change of constitution – Early preparations for EU accession in 2007	– Too short time for debate (only one month) – "Unfair" methods to secure turnout quorum of 50%

The overview shows the large diversity of preconditions and institutional requirements in the seven monitored countries. It is however possible to define a number of shared positive and negative aspects, which the referendums have in common:

+ The EU accession issue has been a top issue for many years in all countries.
- For this reason, however, the EU accession issue cannot be compared directly with other issues (such as the European constitution, for example).
+ The referendum processes have acted as a mirror for the countries concerned, showing more clearly the political, economic and societal progress achieved...
- but also revealing the big problems which still exist, such as the deep mistrust between elected and electors in these countries (with the exception of Malta).
+ In almost all cases, the outcome was decided by a clear majority and a majority of the electorate turned out for the vote, giving the frequently rather discredited referendum tool a new boost for the future and delivering a feeling of common identity in these states.
- However, the legal and political conditions for "free" and "fair" referendums are still not sufficiently developed and require major improvements before the upcoming referendums.

Finally, there is a consensus among observers, promoters, and opponents of EU membership that the existing I&R tools must be not abolished but improved. Working with its many cooperation partners, IRI Europe will do its utmost to contribute to such improvements.
Conclusions:

• I&R has great potential to deliver added value to democracy such as greater legitimacy, transparency, public communication, mutual understanding and, last but not least, integration of highly diversified societies.
• Realizing this potential depends ultimately on the concrete forms and practice; the growing number of referendums alone says little about the quality of these referendums.
• The EU accession referendums are a step forward, since they were successful in the eyes of most people in the new member states and all the referendums did meet the—often very problematic—requirements for validity.

IV. The Convention's Gift: A European Citizens' Initiative

After half a century of European integration, a Convention replaced the former secret diplomacy between states in February 2002, bringing for the very first time an air of transparency and a parliamentarian majority into European Treaty/Constitution-making. Indeed, the Convention assembly offered the possibility for everyone to follow the work, at least in part, even though the powerful presidium, with Valéry Giscard d'Estaing as an even more powerful chairman, did not meet in public.

The final result, presented in July 2003 to the EU heads of state and government in Thessaloniki, provoked highly differing opinions and immediately became the object of a passionate Europe-wide debate. *The* Economist wrote: "There was always a risk that the convention would not design a particularly good constitution. What was harder to imagine was that the convention would produce a text which would worsen the very problems it had been instructed to address. This is what it has somehow contrived to do. In many ways the draft constitution, more than 200 pages long, makes the Union's constitutional architecture harder to understand than it was before. That is an incredible feat."[40] Another European newspaper, the *Financial Times*, was far more positive in its judgment: the constitution was "not perfect but more than we could have hoped for" and "could sow the seeds of a much more federal Europe, where issues such as foreign affairs and law and order are decided on a European rather than a domestic basis and where elections to the much-mocked European parliament would be as important as any national vote."[41]

Even within the Convention Assembly, opinions on the outcome were much divided: for Göran Lennmarker, a Conservative Swedish parliament representative, it was evident that "there has been never more democracy than now."[42] His Danish neighbour Jens-Peter Bonde — one of the longest serving MEPs — had a rather different final comment: "The transfer of more decision making from member states to the Union, concerning criminal justice matters and new areas of domestic policy, will make the Union more remote."[43] Where the one sees giving more power to the common EU institutions as democratic progress, the other argues exactly the contrary. Neither of them has been especially concerned about the right of citizens to participate politically at the European level: Lennmarker even suggested cancelling the article on participatory democracy in the draft constitution.

Nevertheless, on the eve of the last Convention session, a citizens' initiative right was included in the draft constitution, giving citizens for the first time in history a direct-democratic tool at the transnational level. Reuters sent out this message early on June 13:

> "EU-FUTURE, RTE, Datum: 13.6. 00:48, Forum winds up work on historic EU constitution, by Gareth Jones, BRUSSELS, June 13 (Reuters) — Under one of the final amendments accepted by Giscard, EU citizens numbering at least one million spread across a 'significant' number of member states could petition the Commission to submit a proposal on matters where they thought the Union should act."

With this late adoption of a key demand by European democracy NGOs, the Convention opened a small window to transnational agenda-setting from below. It was the fruit of long and arduous work.[44]

The demand for greater and more effective involvement of citizens at the European level is not new. In 1949, before the founding of the EU's predecessor and the final demise of the Coal and Steel Union, Charles de Gaulle declared:

> "I think that the organization of Europe has to proceed from Europe itself. I consider that the start shall be given by a referendum of all free Europeans."[45]

A referendum as the definitive founding act of a political Europe! This is what the Italian European federalist Altiero Spinelli imagined, when in 1964 he proposed the creation of an EU constitution which would have to be ratified by the people in a referendum(s).[46] The supporters of de Gaulle's and Spinelli's ideas had to wait patiently until the time was ripe for more transnational direct democracy, and that did not happen until the end of the '80s.

Since 1988, the European Parliament or its Commission have expressed support for the introduction of direct-democratic elements at the European level in a series of resolutions. The often vaguely formulated resolutions refer to such ideas as "a parallel strategy to allow the popular will to express itself...by popular initiative referendum"[47] and the introduction of EU-wide popular consultations/opinion polls. In December 1993, the Public Liberty and Domestic Affairs Commission expressed its support for the introduction of a "European legislative referendum,"[48] as well as the possibility of citizens' ballots on "Community decisions."[49]

---

40. The Economist, June 21, 2003.
41. Parker, George and Dombey, Daniel, Financial Times, June 20, 2003. P.15.
42. 51st Convention Newsletter by the Democracy Forum, a euroskeptic group in the EP on June 18, 2003.
43. Bonde, Jens-Peter, Alternative Report, THE EUROPE OF DEMOCRACIES.
44. A detailed insider story on how the citizen initiative right finally found its way into the draft constitution is told by Michael Efler in "Transnational Democracy in the Making," IRI Europe, Amsterdam, 2003.
45. De Gaulle, Charles (1970). Discours et messages. Dans l'attente. Fevrier 1946–Avril 1958. Paris: Plon, Vol. II, p. 309.
46. Spinelli, Altiero, Una strategia per gli stati uniti d'Europa, Bologna: Societa editrice il Mulino.
47. EP (1988). Resolution on ways of consulting European citizens about the EU, Brussels: JO C 187/231.
48. EP institutional commission, DOC A2-0332/88.
49. EP Commission, DOC A3-0031/94.

Such impulses from the European Parliament helped to ensure that, before and during the Amsterdam governmental conference, the possibility of introducing a formal right of submission for EU citizens was considered. The then foreign ministers of both Austria (Schüssel) and Italy (Dini) proposed that 10 percent of the citizens in Europe, with signatures from at least three countries, could present a submission to the European Parliament which the Parliament was obliged to consider. This proposal, which was not backed at the governmental conference, did not provide for a subsequent referendum. In relation to the initiative rights which, under the present rules of the EU, belong exclusively to the Commission, the Petitions Committee has recently taken up the Schüssel/Dini proposal and argued for the current right of petition to be upgraded into a right of submission.[50]

After the dramatic changes of 1989 in Europe, NGOs and academic circles began to show more interest in the subject of transnational direct democracy. At more than 20 European meetings over 10 years, the European network organisation "Eurotopia," founded in May 1991, developed methods for involving citizens in a European constitutional process, as well as the first elements of direct democracy in such a constitution.

The appointment of a European Convention was already proposed in the mid-90s. A "double qualified majority" was proposed for the founding referendum on a European constitution: "The Constitution must be accepted not only by a majority of all EU citizens, but also by majorities of citizens in 4/5 of all EU member states."[51] From 1994 onwards, in the run-up to the Amsterdam governmental conference, numerous European NGOs formed a European network under the name of "Inter Citizens Conferences" (ICC): in the so-called "Loccum Declaration" they formulated a set of democratic requirements for a European Charter of Citizens' Rights. This included, for the first time, the right of submission to the European Parliament.[52]

In Germany in the late '90s, the activist NGO "Mehr Demokratie" started to develop a European strategy and concrete proposals. Within the NDDIE network (Network Direct Democracy Initiatives in Europe), which in 2002 changed its name to "Democracy International," a comprehensive set of I&R tools was devised, including a multi-stage right of initiative and an obligatory referendum for alterations to treaties.[53] The draft proposals emphasised that a "constitution is not a prerequisite for the establishment of direct-democratic rights in the EU."

Together with the Dini/Schüssel initiative proposal, the various NGO contributions paved the way for a debate inside and around the Convention on direct-democratic elements in the future EU constitution.[54] Finally a whole package of initiative proposals was launched in the Convention, including amendments by Alain Lamassoure (EPP-ED, France), Johannes Voggenhuber (Green/EFA-Austria), Josep Borell Fontelles (PES—Spain), Sylvia-Yvonne Kaufmann (GUE—Germany), Casper Einem (PES—Austria) and Jürgen Meyer (PES—Germany).

The Meyer proposal, signed by 77 members[55] of the Convention, and launched as I-46, part I, title VI (CONV 724/03) on June 12, managed to break down the last resistance in the Convention presidium and contributed to the late and welcome breakthrough:

"Art I-46 (4): "Citizens of the Union have the right to request the Commission":
"Citizens of the Union may request the Commission to submit any appropriate proposal on matters on which they consider that a legal act of the Union is required for the purpose of implementing this Constitution. Further provisions that particularly regulate the specific procedures and the numbers of signatures that have to be gathered are to be laid down in a European law."[56]

---

50. Koukiadis report, September 2002, Draft Report on European Citizens' Right of Petition, PE 308.157.

51. The Rostock Process, 1991–2004: "On the way to more direct democracy in Europe" (2001), p. 44.

52. Erne, Gross, Kaufmann, Kleger: "Transnationale Demokratie—Impulse für ein demokratisch verfasstes Europa" (Transnational democracy—Suggestions for a democratically constituted Europe'), Realotopia, Zurich (1995). p. 431ff.

53. The proposals are documented in the IRI Regional Forums chapter in "Transnational Democracy in the Making," 2003.

54. Upon invitation by the editors of this publication in cooperation with the (former) MEPs Heidi Hautala and Diana Wallis, as well as Michael Efler the Spokesperson for European Affairs in the German activist NGO "More Democracy," an "informal" Convention working group was founded including Eduarda Azevedo, Péter Balázs, Michel Barnier, Jens-Peter Bonde, John Bruton, Panayiotis Demetriou, Karel De Gucht, Gijs De Vries, Lone Dybkjaer, Alexander Earl of Stockton, Casper Einem, Douglas Stewart, Joschka, Fischer, Michael Frendo, Carlos Gonzalez Carnero, John Gormley, Sylvia-Yvonne Kaufmann, Alain Lamassoure, Jo Leinen, Linda Mc Avan, Iñigo Mendez de Vigo, Jürgen Meyer, Louis Michel, Alojz Peterle, Jacob Södermann

55. members: Akcam, Zekeriya; Amato, Guiliano; Andriukaitis, Vytenis; Athanasiu, Alexandru; Avgerinos, Paraskevas; Belohorska, Irena; Borrell Fontelles, Josep;Costa, Alberto Bernardes; Dam Kristensen, Henrik; De Rossa, Proinsias; Demetriou, Panayiotis; Dini, Lamberto; Duhamel, Oliver; Einem, Caspar; Fayot, Ben; Giannakou-Koutsikou, Marietta; Gricius, Algirdas; Haenel, Hubert; Helminger, Poul; Kaufmann, Sylvia-Yvonne; Kiljunen, Kimmo; Laborda, Gabriel Cisneros; Lequiller, Pierre; Marinho, Luis; Mavrou, Eleni; Oleksy, Jozef; Serracino-Inglott, Peter; Skaarup, Peter; Timermans, Frans; Vastagh, Pal; Voggenhuber, Johannes. alternates: Abitbol, William; Alonso, Alejandro Munoz; Arabadjiev, Alexandar; Basile, Filadelfio Guido; Berger, Maria; Budak, Necdet; Carey, Pat; Carnero Gonzalez, Carlos; D'Oliveira Martins, Guilherme; Eckstein-Kovacs, Peter; Ene, Constantin; Floch, Jacques; Fogler, Marta; Garrido, Diego Lopez; Giberyen, Gaston; Gormley, John; Grabowska, Genowefa; Katiforis, Giorgos; Krasts, Guntars; Kroupa,Frantisek; Lichtenberger, Evelin; Mac Gormick, Neil; Maclennan of Rogart, Lord; Matsakis, Marios; Nagy, Marie; Nazare Pereira, Antonio; Severin, Adrian; Sivickas, Gintauta Speroni, Francesco; Spini, Valdo; Styllanides, Evripides; The Earl of Stockton, Alexander; Vassilou, Androula; Vella, George.observers: Du Granrut, Claude; Sigmund, Anne-Marie; Sepi, Mario.

56. The amendment w as delivered to the presidium with an explanation: "The effect of the above proposal is to bring Europe closer to the people, as Laeken recommended. It represents a large step in the democratization of the Union. It will extend the existing right of petition to a right of the citizens to present legislative proposals to the Commission of the EU. The commission has then to decide whether it will take legislative activity or not. It is very important that the threshold for the signatures that are to be gathered for the European Citizens' Legislative Submission is not too high. A high threshold interferes with the process and effectively allows only powerful organizations the possibility of securing the required signatures."

This last draft amendment built the foundation for the final text in the constitution, presented by the Convention Chairman Giscard on June 13:

Citizen's Initiative — Art. I-46, p 4

A significant number of citizens, not less than one million, coming from a significant number of member states, may invite the Commission to submit any appropriate proposal on matters where citizens consider that a legal act of the Union is required for the purpose of implementing this Constitution. A European law shall determine the provisions regarding the specific procedures and conditions required for such a citizens' request.

As with other promising elements in the Convention's draft constitution (working methods, incorporation of the Charter of fundamental rights, increased transparency in the functioning of the Council), the new citizens' initiative right symbolises a departure from the old-style European Union with closed debates, horse-trading and narrow political considerations. In their actual content and in comparison with established democratic polities at local, regional and national levels, these seem to be very modest steps. Moreover, in October 2003 the governments of the member states will took over the baton.

In respect to the IGC, the very existence of the European citizens' initiative could be threatened by small member states[57] who may believe that "one million signatures" are far too many for their own citizens (the population of Malta is less than 400,000). This critique misjudges the aim and the proposed form of the "initiative right," as it is to be a device for transnational citizens' activities, and because the constitutional provisions demand that the signatures come "from a significant number of member states." Another danger is that proponents of I&R will oppose the new instrument because it will neither automatically trigger a lawmaking process in the EU nor bring about a citizen-initiated referendum.[58] Thus, there was a risk that the achievement of Art. 46.4 could fall between two stools during the IGC. As Heidi Hautala stresses in a contribution to "Transnational Democracy in the Making,"[59] "governments should not be left alone to deliberate on the citizens' right of initiative."

For this reason it was important to start a qualitative debate on the "Citizens' Initiative Right" and to use the generally positive reception of the new instrument to develop it in a citizen-friendly manner, as Victor Cuesta writes in the first IRI Europe assessment of Art. 46.4.[60]

In order to be able to place the new citizens' initiative into a realistic context of development, we have to define what such a European initiative could deliver and what not. Moreover, we have to list the most important criteria which will be decisive for the success of the new tool:

- The European citizens' initiative (ECI) tool is very different from popular initiative rights in countries like Switzerland, Italy or Slovenia. The ECI cannot trigger any referendums. Even the power to trigger proper lawmaking will be filtered through the EU Commission. This is the consequence of the particular structure of the EU, which limits the direct initiative right to the Commission.
- As a step on the way from collective petitions, which are already a frequently used citizens' instrument in the EU, towards full rights to initiate lawmaking and referendums, the ECI could, and perhaps should, be directed through the Parliament to the Commission. The EP could use its informal right of initiative established in Maastricht.
- The ECI will work as a statutory initiative without the possibility of proposing changes to the EU constitution. At the same time, it should be possible to use the ECI also for non-legislative acts such as regulations and recommendations.
- In its initial form, there are very few other restrictions in the ECI (such as the exclusion of certain issues or the form in which the initiative must be presented). In an international comparison of indirect citizen initiatives, the ECI is actually rather user-friendly, requiring only 0.15% of the signatures of the EU electorate.[61]
- With respect to the territorial distribution of the signatures, the Convention has specified that the signatures must come from a "significant number of states." If the EU applies the so-called Massachusetts model (no more than 25% from one county), then the signatories must come from at least five different countries. This hurdle is important to achieve the transnational dimension of the ECI.

---

57. In the Commission for European Affairs of the Finnish parliament ("stora utskottet") such concerns have already be formulated.

58. In the d-europe newsgroup a direct-democracy activist from Bulgaria wrote: "I would vote No to the draft constitution because I don't see real participatory rights in there but only right to beg. The participatory democracy granted by the founding fathers is reduced to participation ONLY in exchange of views, dialogue and consultations but NOT in decision-making..."

59. Hautala, Heidi. "From the petition to the initiative," in Kaufmann et al. "Transnational Democracy in the Making."

60. Cuesta, Victor, "Guide to the future European Citizen Initiative" in Kaufmann et al. "Transnational Democracy in the Making," 2003.

61. Cuesta's comparison shows that indirect initiatives require a bigger part of the electorate in most countries: Latvia 10%, Lithuania 1.47%, Austria 1.23%, Poland 0.25%, European Union 0.15%, and Italy 0.08%.

The experience in many countries is that I&R devices do not work very well because their design is not user-friendly, with high thresholds and the exclusion of important issues from the process. For this reason, it is very important to define and develop the legal provisions for securing the functionality of the new instrument. Using the IRI Europe Country Index on Citizen Lawmaking[62] and Victor Cuesta's assessment in "Transnational Democracy in the Making," we have made a first list of design elements, Convention proposals, and possible developments:

Table 4: Developing the European Citizens' Initiative

Design element	Convention proposal	Possible development
ENTRY HURDLES How many signatures of electors do I have to collect in order to launch an initiative?	"A significant number of citizens, not less than one million"	1,000,000 signatures = 0.2% of all residents in the future enlarged EU (480 million inhabitants)
TIME LIMITS How much time do I have to collect these signatures?	"A European law shall determine the provisions regarding the specific procedures"	8–16 months (in order to allow also the less powerful actors to carry through an initiative process)
LIST OF EXCLUDED ISSUES How many political issues are excluded from the direct-democratic decision making process?	"on matters where citizens consider that a legal act of the Union is required for the purpose of implementing this Constitution"	None. (As the European Citizens' Initiative is limited to the Commission's competences, no further exclusion of issues is advisable.)
TERRITORIAL DISTRIBUTION From how many member states must the signatories come? What is the maximum share of signatures from one country?	"from a significant number of member states"	5–8 states in order to promote the transnational dimension of the initiative issues (the Massachusetts model makes the requirement that no more than 25% of one million signatures can come from any single member state)
COLLECTION AND VERIFICATION OF SIGNATURES How can I collect the signatures? Is there a free collection of signatures with subsequent official verification, or do citizens have to sign in local authority offices and/or under legal supervision?	"A European law shall determine the provisions regarding the specific procedures"	Collection of signatures should be as free as possible, including electronic methods (internet). Verification should be done by member states' administrations by taking random samples.
ROLE OF PARLIAMENT The direct and indirect forms of democracy need to be linked by having the parliament debate all initiatives and giving it the possibility to present counter-proposals.	"may invite the Commission"	European Parliament should have a role in the European citizens' initiative process, without however having the right to stop an initiative.
INFORMING THE ELECTORATE A great deal of effort should be made to ensure that voters are properly informed on the issues and that these can be adequately debated. As an absolute minimum, a voter pamphlet should be provided.	"A European law shall determine the provisions regarding the specific procedures"	A registered citizens' initiative should receive some basic structural resources from the EU to fulfill its mission. A verified and valid citizen initiative should in addition get the resources to inform the whole EU electorate on the law proposal.
FORMAL REQUIREMENTS AND LEGAL STATUS OF INITIATIVE COMMITTEE	"appropriate proposal"	Draft European law. The initiative committee should have the right to withdraw the initiative (if, for example, the EP introduces legislation which partly meets the demand).

As long as the ECI is highly dependent on the goodwill of the EU commission, some sort of "affirmative action" will be necessary in order to build trust for the new tool among the European electorate. The commission has the ambition to present a draft law on the ECI as soon as the new constitution is ratified by the member states.

---

62. Gross & Kaufmann, "IRI Europe Country Index on Citizen Lawmaking," Amsterdam, 2002, p. 5f.

V. The Prospects for a Europe-Wide Constitutional Referendum

In summer 2003 the Convention on the Future of Europe not only adopted a draft constitution, including the already famous Art. 46.4 (citizens' initiative right), but also took note of a resolution signed by 97 Convention members, alternates, and observers, demanding a Europe-wide constitutional referendum on the same day as next year's elections to the European Parliament:

> "We propose that the Convention recommend to the Inter-Governmental Conference that the draft European Constitution be approved not only by National Parliaments and the European Parliament but also by the citizens of Europe in binding referendums. These referendums should take place in accordance with the constitutional provisions of the member states. They should be held simultaneously on the same day, an option being the same day as the European Parliament Elections in June 2004. Those member states whose constitutions do not currently permit referendums are called upon to hold at least consultative referendums. An information campaign must be publicly funded."[63]

Like the "European Citizens' Initiative," the "Europe-wide Constitutional Referendum" proposal was part of a comprehensive development and lobby effort coordinated by IRI Europe and More Democracy/Democracy International within the Convention and backed by the "European Referendum Campaign" in many countries. On June 13 the referendum resolution was signed not only by 97 Convention members from 26 countries, but also by 120 non-governmental organizations from 25 different countries.[64]

The strong support for the referendum resolution in the Convention, including the chairman of the Presidium Valéry Giscard d'Estaing and his deputy Giuliano Amato, can be interpreted as a strong signal to the EU member states in favor of extending the power of ratification to the citizens.

In contrast to the explicitly drafted "Citizens' Initiative," the "Europe-wide Constitutional Referendum" (ECR) was only "adopted" implicitly, as the Convention did not want to interfere directly with the member states' power of deciding how EU Treaties are ratified.

Nevertheless, this call by the Convention and the "European Referendum Campaign" has also been heard by the governments. Besides the three countries which already have some tradition of treaty ratification by the citizens (Denmark, Ireland and France), the prime ministers of other member states without such traditions—such as Portugal, Spain and Luxembourg—have already announced constitutional EU referendums:

> "It's desirable that the ratification of the next Union treaty be preceded by a national referendum that involves all Portuguese in this debate and in this decision," said Durao Barroso, the Prime Minister of Portugal.[65]

> "José María Aznar quiere que la Constitución Europea sea sometida a referéndum en todos los países de la Unión el mismo día que se celebren los comicios europeos: el 13 de junio de 2004."[66]

> "In Luxemburg können die Bürger über die Europäische Verfassung entscheiden. Nach einem Kabinettsbeschluss vom Freitag soll im Verlauf des kommenden Jahres ein Referendum stattfinden. Damit unterstreiche die Regierung, welche Bedeutung sie der Europäischen Verfassung beimesse, sagte Ministerpräsident Jean-Claude Juncker."[67]

A second group of heads of governments has more cautiously indicated the possibility of a constitutional referendum in their countries next year, including Austria, Belgium and Finland:

> "Schüssel machte am Rande des EU-Gipfels allerdings auch klar, dass er sich nicht sperren würde, wenn sich tatsächlich alle anderen zu einer europaweiten Volksabstimmung bekennen würden."[68]

---

63. The text of the resolution was submitted to the Convention presidium as "Contribution 291" by Alain Lamassoure and 36 other Convention members, alternates and observers on March 31, 2003.

64. For a detailed description of these efforts see Thomas Rupp's articles on the European Referendum Campaign in "Transnational Democracy in the Making."

65. "Portugal PM calls for referendum on EU charter," Reuters, June 12, 2003.

66. "Aznar quiere someter a referéndum en los comicios europeos la Constitución de la UE", ABC, Madrid, April 12, 2003. ("José Maria Aznar wants the European Constitution to be submitted to referendum in all the EU countries on the same day as the next EP elections: 13 June 2004")

67. "Luxemburger sollen über EU-Verfassung abstimmen", Associated Press, June 27, 2003. ("In Luxembourg, the citizens will be able to decide on the European Constitution. The Cabinet decided on Friday that a referendum should be held sometime in the coming year. Prime Minister Jean-Claude Juncker said that this demonstrated how much importance the government attached to the European Constitution").

68. "EU-Verfassung: Konflikt um Volksabstimmung," Die Presse, Wien, June 24, 2003. ("Schüssel indicated during the EU Summit that he would not oppose it, if everyone else were to support a Europe-wide referendum.")

"De kans is echter klein dat er een volksraadpleging komt. Premier Guy Verhofstadt ken enkel een referendum aanvaarden als alle lidstaten daaraan deelnemen."[69]

"Vanhanen har föreslagit att Finland ordnar en folkomröstning om EU:s nya grundlag."[70]

A third group of political leaders has tried to exclude the possibility of a constitutional referendum on Europe. This group includes the prime ministers of Slovakia and Sweden and Britain's chief representative in the Convention:

"Our constitution clearly says that a referendum is needed only when we enter a state formation," Dzurinda said, adding that a mandate had been given by the recent referendum on the EU Treaty in Slovakia.[71]

"Den svenske statsminister, Göran Persson, sagde i dag, at der ikke vil blive holdt nogen folkeafstemning i Sverige om den nye EU-forfatning, som nu er under udarbejdelse."[72]

"Labour aims to kill off calls for a referendum on the future of the EU by ensuring the forthcoming restructuring of Europe is mainly a tidying up-exercise," Britain's chief negotiator, Peter Hain, predicted.[73]

The readiness to take note of the referendum issue is impressive. Political leaders have not traditionally been keen to let the people decide, and thus to surrender political control to the citizens. And it is no coincidence that in both Sweden and Britain, where public opinion has forced a referendum on the Euro, the governments are now trying by any means possible to avoid a constitutional EU referendum. The same may be true of the new member states, as is shown by the early "no to a referendum" statement of the Slovak PM Dzurinda.

Just a decade ago, all these countries in which the people now have the opportunity to make a major decision on Europe would still have tried to enter the EU by decision of parliament alone. Today's Europe is fortunately different: EU accession decisions by referendum have become the norm, and we can now witness how European reform decisions by referendum are also about to become the norm.

Few Legal Hurdles, Big Political Challenges

As we have seen in Part Two of this survey ("47 Referendums on Europe"), only three member states, Denmark, Ireland and France, have used the referendum tool for the ratification of treaty reform. But changing the EU from a treaty structure to a constitutional structure means that its new "Basic Law" becomes a natural issue for a referendum in many more countries, where new constitutions and constitutional amendments are subject to referendum (Austria, Estonia, Hungary, Italy, Latvia, Lithuania, Poland and Slovenia). For all the other states, as the German Federal Bureau for Convention Issues pointed out:

"There are neither legal obligations to hold a referendum, nor are there insurmountable legal obstacles in the way of citizens' referendums: as a consequence the political room for maneuver is completely wide open."[74]

A first assessment in 2002 of the prospects for constitutional referendums in the member states revealed the following:

- In a majority of present and future member states—17 out of 25—the prospects for participating in a European referendum can be rated either "good" or "very good." Most of the countries in the "very good" category are medium to small countries.
- The prospects in the large (in part "future") member states, such as France, Germany, Great Britain, Spain, and Poland, are "average" to "good." That means that there are certain legal and/or political problems, but these can be solved.
- In three countries there are serious legal and/or political problems in the way of a European referendum: to this group belong the founder country—Belgium—and the two candidate states Malta and Cyprus.[75]

---

69. "Lidstaten morrelen aan ontwerp Europese grondwet," De Morgen, June 21, 2003.
70. "En skarp men färglös doldis," Hufvudstadsbladet, Helsinki, June 25, 2003.
71. "Dzurinda: Referendum on Constitution not necessary," News Agency of the Slovak Republic, Bratislava, June 20, 2003.
72. "Persson: Ingen svensk folkeafstemning om EU-forfatning," Berlingske Tidende, København, May 27, 2003.
73. "Hain plays down any poll on EU future," The Guardian, May 14, 2003.
74. Report on the prospects for a European Referendum (draft); Office of the German Parliament.
75. Hautala, Kaufmann and Wallis: "The European Referendum Challenge," IRI Europe, 2002, Amsterdam, p. 15

These findings were confirmed and complemented by a study undertaken by the German NGO Mehr Demokratie in June 2003.[76] This report reveals that many member states, especially former Soviet republics like Lithuania, Latvia, and Estonia, have extremely high hurdles for delegating sovereignty to supranational bodies. In Lithuania, for example, Article 148.1 specifies a 75% approval quorum of the electorate in a referendum for the delegation of sovereignty, making such a decision totally unrealistic.[77] For this reason, in Lithuania and in other countries which are still suffering to a certain extent from the trauma of totalitarianism—like Germany or the Netherlands—new laws have been introduced or proposed to make a "constitutional EU referendum" in 2004/2006 legally possible.[78]

One cultural problem with the Convention/civil society demand for a "Europe-wide Constitutional Referendum" is the fact that no common transnational standards for introducing or amending constitutions yet exist. A recent study by IRI advisory board member Dag Anckar and his colleague Lauri Karvonen at Åbo Akademi, Finland, reveals the high diversity of ways in which constitutions are amended.[79] With the help of the data in this study, we can group the 25 EU states according to the degree of power citizens have in constitution making (Table 5):

Table 5: Citizen Influence on Constitution Making in the Member States of the European Union

Level of influence is...	Countries	Methods to adopt & amend constitution
...fairly strong	Denmark, Latvia, Malta, Poland, Slovenia, Spain, (Romania)	Parliament: Qualified majority / Referendum: Simple majority
...fairly good	France	Parliament: Simple majority / Referendum: Simple majority
...rather modest	Austria, Belgium, Cyprus, Czech Republic, Estonia, Finland, Germany, Greece, Hungary, Italy, Lithuania, Luxembourg, Netherlands, Portugal, Slovakia, (Bulgaria)	Parliament: Qualified Majority / Referendum: Not required
...rather weak	Britain, Sweden[80]	Parliament: Simple majority / Referendum: Not required

Table 5 further explains our assessment of the prospects for a "Europe-wide Constitutional Referendum" in the 25 member states until 2006. It is important to underline that a "rather strong" influence on constitution-making does not automatically lead to a constitutional EU referendum, as the political leadership may avoid calling the adoption of the new treaty a constitution at all. It is obvious that the extent to which the ratification process for the new EU treaty/constitution will be the subject of referendums will depend on the political dynamics around the IGC and the level of pressure such institutions as the Convention and the EP, in partnership with European civic society, will be able to produce. The task of IRI Europe in this process will be to provide facts and assessments as well as tools for developing European standards of constitution making for the people and by the people.

Before we look at possible design options for a "Europe-wide Constitutional Referendum," we will assess the current prospects for the referendums to really take place in the 25 old and new member states of the European Union.

76. Efler, Michael, "Volksentscheid über die EU-Verfassung—Verfassungsrechtliche Vorschriften und politische Situation in den Mitglieds- und Beitrittsländern." Mehr Demokratie, Berlin, 2003. (www.mehr-demokratie.de/bu/-pdf/studie_eu-ve.pdf). The "Mehr Demokratie" report is based on research by Marian Zdeb at democracy international: "Study of constitutional conditions and probability of referendums on the EU constitution in 25 European countries," Democracy International, Frankfurt, 2003. www.european-referendum.org/background/refsum.html.

77. "The provision of Article 1 that the State of Lithuania is an independent democratic republic may only be amended by a referendum in which at least three-fourths of the electorate of Lithuania vote in favor thereof." See Krupavicius, Algis, Country Report "Lithuania" in "Transnational Democracy in the Making."

78. In Germany such a proposal has been launched by the liberal group, proposing a special law for the constitutional EU referendum. Cf. Deutscher Bundestag, Drucksache 15/1112.

79. Anckar, Dag and Karvonen, Lauri. "Constitutional Amendments methods in the democracies of the world," Turku University, 2003.

80. However, in the Swedish case the two following parliaments also need a simple majority to amend the constitution, giving the citizens an opportunity for control at the elections.

Table 6: Prospects for Referendums on the New Eu Treaty/Constitution until 2006

Country	Factors in favour of a popular vote	Factors against a popular vote	Probability of popular vote as %	Probability of popular vote in a word	Trend (Early 2004)
Austria	• PM in favour if referendum in all countries • Opposition leader in favour • EU referendum experience	• Limited I&R tradition • PM not in favour if not all countries take part	60%	Open	Unsure
Belgium	• Ruling parties in favour of having a vote • Relatively strong I&R pressure groups	• Almost no I&R tradition or instruments • PM not in favour if not all countries take part	60%	Open	Unsure
Britain	• Growing use of I&R at local and regional level • Non-partisan pressure groups for constitutional referendum • Active media campaign in favour of a vote	• Despite devolution, still one of Europe's most centralized countries • Labour government blocked by internal deadlock on Euro accession	40%	Poor	Negative
Cyprus	• Possibly combined referendum on reunification and constitution • Support by Cypriot Convention members	• No I&R tradition or instruments • Due to the long period without peace on the island: strong leaders, weak citizens	30%	Very poor	Unsure
Czech Republic	• Positive experience with accession referendum, the first in Czech history • Support by ruling parties	• Only single experience with national referendum • Well-established mistrust between elected and electors	80%	Very good	Positive
Denmark	• Art. 20 in constitution demands mandatory referendum for bigger changes to EU Treaty • Government has already confirmed a popular vote		100%	OK	Positive
Estonia	• Depends on the outcome of the upcoming EU accession referendum • Roots of a well-developed I&R system (1918–1939)	• Nordic model of unitary state prevails today • If neighbours (Finland, Latvia) fail to have a vote, Estonia will not have one either	50%	Moderate	Unsure
Finland	• PM and part of government coalition in favour of a EU referendum • Growing importance of pressure group for I&R elements in the Finnish constitution	• Foreign Minister and parts of government are against referendums on principle • Very limited tradition of citizen participation in international affairs	70%	Good	Unsure
France	• Political elite in favour of having a referendum • Tradition of plebiscites on important constitutional questions	• President Chirac tries to avoid referendum • Very little pressure for more I&R in civil society	70%	Good	Positive
Germany	• Promoters in all political camps in favour of the constitutional referendum • Few fears of federal structure of the EU • Well-established regional I&R traditions	• Opponents in all political camps to a constitutional referendum (including the green Foreign Minister and the PM) • Historical misunderstandings used as argument against	50%	Moderate	Negative
Greece	• Government increasingly interested in participatory democracy • Support by Greek Convention members	• Political culture of post-dictatorship mistrust in society • No relevant links to ancient Athenian Agora	40%	Poor	Positive

Country	Factors in favour of a popular vote	Factors against a popular vote	Probability of popular vote as %	Probability of popular vote in a word	Trend (Early 2004)
Hungary	• Citizens groups can demand referendum by initiative • Important steps in international politics are ratified by referendum (Constitution, NATO, EU)	• EU accession not seen as a big success (low participation, poor debate) • No pressure groups for I&R reform in the country	60%	Open	Unsure
Ireland	• EC/EU Treaty reforms must be and have always been ratified by binding referendums		100%	OK	Positive
Italy	• Broad support for an EU constitutional referendum in parliament and government • Only country with EU constitutional referendum experience (1989 on a popular initiative!)	• Unfortunate 50% turnout quorum, which has made 18 out of 53 referendums since 1970 invalid (Law 352) • No referendum allowed on international treaties	70%	Good	Negative
Latvia	• Relatively strong traditions of I&R (8 national votes) • Depends on the outcome of the upcoming EU accession referendum • Constitution makes vote possibly necessary	• No support for European referendum in Convention delegation	80%	Very Good	Unsure
Lithuania	• Relatively strong traditions of I&R (11 national votes) • Positive experience with EU accession referendum	• EU Constitution is seen as a very remote subject to Lithuanian society • Fear of the political elite to lose EU membership again.	70%	Good	Positive
Luxembourg	• Government and parliament have already decided to have a referendum on the constitution	• Small risk of revising the referendum decision taken when the IGC result is known.	90%	Sure	Positive
Malta	• After a very hard fight between the two dominant political parties and another election, both sides accepted the popular decision • Labour opposition in favour of constitutional vote, nationalist government undecided	• Very limited I&R tradition and culture • Small society with very strong political parties	60%	Open	Unsure
Netherlands	• Most parties in favour of a vote • Growing importance of pressure group for I&R elements in the Dutch constitution	• One of the few countries in the world without any national referendum experience at all • Ruling rightist government against I&R	80%	Very good	Positive
Poland	• Positive experience with EU accession referendum • Ready to play an important role in the Union • Efforts to improve I&R instruments in the constitution	• Uncertain support for constitutional referendum in government and parliament • Little public pressure for a constitutional referendum	50%	Moderate	Positive
Portugal	• PM and government ready to put the EU constitution to a referendum • Lessons from unsuccessful EU referendum attempts in 1998	• Little I&R tradition & culture • Some risk of revising the referendum decision taken on June 27, 2003 when the IGC result is known	80%	Very good	Positive

Country	Factors in favour of a popular vote	Factors against a popular vote	Probability of popular vote as %	Probability of popular vote in a word	Trend (Early 2004)
Slovakia	• EU accession referendum conduct has been criticised by both 'yes' and 'no' sides • Right to launch an initiative campaign for EU referendum (12% of electorate)	• PM Dzurinda thinks that EU accession is already mandate for public EU constitution approval • Very large mistrust between politicians and citizens	50%	Moderate	Unsure
Slovenia	• Relatively strong traditions of I&R (7 national votes since 1991 • Possibility of launching an optional referendum with 40,000 signatures	• EU issues do not really fit into legal I&R structures, this gives the parliament more control • 50% turnout quorum uncontested	70%	Good	Unsure
Spain	• Consensus in government and parliament on having a referendum on the constitution	• PM Aznar not very reliable • Risk of revising the referendum decision after the IGC	80%	Very good	Positive
Sweden	• Culture of fairness in referendum processes • After EU accession, Euro membership also voted on by the people	• Ruling social democratic party against I&R on principle (exception: EU commissioner Wallström) • Little understanding for EU as a political community	40%	Poor	Unsure

We can now summarise the second IRI Europe assessment on the prospects for referendums on the EU constitution in the 25 member states of the European Union:

- The overall picture is surprisingly stable. We can forecast rather good referendum prospects in 17 out of 25 member states.[81]
- Expressed as a percentage, the average probability of referendums has risen 5% since 2002 to 65%.
- In the larger member states the referendum probability has risen (with the exception of Britain), whereas in the smaller member states there is a rather negative trend (with the exception of Portugal and Luxembourg). This may indicate that the larger member states are happier with the draft constitution than the smaller ones and, thus, that their governments are more willing to let the citizens decide.

This is our current IRI Europe Referendum Ranking List for a Constitution 2004 Vote in the 25 member states:

1. Ireland	6. Czech Rep.	11. Latvia	16. Hungary	21. Slovakia
2. Denmark	7. Netherlands	12. Slovenia	17. Estonia	22. Greece
3. Luxembourg	8. France	13. Austria	18. Poland	23. Sweden
4. Portugal	9. Italy	14. Belgium	19. Germany	24. Britain
5. Spain	10. Finland	15. Lithuania	20. Malta	25. Cyprus

Preliminary Considerations on the Design of a Europe-Wide Referendum

Assuming that there will be a popular vote on the new EU Treaty/Constitution in all 25 member states, there are a few known facts and many unknown possibilities to consider. As with other electoral and referendum processes, the democratic quality of such a super-referendum will depend on the rules of the game (freedom-dimension) and the conduct of the referendum process (fairness-dimension).

First the main fact. Since there is no legal basis for a European referendum at the European level and since the EU Convention has not proposed such a change in law, a possible Europe-wide vote will be held on the basis of the laws of the member states. European law is founded on uniformity: *de jure* the draft constitution will be rejected if only one referendum in a single member state produces a negative result.

Therefore, the first important question is: What happens if the majority of the voters in one member state say "no"?

To address this possibility, the Draft Constitution of the Convention has included the following article:

---

81. This result is not only confirmed by the Mehr Demokratie/Democracy International study quoted, but also by an assessment published by Time Magazine (June 1, 2003).

Article IV-7.4: Revision of the Treaty establishing the Constitution: If, two years after the signature of the Treaty establishing the Constitution, four fifths of the Member States have ratified it and one or more Member States have encountered difficulties in proceeding with ratification, the matter shall be referred to the European Council."

This article implies that the Constitution may be adopted and can enter into force even if up to five member states fail to ratify. In such an event, the European Council has to decide how to proceed. There seem to be three possible options:

- The Council may decide that the "difficulties encountered" are of a nature which may allow opt-out clauses and special arrangements with the countries concerned, after which a second EU constitutional referendum may be held in those countries. This has already been done: after the Danish "no" to the Maastricht Treaty in 1992, and after the Irish rejection of Nice in 2001.
- The European Council may decide not to adopt the Constitution at all and to continue with the Nice Treaty.
- The Heads of State and Government could decide to establish an inner circle of the 20+ member states which have ratified the constitution and an outer group of members who have not ratified (similar to the EEA Treaty for Norway, Iceland and Liechtenstein).

It is still very hard to see how these options might be carried out in practice. For the first time, however, the draft constitution opens the possibility of "entry into force" by qualified majority. Furthermore, the Convention's draft constitution also provides for the very first time for a right of withdrawal from the EU:

Article I-59: Voluntary withdrawal from the Union: Any Member State may decide to withdraw from the European Union in accordance with its own constitutional requirements. This Constitution shall cease to apply to the State in question from the date of entry into force of the withdrawal agreement.

The new withdrawal option makes it clear that the European Union is an "intentional" political community. Furthermore, the option enables withdrawal from the EU after failing, for example, to ratify a constitutional amendment in a referendum.

Articles IV-7.3 (4/5 majority) and I-59 (withdrawal) of the draft constitution do not provide any specific instruments for a future European referendum, but neither do they create any new hurdles for such a popular vote in the EU.

As Jürgen Meyer and Sven Hölscheidt outline in an article for "Transnational Democracy in the Making," there are three possible steps to a European Referendum method:[82]

- Step One: national referendums (in accordance with their own requirements) on the constitution in as many member states as possible on the same date (the same day as the EP elections is proposed) = this would be the Europe-wide EU constitutional referendum recommended by the Convention/Civil Society resolution.
- Step Two: a Europe-wide referendum (with simple majority, but held in accordance with the requirements of the individual member states; similar in system to the EP elections) in addition to the country-by-country ratification, which may be done by parliament or by popular vote = this would be a combination of a pan-European and a country-by-country ratification process and would imply a double (possibly even qualified) majority regime.
- Step Three: a European referendum. In such a referendum the votes would be counted twice. First, a majority of all participants would be counted and then a (possibly qualified) majority of the votes in the member states = this model of double majority referendums is well known in federal polities such as Switzerland and Australia.[83]

It is not at all sure today whether the EU constitutional referendum(s) in the next few years will even fulfill the basic requirements of Step One: referendums in all member states on the same day as the next EP elections. In addition, there are countries like Britain, where referendums on the same day as elections are forbidden.[84] However, the very strong trend towards more direct democracy by initiative and referendum offers an opportunity for developing the way towards "fair" and "free" referendums at the EU level as well. As with popular votes within countries, consideration should be given to the IRI Europe Referendum Draft Checklist:

---

82. Meyer, Jürgen and Goldschmidt, Sven, "Three ways to organize a European wide constitutional referendum," in "Transnational Democracy in the Making."

83. Andreas Gross proposes in his contribution to "Transnational Democracy in the Making" to establish the following double majority requirement in a Europe-wide referendum: simple majority of the voters, 2/3 majority of the member states.

84. For an overview of the reasons for/against having referendums combined with elections see Nigel Smith's contribution to "Transnational Democracy in the Making."

a) Legal and Constitutional Basis: Trigger function? Binding/consultative? Quorums/thresholds? Compulsory voting? Registration (citizens/non-citizens)? Secrecy of ballot? Appeal against the result? Counting procedures? Voting: how, where (mail, e-voting)?

b) Timing: Who sets the date? One day or more? Weekend, weekday? Length of time between announcement and ballot day? Referendum on same day as other votes/elections? "Domino effect" on other countries? Designated time period before another vote may be held on the same subject?

c) Financial rules: Spending limits? Disclosure? "Affirmative action" to help underfunded campaigns? Transparency in use of tax money?

d) Campaign rules: Managed by referendum commission or another independent body? The role of the media: focused primarily on "latest poll," not debating the issues? International interference? Role of government, civil servants, political parties? Do the rules enhance the culture and practice of democracy?

Chapter Three

Country-by-Country Overview

Austria

The I&R laws of 1958 and 1963 were enacted as a result of public pressure when the majority coalition of the ÖVP (Austrian People's Party) and the SPÖ (Social Democratic Party) was seen as unresponsive to citizens' demands.

Since 1964, 27 out of 29 citizens' initiatives have reached the required threshold to oblige their consideration by the first chamber of parliament (National Council/Nationalrat), but only three of the "formally successful" initiatives have been converted into legislation.

To date there have been two national referendums: in 1978 on a national law about the peaceful use of nuclear power (result: decision to prevent the Zwentendorf nuclear power station from going on-stream) and in 1994 the constitutionally mandatory referendum on the law allowing Austria's accession to the European Union.

- Population: 8,139,000
- Area: 83,858 km²
- Capital: Vienna (Wien)
- Official languages: German (92%); in some districts/regions: Slovenian, Croatian
- Religion: Roman Catholic (78%), Muslim (5%), Protestant (5%)
- Political System: Republic (since 1918), federal structure with nine autonomous regions (Bundesländer)
- Constitution: October 1, 1920 (without Referendum)
- Membership: EU
- GNP/Capita: $26,730
- Human Development Rank: 16
- I&R practice: two nationwide referendums (since 1945); 29 citizens' initiatives (since 1964); 27 reached threshold.

Types of Initiative and Referendum

I. National Level

At the national level, Austria has the referendum, the popular/citizens' initiative and the popular consultation/consultative referendum.

a. Compulsory Referendum
A referendum is obligatory if:

- a proposal for a complete or partial revision of the constitution has been submitted by at least one third of the members of the National Council (the first chamber of the Parliament), or
- a majority of the National Council decides to submit a law to a national referendum. A referendum is not possible on the basis of a referendum initiative; i.e. even an appropriately supported popular initiative does not automatically lead to a referendum.

b. Popular Initiative (Petition)
The subject of a Citizens' Initiative (C.I.) must be a proposal relating to a law. To be launched, it requires a minimum of about 8,000 signatures of registered voters (0.1% of the population), who must be Austrian citizens. The signatures are given at the local authority offices and must be verified by the production of an identity card.

A C.I. submission does not have to be precisely formulated; the final wording is determined by the Ministry of the Interior on the basis of the submission or proposal which has been presented. A C.I. proposal can be submitted by a group of voters or by a political party organization. Since 1999, it is no longer possible for a proposal to be submitted by members of the National Council.

Once the required minimum of about 8,000 signatures has been collected, the Interior Ministry decides on the period of time to be allowed for the general collection of signatures. It is open to any Austrian citizen whose main place of residence is Austria to support the initiative (proof of identity by identity card/passport is required).

C.I.s which succeed in gaining more than 100,000 signatures must be considered by the National Council. However, the N.C. is not obliged to change an existing law or enact a new one as a result of a C.I.: from 1964 until August 2002, only three of 27 "formally successful" C.I.s had been converted into law. A "Welfare State" (Sozialstaat) C.I., initiated by a non-partisan committee for the purpose of having the "welfare state principle" formally inscribed in the Austrian constitution, received 717,000 signatures (12.2% of the electorate) in April 2002. However, like the "Temelin Veto" initiative of January 2002 launched by the FPÖ (Freiheitliche Partei Österreichs), which gained 915,000 signatures, the "Welfare State" initiative will not become law.

The most recent popular initiative, a constitutional law against the purchase of interceptor planes, was initiated by a small extra-parliamentary group and gained 625,000 signatures (10.7% of the electorate) in July and August 2002. The government, however, had decided some weeks before to buy new interceptor planes, and calls for a referendum by the opposition Socialist and Green parties were not accepted.

A C.I. must be a law-making submission to the National Council. Other than this, there are no restrictions as to content or subject matter. There are no limits to the number of C.I.s which can be submitted in any year or any legislative period.

c. Popular Consultation/Consultative Referendum

According to Article 49 of the Austrian Constitution, a popular consultation can be launched by a decision of the National Council or of the national government "on a subject of fundamental and national significance within the competence of the national legislature." This instrument has so far never been used in Austria. Although the coalition government (of the ÖVP and FPÖ) decided in September 2000 to initiate a consultation on lifting the measures taken against Austria by the other 14 EU member states (resulting from the participation of the FPÖ in the government), the subsequent decision of the "White Book" to lift the sanctions forestalled its implementation.

II. Regional Level

In eight of Austria's nine federal regions ("Länder")—the sole exception is Salzburg—citizens have the right to submit proposals for legislation (Volksbegehren), and most of them also have provisions for consultative referendums on matters of state (Land) governance. Legislative proposals require the signatures of between 2% and 5% of the electorate; consultative referendums, between 2% and 11% of the electorate.

In only two of the states, Upper Austria and Styria, does a sufficiently well-supported C.I. (10–11% of the electorate) automatically lead to a referendum. Referendums resulting from decisions of the state (regional) parliaments (Landtag) are possible in all the states, but they are rarely used.

III. Local Level

At the local (communal) level, there is neither referendum nor C.I., since the communes have no legislative competence. However, all states have consultative referendums on issues of communal politics which can be launched by a decision of the local council or as an initiative by a small percentage of the local residents. Only in rare cases (e.g. on a proposal to amalgamate communes) is the result of a consultative referendum binding.

IV. Practical Guide

Citizens do not have the right to launch a referendum by means of a citizens' referendum initiative. A popular initiative (Volksbegehren) must be submitted to the National Council in the form of a specific legal proposal. The initiative committee has to define the aim of the initiative and submit a text for legislation, and the intention to launch an initiative is conveyed to the Interior Ministry.

Reaching the minimum of about 8,000 signatures necessary to officially launch the popular initiative requires the cooperation of several initiative groups, the support of the mass media, and/or the support of a political party. There is no financial support from the state for those launching a popular initiative.

Referendum, popular initiative and consultative referendum are all anchored in the national constitution (Articles 43, 44 and 60 for the national referendum; Articles 41 and 42 for the popular initiative; Article 49 for the consultative referendum), and referendum and popular initiative have been constitutionally guaranteed since 1920. However, the appropriate enabling laws were passed only in 1958 (for the national referendum) and 1963 (for the popular initiative), and there have been various amendments, most recently in 1999, to the law enabling popular initiatives. The law establishing the consultative referendum was passed in 1989 along with other constitutional amendments.

V. Trends

Public pressure from the mass media and criticism from scientists and reformist politicians led to the referendum and popular initiative laws of 1958 and 1963. The criticism was caused by the growing indecisiveness of the majority coalition of the ÖVP (Austrian People's Party) and the SPÖ (Austrian Socialist Party) and by the stagnation of the political system, which reformers hoped to counter by promoting more direct democracy. During the 80s and 90s, the opposition FPÖ and Green parties supported the extension of direct democracy, and the FPÖ demanded the establishment of a right to a referendum initiative.

The February 2000 manifesto of the ruling ÖVP/FPÖ coalition does in fact provide for the introduction of the referendum initiative: if a popular initiative (Volksbegehren) is supported by at least 15% of the electorate, a national referendum becomes mandatory—unless, within 9 months after this threshold is reached, the National Council has introduced legislation which implements the content of the initiative. However, the coalition also proposes to restrict the subject matter of the popular initiative by removing from its compass constitutional changes, EU and other international obligations, and issues which would commit the country to extra expense or would affect national rights. Since the opposition SPÖ and Green parties are against these restrictions, it will be impossible to achieve the two-thirds parliamentary majority which is required to ratify any change to the national constitution.

There have been very few opinion polls to test general attitudes to direct democracy within Austria. The most recent poll known to the author dates from December 1997 (Institut fuer empirische Sozialforschung, N=2,000). 58% of those polled stated that they felt able to pursue their interests either very well or well through referendums and popular initiative. 55% of them had already taken part in a popular initiative, and 31% said that they would do so again. 63% agreed with the statement that being able to vote regularly and directly on important issues was more important than electing representatives.

To date there have been two national referendums: in 1978 on a national law about the peaceful use of nuclear power (result: decision to prevent the Zwentendorf nuclear power station from going on-stream) and in 1994 the constitutionally mandatory referendum on the law allowing Austria's accession to the European Union (result: agreement to accession).

Since 1964, 27 out of 29 popular initiatives have reached the required threshold to oblige consideration by the National Council (before 1981 this was 200,000 signatures; after 1981, 100,000). The level of support varied from 1.3% of the electorate to 25.7%. Only three initiatives in the 1960s actually became law, two of them due to the fact that the SPÖ, which had hitherto been in opposition, came to power in 1970 and was able to implement its demands.

The reason popular initiatives have generally failed to achieve practical success is that their support normally comes from opposition parties or extra-parliamentary groups; the parliamentary majority of the ruling parties does not support legislative initiatives from the opposition, which are frequently aimed at attacking government policy. Popular initiatives primarily serve the function of stimulating debate on political issues which are being ignored by the government, or of heightening the political profile of opposition parties or extra-parliamentary groups.

One exception to this general rule was the popular initiative against the Temelin nuclear power station in the Czech Republic, which was launched by one of the ruling parties—the FPÖ—against the wishes of its coalition partner, the ÖVP, and which succeeded in obtaining the support of 15.5% of the electorate in January 2002. However, the content of the initiative will not be implemented, since there is no parliamentary majority in favor of making the Czech republic's accession to the EU conditional on shutting down Temelin. Under the current laws, popular initiatives launched solely by extra-parliamentary groups have no realistic chance of becoming law.

Main author: Christian Schaller

Constitutional Requirements for Legislation

Chapter 1: General Provisions
Part D: Federal Legislative Procedure
Article 41 (Bills):
(1) Legislative proposals are submitted to the House of Representatives either as motions by its members or as Federal Government bills. The Senate can propose legislative motions to the House of Representatives through the Federal Government.

(2) Every motion proposed by 100,000 voters or by one sixth of the voters in each of three States shall be submitted by the main electoral board to the House of Representatives for action. The initiative must be presented in the form of a draft law.

Article 42 (Objection):
(1) Every enactment of the House of Representatives shall be conveyed without delay by the President to the Senate.
(2) Except as otherwise provided by constitutional law, an enactment can be authenticated and published only if the Senate has not raised a reasoned objection to this enactment.
(3) This objection must be conveyed to the House of Representatives in writing by the Chairman of the Senate within eight weeks of the enactment's arrival; the Federal Chancellor shall be informed thereof.
(4) If the House of Representatives in the presence of at least half its members carries its original resolution a second time, this shall be authenticated and published. If the Senate resolves not to raise any objection or if no reasoned objection is raised within the deadline laid down in Paragraph (3), the enactment shall be authenticated and published.
(5) The Senate can raise no objection to resolutions of the House of Representatives relating to a law on the House of Representatives' Standing Orders, the dissolution of the House of Representatives, the appropriation of the Federal Budget estimates, the sanction of the final Federal Budget, the raising or conversion of federal loans, or the disposal of federal property. These enactments of the House of Representatives shall be authenticated and published without further formalities.

Belgium

Belgium is one of the very few countries in Europe where there is no possibility of having referendums at the national level. However, I&R has been debated in the parliament on several occasions since 1983. During the nineties, there was renewed interest in direct democracy.

The current liberal Prime Minister is promoting the introduction of I&R at all levels, but these intentions are boycotted by Walloon socialists. Polls show that a large majority of Belgian citizens favor I&R in EU affairs.

- Population: 10,204,000
- Area: 30,528 km²
- Capital: Brussels (Brussel/Bruxelles)
- Official languages: Flemish (57%), French (42%), German.
- Religion: Roman Catholic (81%)
- Political System: Monarchy (1830), federal structure with three autonomous regions.
- Constitution: 1831 (without referendum)
- Membership: EU, NATO
- GNP/capita: $25,520
- Human Development Rank: 6
- I&R Practice: two Plebiscites—after WWI on the annexation of a German-speaking region and after WWII (1950) on the return of the King.

Types of Initiative and Referendum

The idea of direct democracy was already present in Belgium in the 19th century. When the Socialist Party was founded in 1885, the first article of its program was formulated as follows:

Article one: "Universal voting rights. Direct law-making by the people, i.e. ratification and initiative for the people in the field of legislation, secret and obligatory voting. Elections should take place on Sunday."

The principle of "one man, one vote" was realized after World War I. Curiously, this was done before the constitution was changed (the so-called "coup van Loppem"). The Belgian élite, among them King Albert I, were anxious to make concessions to the working class, probably because they feared a socialist revolution. It was determined that elections would take place on Sundays and would be obligatory: these were socialist demands, because non-obligatory elections taking place on a working day would allow the capitalists to intimidate their workers. After the Second World War, voting rights were also accorded to women.

The socialist party thus realized its entire first article, except for direct democracy. This does not mean that direct democracy is now a major goal for the socialists; on the contrary, the Parti Socialiste opposes the introduction of direct democracy, at least at the national level.

Direct democracy has been debated in the parliament on several occasions, for instance in 1893, in 1921 and in 1970. These discussions took place when the constitution had to be altered in other respects, and they never resulted in legislative initiatives. Belgium remains a strictly representative regime to this day, especially at the federal and regional levels.

I. National Level

After the First World War, the German-speaking region of Eupen-Mamédy was annexed by Belgium. This annexation had to be approved by the local population. However, people wanting a return to Germany had to make their names public, and those who did not were assumed to prefer the annexation.

The "referendum" was thus a complete farce: only 209 locals dared to resist the annexation, and officially, the population of the annexed region was assumed to have preferred annexation by 33,455 votes to 271. During the Second World War (1940–1945), the region returned to Germany, but thereafter it was incorporated again into Belgium. Today the region is officially bilingual (German and French).

After the Second World War, the Belgian population was divided concerning the return of King Leopold III. Because the Belgium constitution does not allow for direct democracy, the plebiscite held on the question on March 12, 1950, had only a consultative character. Moreover, the political parties were divided on its interpretation: the socialist party declared that it would accept the return of the king only if two thirds of the voters preferred this outcome, while the Christian-Democrats declared that a simple majority would be sufficient. A majority of the people voted for the return of the king. However, the French-speaking south of the country (Wallonia), with its traditional socialist strongholds, voted against the return of Leopold III and refused to accept the result of the plebiscite.

There were serious riots, and finally the king abdicated, and his son Baudouin I became the new king. This episode in Belgian history, known as "the royal question" ("de koningskwestie" or "la question royale") was very traumatizing because it so clearly divided the Northern and Southern parts of the country. To this day, it is still invoked by many politicians as proof that direct democracy is impossible in Belgium.

The elections of 1999 brought to an end the coalition of Christian Democrats and socialists and began a new federal coalition of liberals, socialists and greens. After the elections in summer 2003 the liberals and socialists continued their cooperation, but the greens left the government. The same coalition was installed at the regional level, with the nationalist Volksunie also being part of the Flemish coalition. In both the federal and regional coalitions, there is the expressed intention of promoting direct democracy. However, these intentions are boycotted by some, especially the Walloon socialists, who openly oppose the introduction of direct democracy at the federal level.

II. Local Level

There have been some official letters emanating from the minister of interior affairs, indicating that communities can organize referendums on strictly local questions. Some of these letters even date from the 19th century. Sporadically, such local referendums have indeed been held: for example, there was a referendum in the Flemish village of Tessenderlo on the establishment of an industrial plant presenting pollution risks (March 25, 1979), and in the Walloon villages of Andenne (October 1st, 1978) and Florenne (June 27, 1982), on the creation of a nuclear plant and a military installation respectively. During the nineties, there was a modest boom in local referendums: Mons (September 17, 1995), Ath (October 1995), Liège (October 9–14, 1995), Mouscron (December 19–23, 1995), La Louvière (February 11, 1996), Namur (June 2, 1996), Ciney (October 13, 1996), Genk (October 13, 1996), Begijnendijk (June 29, 1997), and Beauraing (June 28, 1998). Many of these referendums were organized according to local regulations. Sometimes, non-Belgian citizens were allowed to take part.

There have been some successful referendums, including those in the towns of Ghent and Sint-Niklaas. However, other local initiatives have ended traumatically. In Ghent, a second initiative to introduce free public transport (which exists in Hasselt, another Flemish town) was bluntly rejected by the local politicians, who instead organized a meaningless referendum (April 25, 1999) on the "improvement of public transport" which attracted few voters. As a consequence, the votes were not counted and the ballot papers were destroyed. In many cases, the participatory thresholds have induced boycott actions: this has occurred in Genk, Gent, and Sint-Niklaas. In one case, the local political majority devised a participation quorum that was more stringent than the threshold set by law (Boechout, June 28, 1998).

III. Trends

During the nineties, there was renewed interest in direct democracy. This was, to a great extent, the work of the current prime minister of Belgium, Guy Verhofstadt. As an opposition leader, he promoted the idea of direct democracy and made the referendum one of the main issues in his election campaign of 1995.

In that same year, a law was made introducing the referendum in Belgium at the communal level. However, the referendum was extremely restricted. Not only was it merely consultative, it was also non-obligatory: when the citizens had collected signatures, they could still only make a request for the consultative referendum to be held. The law had yet another peculiarity: it imposed a participatory quorum of 40% and introduced the drastic measure that if this threshold is not reached, the votes are not counted and the ballot papers are destroyed. Thus Belgium is one of the few countries on this planet where uncounted votes are burned in the name of democracy.

In 1998, the law was changed: the communal referendum can be compelled, but it remains consultative. Moreover, the number of signatures required for obtaining a referendum has been raised to a planetary record: in smaller towns, 20% of the *inhabitants* (not the voters!) have to sign in order to hold a referendum.

IV. Polls

There have been several polls concerning the referendum. In 1996, there was a national poll showing that 67% of the population wanted a referendum on the European treaty (with only 15% opposing such a referendum; see Le Soir 3/30–31/1996). Le Soir wrote: "Près de sept personnes sur dix réclament une consultation. Ils ont cependant peu de chance d'être entendus. Malgré les propositions des partis écologiste et libéral, le Premier ministre a déjà exclu la tenue d'une consultation, préférant privilégier l'approche parlementaire." ("Almost seven out of ten people want a referendum. However, they have little prospect of being listened to. Despite the proposals from the green and liberal parties, the prime minister has already ruled out a referendum, preferring to favor the parliamentary approach.")

Another poll, taken by *Het Nieuwsblad* on April 27, 1998, showed that 58.4% of the Belgian population wanted a referendum on the further unification of Europe and only 17.7% opposed it. However, in the same newspaper the then minister of external affairs, Erik Derycke, expressed his opposition to the idea of a referendum because the citizens did not trust the Euro. More recently, a poll among the Flemish population revealed that 71% of the citizens want direct democracy at the federal and regional levels, whereas only 5% oppose this idea (*Knack*, October 7, 1998, p. 29).

Main author: Jos Verhulst

Constitutional Requirements for Legislation

Title VIII: Revision of the Constitution
Article 195 (Declaration, Dissolution, New Houses Debate):
(1) The federal legislative power has the right to declare a warranted constitutional revision of those matters which it determines.
(2) Following such a declaration, the two Houses are dissolved by full right.
(3) Two new Houses are then convened, in keeping with the terms of Article 46.
(4) These Houses legislate, in common accord with the King, on the points submitted for revision.
(5) In this case, the Houses may debate, provided only that two-thirds of the members comprising each House are present; and no change may be adopted unless approved by a two-thirds majority.
Article 196 (Restrictions):
No constitutional revision may be undertaken or pursued during times of war or when the Houses are prevented from meeting freely on federal territory.
Article 197 (Permanent Regency):
During a regency, no changes may be made to the Constitution regarding the constitutional powers of the King and Articles 85 to 88, 91 to 95, 106, and 197.
Article 198 (Editorial Changes):
(1) In agreement with the King, the Constituting Chambers may change the numerical order of articles and of sub-articles of the Constitution, sub-divide the latter into titles, sections, and chapters, modify the terminology of dispositions not submitted for revision to make them consistent with the terminology of new dispositions, and ensure the concordance of French, Dutch, and German constitutional texts.
(2) In this case, the Houses may debate, provided only that two thirds of the members comprising each House are present; and no change may be adopted unless approved by a two-thirds majority.

Britain

The British "Constitution" is an unwritten collection of statute law, common law and conventions. The democratic system is very weakly representative; British democracy has been described as an "elective dictatorship."

All national and regional referendums since 1975 have been imposed by government: they were in fact plebiscites. Within the last few decades there have been approximately 35 referendums held in towns and districts. Six referendums in Scotland, Northern Ireland and Wales dealt with devolution. At the local level, the Local Government Act of 2000 enables citizens, for the first time, to initiate and carry out a referendum process.

- Population: 59,756,000
- Area: 242,910 km²
- Capital: London
- Official language: English. Further indigenous languages are Gaelic and Welsh.
- Religion: Anglican (56%), other Protestant (15%), Roman Catholic (13%).
- Political System: Parliamentary Monarchy, with three regions (Scotland, Wales and Northern Ireland) enjoying devolved powers (1999), as well as Crown Dependencies (Channel Islands, Isle of Man) and Dependent Territories.
- Membership: NATO, EU (not EMU)
- GNP/Capita: $24,160
- Human Development Rank: 13
- I&R Practice: One nationwide Referendum (6/5/1975): EU-membership.

Types of Initiative and Referendum

The U.K. is nominally a constitutional monarchy—although it has no written constitution and the monarch has largely symbolic status.

By law, the monarch is head of the executive, head of the judiciary, commander-in-chief of the armed forces, and the "supreme governor" of the established Church of England. However, as the result of a long process of change, the monarch's formerly absolute power has been progressively reduced and the King or Queen acts exclusively on the advice of the government ministers. The UK, therefore, is governed by "Her Majesty's Government" in the name of the Queen.

The monarch formally appoints the Prime Minister and other government ministers, judges, officers in the armed forces, governors, diplomats, bishops and some other senior clergy of the Church of England and confers peerages, knighthoods and other honors. Paradoxically, though the monarch is also referred to as "the sovereign," practical sovereignty is now held to be invested in Parliament (although a prominent constitutional expert, Albert Venn Dicey (1835–1922) called the referendum "the people's veto" and stated: "the nation is sovereign and may well decree that the constitution shall not be changed without the direct sanction of the nation").

In most respects, the U.K. functions as a parliamentary representative democracy. Until 1999, there was only one parliament, at Westminster, with two chambers: the House of Commons and the House of Lords. In 1997, referendums were held in Wales and Scotland on the proposals for national assemblies: 74% of the votes were in favor in Scotland and 50.3% in Wales.

The referendum in Northern Ireland held a year later was more complex: the vote linked the proposal for a new Northern Ireland Assembly to approval of the peace agreement concluded in April 1998 in Belfast (known as the "Good Friday Agreement"). Simultaneous referendums were held in Northern Ireland and the Irish Republic in May 1998, both of which secured large majorities in favor of the Good Friday Agreement and the linked proposal for a National Assembly: 71.1% "for" in Northern Ireland; 94.3% "for" in the Irish Republic.

In 1999, Scotland, Wales and Northern Ireland were granted certain devolved powers and received their own representative assemblies: the Scottish Parliament, the National Assembly for Wales, and the Northern Ireland Assembly.

The Scottish Parliament is unicameral, with 129 members (MSPs) elected for a fixed term of four years by the "additional member" system of proportional representation (each voter has two votes: one vote for a constituency MSP and one "regional" vote for a registered political party or an individual independent candidate)—which allowed the election of the first and so far the only Green member of parliament at either Westminster or Edinburgh.

The devolved responsibilities of the Scottish Parliament include: health; education and training; local government; housing; economic development; many aspects of home affairs and civil and criminal law; transport; the environment; agriculture, fisheries and forestry; sport and the arts. In these areas, the Scottish Parliament is also able to amend or repeal existing acts of the UK Parliament and to pass new legislation of its own.

The U.K. government retains responsibility for overseas affairs; defense and national security; overall economic and monetary policy; energy; employment legislation; and social security. The Secretary of State for Scotland has a seat in the Cabinet and represents Scottish interests within the UK Government through the Scotland Office. The Scottish Executive is the devolved administration and has responsibility for all public bodies whose functions and services have been devolved to it. Since the first elections in May 1999, the Executive has been run by a partnership between Labour and the Liberal Democrats.

The National Assembly for Wales (60 members elected on the "additional member" system) has responsibilities similar to those of the Scottish Parliament, but it cannot enact separate primary legislation. The Northern Ireland Assembly (108 members elected on the single transferable vote system) also has restricted devolved powers.

The new system incorporates a certain amount of overlap in terms of political representation: all parts of the U.K. continue to send Members of Parliament to Westminster (the House of Commons has 659 members), while Scotland, Wales and Northern Ireland also elect separate representatives to their national assemblies. Thus Scotland elects 129 MSPs (Members of the Scottish Parliament) to its parliament in Edinburgh as well as sending 72 MPs to Westminster; Wales has 40 Westminster MPs and 60 seats in its own Assembly; Northern Ireland has 18 Westminster MPs and 108 seats in its Assembly. In addition, the U.K. sends 87 MEPs (elected by proportional representation) to Brussels (71 from England, 8 from Scotland, 5 from Wales and 3 from Northern Ireland).

Unlike Wales, Scotland, and Northern Ireland, England has no separate elected national body exclusively responsible for its central administration. Instead, a number of government departments look after England's day-to-day administrative affairs, while a network of nine Government Offices for the Regions, each with a Regional Development Agency, is responsible for carrying out government programs regionally. The local government areas do not coincide with the boundaries of the Regions. Successive reforms since 1974 have changed the old system of division into the traditional "counties," and the current system represents a typical compromise: 42 county councils remain alongside the 46 new unitary or "single-tier" authorities, most of which are larger cities.

In London there is a Greater London Authority (with an elected Mayor), a City of London Council, and 32 borough councils. There are six Metropolitan County Areas with responsibilities divided among 36 district councils. The non-Metropolitan Counties have two-tier systems of county and district councils. County Councils are responsible for transport, planning, highways and traffic regulation, education, consumer protection, refuse disposal, fire services, libraries, and personal social services. The District Councils look after environmental health, housing, local planning applications, and the collection of household waste.

Below the district council level there are more than 10,000 parish councils in England, which have extremely limited powers. They provide and manage such local facilities as allotments and village halls and act as agents for certain District Council functions. They also function as forums for the discussion of local issues.

Scotland has 32 single-tier councils, many of them based on old shire divisions. They are responsible for all local government services. Community councils gather the views of local communities and represent them to the local authorities. Wales has 22 single-tier councils and 750 community councils whose powers are similar to those of the English parish councils.

Northern Ireland has 26 district councils with limited executive functions.

The various councils are all composed of elected members. A presiding officer (in England and Wales usually a mayor, in Scotland a provost) is elected annually. Councilors are elected for four years. Whole council elections are held every four years in all county councils in England, all borough councils in London, and about two thirds of non-metropolitan district councils. In the remaining districts (including all metropolitan districts), one third of the councilors are elected in each of the three years when county council elections are not held.

Unitary authorities in non-metropolitan districts and London boroughs have a pattern of elections similar to that in metropolitan districts. In Scotland, whole council elections are held every three years. In Wales, whole council elections are held every fourth year. County, district and unitary authority councilors are paid a basic allowance but may be entitled to additional allowances and expenses for attending meetings or taking on special responsibilities.

I. Political System

Counties in England are divided into electoral divisions, each returning one councilor. Districts in England and Northern Ireland are divided into wards returning one or more councilors. In Scotland the unitary councils are divided into wards and in Wales into electoral divisions; each returns one or more councilors. Parishes (in England) and communities (in Wales) may be divided into wards, each returning at least one councilor. In Northern Ireland, district councils are elected by proportional representation.

The procedure for local government voting in Great Britain is broadly similar to that for parliamentary elections. Eligibility rules for voters are also similar to those for parliamentary elections, except that citizens of other EU member states may vote. To stand for election, a candidate must either be registered as an elector or have some other close connection to the electoral area in which he is a candidate.

The electoral arrangements of local authorities in England are kept under review by the Local Government Commission and in Wales and Scotland by the Local Government Boundary Commissions. Electoral arrangements for parishes and communities in England and Wales can be reviewed by local councils.

a. Decision-Making in Local Authorities

In most authorities the governments are based on one of three executive frameworks: a mayor and cabinet, a council leader and cabinet, or a mayor and council manager. Council constitutions must include rigorous arrangements for the review and scrutiny of the councils' policies and decisions. Although some decisions—such as the acceptance of policies and the budget—are reserved for the full council, most decisions relating to the implementation of policy are made by the executive. The executive is also responsible for preparing the policies and budget to propose to the council. Decisions may be made by the executive collectively, by individual members of the executive, by committees of the executive, or by officers of the authority. The executive is also able to delegate decision-making to area committees and to enter into partnership arrangements with other authorities.

New arrangements, introduced by the Local Government Act of 2000, ensure that people know who in the council is responsible for making decisions, how to make their input into decision-making, and how to hold decision-makers accountable. The Local Government Act of 2000 also includes the right of the public, including the press, to be present at meetings of the executive when key decisions are being discussed. The public has access to agendas, reports and minutes of meetings, and certain background papers. Local authorities must publish a Forward Plan setting out the decisions which will be made in the coming months. Only in limited circumstances may local authorities withhold papers or exclude the press and public from meetings.

b. Local Government Complaints System

Local authorities are encouraged to settle complaints through internal mechanisms, and members of the public often ask their own councilors for help in this. Local authorities must also appoint a monitoring officer, whose duties include ensuring that the local authority acts lawfully when carrying out its duties.

Complaints against inefficient or badly managed local government may be investigated by independent Commissions for Local Administration, often known as the "Local Ombudsman Service." There are three Local Government Ombudsmen in England and one each in Wales and Scotland. A report is issued on each complaint fully investigated and, if injustice is found, the Local Ombudsman normally proposes a solution. The council must consider the report and reply to it. In 2000–1 the Local Government Ombudsmen for England received 19,179 complaints, a 9% increase over the previous year.

In Northern Ireland, the Commissioner for Complaints deals with complaints alleging injustices suffered as a result of maladministration by district councils and certain other public bodies.

c. Pressure Groups

There is a huge range of pressure groups, covering politics, business, employment, consumer affairs, ethnic minorities, aid to developing countries, foreign relations, education, culture, defense, religion, sport, transport, social welfare, animal welfare, and the environment. Some have over a million members (many times more than even the largest political party!); others only a few. The existence of so many pressure groups in the U.K. is a direct result of the almost total absence of participatory democracy and the perceived failure of the representative system to be responsive to the concerns of ordinary citizens. Where formal channels are lacking, people are forced to petition and campaign through informal means—in effect begging the government to listen to their concerns, a system little changed in essence since the Middle Ages.

Pressure groups operating at a national level may affect how the U.K. is governed. With the decrease in legitimacy as voting percentages decline, governments become sensitive to public pressure and are careful not to alienate voters by unpopular policies. Increasingly, citizens have come to be seen by government—and to see themselves—as consumers of political products and amenable to exactly the same kinds of approaches companies use to woo customers, including advertising, packaging, and consumer research (opinion polls).

Lobbying—approaching members of Parliament directly—has significantly increased in recent years. Many pressure groups employ full-time parliamentary workers or liaison officers whose job is to develop contacts with MPs and peers sympathetic to their cause and to brief them when issues affecting the group are raised in Parliament. Some public relations and political consultancy firms specialize in lobbying Parliament and Government. They are employed by pressure groups and by British and overseas companies and organizations to monitor parliamentary business and to promote their clients' interests.

d. Democracy?

Although it promised before the 1997 elections to introduce proportional representation for national elections if elected, the ruling Labour Party has conveniently forgotten its promises. Two landslide victories have given it a taste for virtually unchecked power which it is reluctant to lose. The existing FPTP ("first-past-the-post"—a metaphor taken from horseracing) system is manifestly unfair. In the last two national elections, in 1997 and 2001, the voting was as follows:

Year — 1997
Electorate: 43,846,000 / Votes counted: 31,286,000 / Percentage: 71.4%

Distribution of the 659 seats contested

Party	% of votes cast	Number of seats won	% of seats won	Seats if pure PR
Labour	40.1	418	63.45	264
Conservative	25.0	165	25.0	164
Liberal Democrats	14.4	46	7.	95
Scottish Nationalists	4.1	6	.91	27
Plaid Cymru (Welsh)	2.3	4	.6	15
Others	14.1	20	3.0	93

Year — 2001
Electorate: 44,403,000 / Votes counted: 26,367,000 / Percentage 59.4%

Distribution of the 659 seats contested

Party	% of votes cast	Number of seats won	% of seats won	Seats if pure PR
Labour	40.7	412	62.5	268
Conservative	31.7	166	25.18	208
Liberal Democrats	18.3	52	7.9	120
Scottish Nationalists	1.8	5	.76	12
Plaid Cymru (Welsh)	.7	4	.6	5

The most obvious point is that the Labour Party had no overall majority in either election, and that with proportional representation it would have had to enter into coalition with another party (probably the Liberal Democrats) in order to create a government. The other main point is that there is massive discrimination against minority parties. For example, in the 2001 general election, the Green Party secured 2.85% of the total votes: on a simple proportional basis, this would have given them 17 parliamentary seats. In fact, they got none. In a representative system, proportionality is surely *a sine qua non* of democracy.

The legitimacy of government is questionable when, as in 2001, the ruling party is elected by only 40% of less than 60% of the electorate, i.e. by less than 25% of the total electorate, and when six out of ten of those who did vote, voted against the party which "won" the election.

e. Turnout

Voter turnout in all types of elections has decreased badly over the last ten years or so. Turnout in general elections was 78.7% in 1959, 71.4% in 1997, and 59.4% in 2001. Turnout in local elections (always lower than in general elections) was 47.2% in 1990, 41.38% in 1995, 29.6% in 2001, and 35% in 2002. In European Parliament elections (1999), turnout was 23.1%, lower than in any other EU country.

Turnout in the new "mayoral referendums" averaged 29%, with a high of 74% and a low of 10%: about the same as in normal local elections. There was no significant difference in turnout when the referendum had taken place as a result of a local petition, which it had in 5% of local electors in England and 10% in Wales.

Government Response to Voter Alienation

Concerned with the continuing decline in electoral turnout, the government approved 38 pilot schemes in some 32 local authorities, designed to assess the impact of changes to electoral procedures. Various options were tested:

a) electronic voting
b) early voting at designated polling stations (i.e. before the official voting day)
c) weekend voting
d) extended voting hours
e) use of mobile polling stations
f) postal voting

Of these options, postal voting appeared to have the most positive impact on turnout: in the May 2002 local council elections in England, it doubled the turnout in some areas.

Expressions of concern from politicians about low voting figures are now fairly routine, but only one of the major parties, the Liberal Democrats, has made any sort of commitment to direct democracy. And it appears that even this party envisages a non-binding, petition-based form of I&R.

Chris Patten, EU Commissioner for External Relations and former Conservative MP, recently spoke of the need for much greater democratic accountability, especially in European politics. However, it is clear that he saw this as offering more convincing post-hoc explanations of decisions already taken by EU institutions rather than allowing citizens to be directly involved in the decision-making: "… when we've decided what needs to be done at the European level, we [i.e. the EU officials and politicians] have to make sure that it is properly accountable democratically." He also spoke in a public-relations kind of way about the "need to address people's concerns."

II. National Level

"I could not consent to the introduction into our national life of a device so alien to all our traditions as the referendum," said Clement Attlee, British Prime Minister 1945–1951. Apart from the relatively trivial right to opt for election of a local mayor by referendum, by which the official party candidates in at least two cities have been defeated by local independents, British citizens have no statutory right of referendum. All referendums so far have been "gifted" by government, and each of them has required separate legislation. Nonetheless, the fact that the referendum is being used more frequently in Britain will inevitably have positive consequences for the public's experience of and attitude towards democracy. This is Britain's referendum record so far:

1973 — Northern Ireland border poll: 98.9% in favor of remaining within the U.K.
1975 — Referendum on renegotiated terms of entry to E.C. (the only UK wide referendum so far): two to one in favor of entry.
1979 and 1997 — Referendums on devolution in Scotland and Wales (the first unsuccessful; the second successful in both countries).
1998 — Referendum on proposals for a Greater London Authority with an elected mayor: 72% in favor. Northern Ireland referendum on the "Good Friday" peace agreement: more than 70% in favor; turnout 81% (a simultaneous referendum on the same issue in the Irish Republic produced an overwhelming 94% in favor).
1999 and 2001 — Local council tax referendums in a number of English cities.
2001 and 2002 — Referendums on mayoral elections.

The Labour government has promised future referendums on conversion to the Euro, English regional assemblies, the future of Gibraltar, and voting systems/proportional representation. These referendums were promised in 1997, but there has been no action to date.

III. Trends

There are currently no signs of radical change being seriously considered by any of the major parties. The Labour Party is enjoying a second term with a massive parliamentary majority and is not anxious to undermine its electoral success. Despite devolution in Scotland, Wales and Northern Ireland, the actual trend is towards greater and greater centralization and manipulation of power by government. The Conservative Party recently announced a solid commitment to retaining the current political system: it has also benefited in the past from the inequities and iniquities of the majority system and hopes to use them to its advantage in the future. As mentioned above, the Liberal Democrats have expressed a commitment to introduce some form of I&R if they ever form a government, but have done nothing to promote the idea since their manifesto pledge in 2001.

I&R is not on the political, public or media agenda. It is doubtful if even 1% of the electorate would be able to say what "direct democracy" means.

There are a number of smaller and larger pressure groups, including "Charter 88," which campaign for electoral reform and greater democracy, but there is no active group specifically campaigning for I&R. The main hope is that I&R will be incorporated into EU law in the not-too-distant future and that Britain will then be forced to take it seriously, and another cause for optimism is Britain's increasing use of referendums. However, we cannot discount the possibility that more reactionary and regressive forces in Britain will gain the political upper hand and even engineer Britain's withdrawal from the EU.

Main author: Paul Carline with additional remarks by Michael Macpherson

Legislative Requirements

Despite the extremely unfavorable environment for I&R in Great Britain (no rights of initiative or referendum except for the recently introduced right to petition for a referendum on whether to directly elect the mayor and a right of petition to the Scottish Parliament), a recent Act, the "Political Parties, Elections and Referendums Act of 2000," provides the legal framework for the future conduct of major referendums in the UK. The Act applies to referendums held across the UK, to referendums held in Scotland, Wales, England or Northern Ireland, or to regional referendums within England. So far, no referendums have been held under this Act.

The Act also establishes an Electoral Commission with the following main functions:

- to comment on the referendum question
- to register campaign groups and regulate campaign fund-raising and expenditure
- to certify the result of the referendum(s)

The wording of a "referendum" question will ordinarily be specified in the Bill providing for the referendum, i.e. these are not genuine referendums, but plebiscites in which the question is proposed by government. The Commission must consider the wording of all referendum questions and can publish a statement of its views, if any, as to the intelligibility of a ballot question: how effective the question is in presenting the options clearly, simply and neutrally.

Any campaign groups, including political parties and individuals, who intend to spend more than... 10,000 on referendum expenses must register with the Commission as a "permitted participant." A total spending limit of... 500,000 will then apply. Higher limits apply to registered political parties and to any "designated organizations."

The Commission has the power to designate *one* permitted participant to represent each possible outcome of a referendum as a "designated organization." Permitted participants may apply to the Commission for designation, but if no applicants are considered to be properly representative, the Commission may decide not to designate anyone. If the Commission designates a campaign group for one outcome, it must also designate groups for the other outcomes. Designated groups are eligible for certain types of assistance, including referendum broadcasts and the free postal delivery of a leaflet to each household in the referendum area.

The chairman of the Commission will be the Chief Counting Officer or will appoint someone else to carry out this role, and will be responsible for overseeing the conduct of the referendum and for certifying the result. He appoints officers in the relevant local referendum areas who are responsible for organizing and for counting votes in their respective areas. In Northern Ireland, the Chief Electoral Officer is responsible.

The active period for any particular referendum will usually be specified in the referendum legislation and last from a minimum of ten weeks to a maximum of six months. Using the minimum (10-week) scenario, applications for status as designated organizations must be made within the first four weeks. The Commission then has two weeks in which to make a designation, if any. There is then a campaign period of four weeks before the day of the poll.

Financial controls apply throughout the referendum period, and all campaign materials must contain details of who has produced and printed them.

There is a restriction on referendum publications issued by Government, local authorities, and other publicly funded bodies during the final four weeks of the referendum period: materials may be made available only to those who specifically request them. This restriction does not apply to the Commission, which is allowed to run a voter awareness and engagement campaign during this period.

The Regional Assemblies (Preparations) Bill of November 14, 2002 provides for referendums on elected regional assemblies. The draft legislation:

- states that those who may vote in a referendum are electors entitled to vote in local government elections in the region

- provides for the setting of the date for the referendum
- specifies how the question to be asked at any referendum shall be worded
- stipulates that where a region has held a referendum resulting in a "no" vote, a second or subsequent referendum cannot be held for at least another 5 years
- provides for local government reviews before any referendum.

Bulgaria

No nationwide referendum has taken place since Bulgaria became a Parliamentary Democracy again in 1991. However, in 2005 a nationwide referendum will be held about EU membership.

The legal provisions for direct participation by the people are very restricted and exclude constitutional amendments, parliamentary issues, financial issues, and competences of the Courts.

The citizens have more power at the local level, where they can trigger a referendum. However, the threshold of 25% to qualify a local initiative is too high. In practice, local referendums are only held to decide territorial questions such as the division or unification of municipalities.

- Population: 8,257,000
- Area: 110,994 km²
- Capital: Sofia (Sofija)
- Official language: Bulgarian
- Religion: Orthodox (86%), Muslim (13%)
- Political System: Republic (since 1990)
- Constitution: June 13, 1991 (without referendum)
- Membership: Candidate to NATO and EU
- GNP/Capita: $ 6,890
- Human Development Rank: 57
- I&R Practice: Three nationwide referendums: Charges against war criminals, 1922; Republic vs. Monarchy, 1946; Socialist Constitution, 1971.

Types of Initiative and Referendum

There are four different I&R institutions in Bulgaria:

- national referendum
- local referendum
- popular assembly (meeting)
- initiative

The instruments of I&R can be found as a principle in the Bulgarian Constitution: Article 84, Paragraph 5 of Chapter III — "National assembly" — and Article 136, Paragraphs 1 and 2 of Chapter 7 — "Local self-government and local administration."

A special law regulating I&R instruments was enacted on November 22, 1996, and was changed in 1999. Under the amended law, the four forms listed above — national and local referendum, popular assembly and initiative — provide for the direct participation of the citizens in the state government.

I. National Level

At the national level there is only the national referendum. By means of the national referendum, the citizens can decide/vote on basic issues that are in the competence of the National Assembly. They cannot vote through national referendums on issues related to:

- changing the Constitution;
- the competence of the Great National Assembly;
- the national budget;
- the competence of the Constitutional court and other juridical institutions.

A national referendum can be called if requested by:

- 1/4 of all members of Parliament;
- the Council of Ministers;
- the President.

After one of these institutions has proposed a referendum, the National Assembly votes to decide whether it shall be held. The referendum in Bulgaria is binding: a decision made through it is obligatory. No national referendum has been held since 1989.

II. Local Level

At the local level there are three instruments of direct democracy: referendum, assembly, and petition.

a. Referendum

This referendum is called only on local issues that are in the competence of the local authorities. For instance, through a local referendum citizens of one municipality can vote on:

- loans from banks and other financial institutions;
- the sale or rent of municipal property;
- issues concerning the local infrastructure and other projects requiring investment.

A local referendum can be called if requested by:

- no less than 1/4 of the voters,
- no less than 1/4 of the municipal council,
- the mayor, or
- the regional governor.

The municipal assembly regulates the manner and the form in which this referendum will be held. There are many local referendums in Bulgaria, most of which are held to determine the boundaries of a municipality or the division or unification of municipalities.

b. Assembly

This is almost the same as the local referendum: the difference is that it involves fewer people and decides smaller issues. It is usually held in villages in which most of the people know one another.

c. Petition

Through the petition, people can make proposals to the municipal council. These proposals concern problems in the municipality or the district. An initiative can be launched by a minimum of 100 voters or, where the population is less than 200, by a minimum of 1/5 of the voters.

III. Trends

a. History of I&R in Bulgaria

National referendum: Three national referendums have been held in recent Bulgarian history. In brief:

- 1922 — first referendum. In this referendum the Bulgarian people voted to assign the blame for the national catastrophes to the old bourgeois parties.
- 1946 — second referendum. In this referendum the Bulgarians voted to replace the monarchy with a republican government.
- 1971 — third referendum. This referendum confirmed the socialist constitution.

A fourth national referendum on joining the EU will soon be necessary. Bulgaria is already negotiating to enter the European Union.

I&R at the local level: Examples of local direct democracy are many, and there is a stable trend for it to be used more frequently. But it is used for only one purpose: the definition of boundaries.

b. Polls

Overall, there is little popular awareness of direct democracy. We will present the results of two polls taken by our organization, but is important to note that these results are not representative of all the Bulgarian people. These are limited polls with only one aim: to record the opinions of people chosen at random in Sofia and Razgrad about civil participation and the instruments of direct democracy.

- First inquiry: October 2000, Sofia. Results (unrepresentative): the poll included 22 questions about politics, the authorities, attitudes to direct democracy, and EU, asked of citizens aged 20 to 50 who were chosen at random. In summary, most of those asked did not want to vote for candidates (MPs) to represent their interests, but neither did they want to take the responsibility of becoming part of the decision-making process, which is the purpose of direct democracy. Most of the people asked were willing to be involved in deciding difficult day-to-day questions. However, although a majority of those polled did not support direct democracy as a form of participation in public life, a majority did support a referendum on joining the EU.
- Second inquiry (direct democracy and civil participation): April 2001, Razgrad. Results (unrepresentative): The inquiry contained 12 questions about direct participation in public life and the responsibilities of being a citizen and was aimed at 53 randomly chosen citizens aged 18 to 50. This poll showed high motivation to vote, defined by a high level of interest in local politics and local authorities. At the same time, this high level of voter interest is accompanied by ignorance of the meaning of direct democracy. Most of the people asked felt that referendums should be held on measures dealing with such questions as crime, improvement of the infrastructure, and social or ethnic tension, but the citizens hesitated to answer questions concerning their own individual responsibility.

For example, the question "Would you participate in an event organized by other people?" got mostly neutral answers, such as "Yes, but only if this event has social benefit" or "No, if this event is of a self-seeking nature." At the same time, almost all of the people asked said that they would definitely organize an event whose purpose was to clean up their residential area.

These polls showed a lack of civil knowledge, but showed at the same time that in certain situations and on certain topics and issues, people do want to be active and participate in the decision-making process. According to our analysis, people do not know enough about the opportunity to use the instruments of direct democracy. This problem should be addressed not only by the state institutions, but also by all the NGOs and civil organizations that are working to spread civic values and build a stable society in Bulgaria.

Main author: Nelly Ivanova Sirakova

Constitutional Requirements for Legislation

Article 45 (Petition):
Citizens have the right to lodge complaints, proposals, and petitions with the state authorities.
Article 87 (Initiative):
(1) Any Member of the National Assembly or the Council of Ministers shall have the right to introduce a bill.
(2) The State Budget Bill shall be drawn up and presented by the Council of Ministers.
Article 136 (Election, Referendum):
(1) A municipality is the basic administrative territorial unit at the level of which self-government shall be practiced. Citizens shall participate in the government of the municipality both through their elected bodies of local self-government and directly, through a referendum or a general meeting of the populace.
(2) The borders of a municipality shall be established following a referendum of the populace.
(3) A municipality shall be a legal entity.
Article 150 (Initiatives):
(1) The Constitutional Court shall act on an initiative from not fewer than one-fifth of all Members of the National Assembly, the President, the Council of Ministers, the Supreme Court of Cassation, the Supreme Administrative Court, or the Chief Prosecutor. A challenge to competence pursuant to Paragraph (1.3) of the preceding Article may further be filed by a municipal council.
(2) Should it find a discrepancy between a law and the Constitution, the Supreme Court of Cassation or the Supreme Administrative Court shall suspend the proceedings on a case and shall refer the matter to the Constitutional Court.

Czech Republic

Czech citizens have experienced only 30 years of democracy during the last 100 years and are suffering from a lack of trust in their own ability.

The ruling Social Democratic Party has proposed a legislative popular initiative. According to this draft law, the support of 300,000 citizens would trigger a nationwide vote.

At the local level, many important issues are excluded from the referendum option. Additionally, the proponents of a measure must present a financial plan to meet the costs of implementing it.

In the I&R debate, I&R is often confused with the direct election of the President and/or local mayors.

Because a referendum about EU membership has become a Europe-wide standard, the Czechs got their first opportunity to decide an issue in 2003.

- Population: 10,292,900
- Area: 78,865 km²
- Capital: Prague (Praha)
- Official languages: Czech (96%). Other languages: German, Slovakian.
- Religion: Roman Catholic (39%), Protestant (2,5%)
- Political System: Republic (since 1993)
- Constitution: 1993 (without Referendum)
- Membership: EU and NATO (2004)
- GNP/Capita: $14,720
- Human Development Rank: 32
- I&R practice: The Czech Republic had its first nationwide referendum in June 2003.

Types of Initiative and Referendum

An independent Czech state was reconstituted in 1918, after the end of WWI. It was a unitary state of Czechs and Slovaks in which Czechs, Moravians and Slovaks were considered members of one and the same Czechoslovak nation. The political system of that state was parliamentary democracy headed by the first President, T. G. Masaryk. General suffrage, including women's suffrage, arose from the establishment of that state, or more precisely from the adoption of the first constitution in 1920.

The right to referendum was also included in that constitution. However, although the first draft proposed the adoption of the Swiss model, i.e. the people's right to initiate referendums and pass laws, the final version of the constitution included only the right of the Government to address people directly, and this right has never been used.

In 1989, the communist regime established after 1948 was abolished. In 1993, Czechoslovakia split into the Czech and Slovak Republics. In 2000, the first elections were held in the 14 newly established regions.

The current constitution, adopted in 1993, allows direct popular decision-making if so stipulated by constitutional law, but so far, such a law has not been passed. The proposals put forward by the Czech Social Democratic Party have been rejected three times by the Parliament, mostly due to votes cast by the right-wing parties. One of the parties most opposed to the referendum is the liberal right-wing ODS; a somewhat more moderate opponent is the US, also right-wing. Successful negotiations were held to pass a law which would organize a single referendum on the issue of joining the EU but which would admit no other referendums.

I. National I&R

A special law made the EU accession referendum possible, but otherwise it is not possible to hold nationwide referendums. Because of resistance by right-wing parties, the constitutional law necessary for this purpose has not yet been adopted.

II. Regional I&R

Referendums are not possible at this level.

III. Local Level

Czech law permits the holding of popular referendums only at the level of communes, towns and town districts: Law No. 298/1992, updated by Law No. 132/2000 of the code.

The right to vote is reserved for citizens age 18 or older, whose permanent place of residence is the commune in question. It is not permitted to hold a referendum concerning:

- the communal budget;
- local duties;
- election and recall of the mayor, deputy-mayor, communal council and members of other authorities elected by the council;
- proposals which contradict generally binding legal regulations;
- issues treated by administrative processes;
- issues which were subjected to a referendum during the preceding 24 months;
- issues decided by the council during the last six months;
- issues decided by the council after a referendum proposal has been presented, unless the petitioner presents a new justification for his/her proposal within 2 weeks after receiving the decision of the council; or
- the splitting of the commune, if this would result in the establishment of a commune having less than 300 permanent residents.

The proposal to hold a referendum can be presented by a citizen who obtains a sufficient number of signatures. For communes and town districts, this number is:

- Fewer than 3,000 inhabitants — 30% of qualified voters
- 3,001 to 20,000 inhabitants — 20% of qualified voters
- 20,001 to 200,000 inhabitants — 10% of qualified voters
- More than 200,001 inhabitants — 6% of qualified voters.

The referendum proposal has to contain: the wording of the question; petition forms including the name, address and I.D. number of every supporter of the proposal; information about the exact area concerned; and the initiator's identification data. The referendum proposal also has to contain an economic analysis of the cost incurred if the proposal presented is approved by referendum, and an indication of resources by which the cost would be covered.

This last mentioned requirement, in particular, potentially hampers the use of local referendums in the Czech Republic. In many cases, it is difficult for a citizens' initiative to express in figures the cost of a proposed measure or the cost incurred if a referendum were to reject the solution presented by the local council.

To date, only about five local referendums have been held in the Czech Republic.

IV. Practical Guide

Information on holding a local referendum is published on the website of the Ministry of Interior of the Czech Republic. The wording of the laws which govern the process can also be found there. It is also possible to contact the Ecological Legal Service, which is an association of lawyers who volunteer to give legal advice to citizens' initiatives, especially with regard to environmental causes but also concerning local referendums. Their Internet address is www.i-eps.cz.

The Czech Movement for Direct Democracy can be found at www.pdemokracie.ecn.cz. In addition to the right to popular initiative and referendum, this movement also advocates the citizens' right to demand the recall of representatives and MPs at both local and national levels.

V. Trends

As mentioned above, it is the liberal right-wing parties which especially oppose the referendum: at present the ODS, the US, and the ODA, which used to be influential but is no longer so. The Christian Democratic Union — the Czech People's Party — used to oppose I&R as well, but more recently (2001) its president has begun to speak of the merits of direct democracy.

In the Czech Republic, direct democracy is often misunderstood as referring to the direct election of the president, who is now elected by parliament. The author of this text does not consider direct presidential election as a direct-democracy instrument because it does not in any way strengthen public control of political power. Rather, it could tend to renew the cult of strong personalities, leaders who stand above the citizens.

The Social Democratic Party generally supports the referendum, but there are voices even within this party which reject it, especially if initiated by independent citizens. Consequently, the support given to the idea of I&R by this party is rather weak. It does not promote direct decision-making by the people.

On the other hand, the citizens' right to I&R is amply promoted by the KSCM, the successor organization of the KSC (Czech Communist Party). In 1948, the KSC established a totalitarian regime in Czechoslovakia, a regime which lasted under its leadership until 1989. The KSCM is generally considered a party which has not sufficiently disavowed its totalitarian past; nevertheless, it obtained 18% of the votes at the last election in June 2002.

Besides these parliamentary parties, there are many groups whose programs contain passages concerning direct democracy, including statements about the right of citizens to I&R. These groups are scattered across the whole political spectrum, from the Anarchists to the Neo-Nazis who claim adherence to the legacy of Adolf Hitler. Neo-Nazi and extreme right-wing groups see in the referendum an instrument for the establishment of their own power and the promotion of their authoritarian and racist programs. Their membership is no more than a few hundred, but they enjoy considerable support from abroad. The anarchist groups consist of young people, mostly between the ages of 16 and 25. They are often characterized by ideological intransigence and sectarian isolation, which makes their impact on public opinion rather negligible.

A special case are Czech environmental groups which, so far, have rejected the methods of direct democracy in principle but were willing to initiate large-scale petitions demanding a single referendum concerning the closure of the Temelin nuclear plant. At present, a majority of public opinion is on their side. However, they are still not willing to cooperate in efforts to promote the citizens' right to I&R. They tend to distrust the citizens and consider them unqualified and easily manipulated.

The Czech media completely support the ruling elite and refuse to publish anything about direct democracy. The only exceptions are certain IT periodicals, whose impact is very limited.

The Czech Republic has been deeply affected by the events of WWII. The Nazi occupation lasted from 1939 to 1945., and as early as February 1948, the Communists seized power and established a totalitarian regime. This means that Czech citizens have experienced only 20 years of democracy, from 1918 to 1938.

Thus, the most important task is to counteract this totalitarian heritage, which manifests itself in many forms. Citizens have very little trust in their own ability, almost no mutual solidarity, and little of the belief in citizen involvement which would encourage them to promote direct democracy. Most of all, they have little faith that a new generation will arise which is not scarred by the totalitarian regime.

On June 13–14, 2003, for the first time in their history, the Citizens of Czech Republic had the opportunity to participate in a parliamentary referendum: to decide whether or not their country should join the EU. More than 55% of the population participated in the referendum, and 77.3% of the participants approved the accession of Czech Republic to the European Union. This referendum can be regarded as the first successful step towards a more democratic society in a country whose citizens have virtually no experience of direct participation in public affairs and are still not convinced that the man in the street can change anything in the political sphere. At the same time, the event also confirmed our observation that the proponents of direct democracy will have to overcome many obstacles, especially the strong resistance of politicians belonging to parliamentary parties and, in general, of all members of the so-called power elite.

In the referendum on the country's accession to the EU, pressure from abroad played an important role. It no longer seems possible for any country to join the EU without its being sanctioned by the citizens in a referendum, and even the most inveterate political opponents of referendum had to admit that such an "important issue" should be decided by the citizens. As a result, an ad hoc bill was passed sanctioning a referendum on the accession of Czech Republic to the EU: a law which expired immediately after the accession referendum had been held.

Since the Czech referendum law was limited to one specific case, the MPs did not establish any special conditions for the validity of the result. The politicians agreed that, in this particular case, they would respect the people's voice. The referendum was thus acknowledged as binding: had the voters rejected accession to the EU, the MPs could not have ignored their decision. A second referendum on the same issue could take place two years after the first.

The politicians originally discussed a minimum 50% participation requirement, but at the end, they did not adopt this option. They feared that participation might not be sufficient, since the communal and Senate elections did not achieve a participation rate exceeding 30%. Even the date of the referendum became an issue: should one day or two days be reserved for voting, and should the election be on a weekday or weekend? At the last moment, the politicians decided that it would be best to hold the referendum on Friday and Saturday mornings, before people would leave for the weekend.

The approximate date of the referendum had been decided more than one year earlier by the representatives of the so-called Visegrad Four. In the Czech Republic, there were fears of skepticism, so it was decided that the Czechs would vote only after the integration votes had taken place in Hungary, Slovakia, and Poland, whose citizens were considered more EU-friendly. Politicians expected that a positive outcome of referendums held in the neighbouring countries would influence Czech voters as well.

The voting itself proceeded without much surprise. The European integration issue is one of few areas in which the opinion of the majority of the public coincides with the opinion of the Government. This very fact hallmarked the voting as almost a formal act. Many observers were surprised by the relatively high participation rate (over 55%), which approached that of the latest parliamentary election. Accession to the EU obtained fairly equal support on the part of all segments of the population: people living in the country and in towns, seniors and first-time voters, academics and those who had only received basic education. Only the voters of the Communist Party largely rejected EU membership.

Main author: Milan Valach with comments by Veronika Valach.

Constitutional Requirements for Legislation

Chapter One Basic Provisions
Article 9 (Constitutional Laws):
(1) The Constitution may be amended or altered solely by constitutional laws.
(2) Any change in the fundamental attributes of the democratic law-abiding state is inadmissible.
(3) Legal norms cannot be interpreted as warranting the removal or threatening of the foundations of the democratic state.

Denmark

The compulsory referendum in Denmark plays a very important role, as it introduced an I&R dimension to the European integration process.

A minority of the Parliament has the right of legislative initiative, which triggers a nationwide referendum, but this right is not used. There are no provisions for citizen-initiated referendums, and it does not seem likely that the political parties in Parliament will extend I&R rights to the citizens in the near future.

At the local level, more than 160 referendums were held between 1970 and 2002. The most prominent issues for citizens' decisions were schools, infrastructure, and territorial questions. Even though the local citizen decisions are *de facto* only advisory, they have an important impact on the political decision-making process.

- Population: 5,301,000
- Area: 43,094 km²
- Capital: Copenhagen (København)
- Official languages: Danish (97%), German
- Religion: Lutheran (90%)
- Political System: Parliamentary Monarchy (since 1953), with the autonomous regions of Greenland and the Faroe Islands (both have their own parliaments).
- Constitution: June 5, 1953 (referendum, 78% Yes)
- Membership: EU, NATO
- GNP/Capita: $ 29,000
- Human Development Rank: 11
- I&R practice: 19 nationwide referendums (since 1916), 6 regional votes (Greenland, Faroe Islands, Slesvig)

Types of Initiative and Referendum

The government of Denmark is relatively decentralized. In addition to the central state administration, Denmark is divided at a regional level into 14 counties plus the metropolitan areas of Copenhagen and Frederiksberg, and at a local level into 273 municipalities. The Local Government Reform of 1970 transferred many of the state tasks to counties and municipalities, which today administer approximately 33% of the gross national product and employ almost 75% of the public servants. Each of the counties and municipalities has its own administration, led by a popularly elected council which is headed by a mayor chosen by the council. Elections for county and municipal councils take place every four years.

The Faeroe Islands have had home rule since 1948; Greenland, since 1979. Both have their own parliaments and governments, but the Government in Copenhagen is responsible for their foreign and defense policies. Negotiations are being held between the Government of the Faeroe Islands and the Danish Government on releasing the Faeroe Islands from the Danish realm. An independence referendum on the Islands, scheduled for May 25, 2001, was cancelled, and at the last elections (April 30, 2002) the pro-independence parties lost their majority in the Parliament (the Lagting).

An electoral hurdle of only 2% means that the party landscape is relatively fragmented, with small parties of the Center entering into various alliances with the larger parties to their right and left on the political spectrum:

The Liberal Party (with historical origin among Danish farmers) is the strongest political force in the country, with approximately one third of the parliamentary seats (57).

The second largest party is the Social Democratic Party (52), followed by the right-wing Danish People's Party (22) and the Conservative People's Party (16).

The smaller parties of the Center are the Radikale Venstre (Social-Liberal Party, 9 seats) and the Christian People's Party (4).

The new Red-Green Alliance (4) entered the Folketing on September 21, 1994; since then it has been competing on the left of the party spectrum with the Socialist People's Party (12), which split from the Communists in 1956 and is closer to the center than the Red-Green Alliance.

In addition, there are two Eurosceptic movements: "People's Movement against the European Union" and the "June Movement." They run for office only in the European Parliament and do not run for office in the Folketing.

Traditionally, Denmark has often been governed by minority governments; there have only been three majority governments since the Second World War. The need to compromise, which any minority government faces, has left its mark on Denmark's parliamentary culture.

In the Folketing elections held on November 20, 2001, the parties right of center won a majority. The ruling coalition of Liberal and Conservatives (together 73 seats) is supported by the Danish People's Party.

In the first 37 years after the Second World War, Denmark established a far-reaching social security system: it introduced a state pension, grants for all young people under the age of 18, and comprehensive social benefits in all spheres of life.

In spite of critical discussions on the future of the welfare state, the dominant view seems to be that high taxes and contributions are justified in order to guarantee the existing high level of state care. Social assistance payments are dependent on recipients' participation in "social activation" measures.

I. National Level

The *Danish Constitution* requires or enables national referendums in a number of instances. On the other hand, there exist no means for national initiatives.

In the following paragraphs, the different legal provisions concerning the national referendum shall be briefly described. The outcome of these referendums is binding.

1. To *change the Danish Constitution,* a number of prerequisites must be fulfilled; one of them is approval in a mandatory referendum by a majority of the voters. This majority must comprise no less than 40% of the total electorate (Constitution, Section 88).

2. Section 42 provides for a facultative legislative referendum. This article enables a minority of one third of the Parliament's members, i. e. 60 members, to *postpone the final passing of a bill and to decide that the bill must be subject to a referendum*—and that the bill must obtain a majority among the voters before it can go into effect. Section 42 contains detailed regulations, one of which is that votes in the referendum shall be cast for or against the bill. For the bill to be rejected, a majority of the electors who vote and no less than thirty (30) percent of the total electorate must vote against the bill. Certain bills cannot be submitted to decision by referendum, e. g. finance bills, government loan bills, civil servants' bills, salary and pension bills, naturalization bills, expropriation bills, direct and indirect taxation bills, and bills introduced for the purpose of discharging existing treaty obligations.

3. *Alteration of the age qualification for suffrage* requires a mandatory referendum (Section 29). A bill passed by the Folketing for the purpose of such alteration can come into effect only after having been submitted to a referendum in accordance with Sub-section 5 of Section 4 of the Constitution.

4. A mandatory legislative referendum is required for *any act which delegates powers vested in the authorities of the realm under the Danish Constitution to international authorities* set up by mutual agreement with other states for the promotion of international rules of law and cooperation.

For the enactment of a bill which delegates such power to international authorities, a majority of five sixths of the members of the Folketing shall be required. If this majority is not achieved, but the majority required for the passing of ordinary bills is obtained, and if the government wishes to retain the bill, it shall be submitted to the electorate for approval or rejection (Section 20).

5. A facultative and binding referendum is required on *bills concerning the entering of international treaties involving renunciation of sovereignty* (Section 42, Subsection 6, cf. Section 19).

6. Finally, it should be mentioned that facultative referendums may be arranged in other instances even if the constitution does not provide for them. Unlike the types of referendums which are provided for in the constitution, such referendums will be of a consultative character only, because they do not bind the authorities that are constitutionally responsible and empowered.

In comparison with many other countries, the institution of referendum is very explicitly regulated in the Danish constitution.

Denmark is one of the countries with the largest number of referendums. Between 1915 and 2000, nineteen referendums have taken place in Denmark. Three of these were mandatory constitutional referendums (1920, 1939 and 1953). Four were facultative referendums on land property regulations; five were mandatory referendums concerning the age of suffrage; four were mandatory referendums concerning the EEC or EU (Denmark's joining of the EEC, 1972; Maastricht Treaty, 1992; Amsterdam Treaty, 1998; European single currency, 2000). Finally, three were facultative referendums: a consultative referendum concerning the sale of the Danish West Indies to the USA (1916), a consultative referendum concerning the European Single Market (1986), and a binding referendum in 1993 about the Maastricht treaty with the Danish opt-outs (the Edinburgh Agreement).

II. Regional and Local Level

Danish law does not provide any formal rules enabling local referendums or initiatives.

However, a large number of local consultative referendums have taken place over the years. Between the municipality-reform of 1970 and 2000, more than 160 local referendums have been held in approximately 80 municipalities. A total of 88 of the local referendums have been about the closure of local public schools. In addition, there have been referendums concerning various construction projects (24 referendums), road closures (9 referendums), and boundary regulations between municipalities.

The results of a local referendum of this kind are not formally binding. However, the results have an important impact on the political decision-making process.

III. Trend

Since 1975, a few of the political parties in the Folketing have tried to convince the major parties to enact legislation which would give the voters the opportunity to initiate local referendums in specific areas within the municipal competence.

In recent years there have been several debates on whether the use of referendums should be increased. One of the options would be to introduce a bill which would enable the local municipal councils or the voters to initiate referendums of a legally binding character.

In 1975 and again in 1996 a bill was proposed, which would enable a certain percentage of voters in a municipality or a county to require a binding referendum on a local question. A vast majority in the Folketing rejected these bills. However, in summer 2003, former Foreign minister Niels Helveg Petersen launched a new attempt to establish proper I&R rules in the Danish Constitution, and these proposals have met rather positive responses. In autumn 2003, the opposition parties in the Danish Parliament launched an initiative for a referendum on the environmental laws. Finally, Danish Prime Minister Anders Fogh Rasmussen announced a referendum on the new EU constitution in 2004.

The Danish political parties have expressed their views in their most recent political manifestos. Several parties support the idea of allowing a larger number of consultative or advisory local referendums.

A few public surveys or opinion polls have been carried out. They seem to indicate that approximately one half of the voters are in favor of more initiatives and referendums, while almost the same number of voters are opposed.

Main author: Steffen Kjaerulff-Schmidt.

Constitutional Requirements for Legislation

Part X: Constitutional Amendments
Section 88 (Constitutional Amendments, Electors' Vote):

When the Parliament passes a Bill for the purpose of a new constitutional provision, and the Government wishes to proceed with the matter, writs shall be issued for the election of Members of a new Parliament. If the Bill is passed unchanged by the Parliament assembling after the election, the Bill shall within six months after its final passing be submitted to the Electors for approval or rejection by direct voting. Rules for this voting shall be laid down by Statute. If a majority of the persons taking part in the voting, and at least 40 per cent of the Electorate, have voted in favor of the Bill as passed by the Parliament, and if the Bill receives the Royal Assent, it shall form an integral part of the Constitution Act.

Estonia

In the first Estonian Constitution (1920), I&R institutions were very strong and included citizen-initiated referendums: a legislative initiative with 25,000 signatures triggered a binding ballot. But in practice, I&R never worked in Estonia because authoritarian forces gained power and changed the system towards a plebiscitary model in the 1930s. This old trauma, along with an orientation towards the strictly non-I&R countries of Scandinavia after independence was regained in 1991, led to the establishment of an almost purely representative system. However, the compulsory referendum for constitutional change and the EU accession referendum in September 2003 have changed the pattern. A further trend towards more I&R in Estonia is the strong commitment to e-democracy.

- Population: 1,450,000
- Area: 45,227 km²
- Capital: Tallinn (Reval)
- Official languages: Estonian (62%); other language: Russian (35%)
- Religion: Lutheran, Russian-Orthodox
- Political System: Republic (since 1991)
- Constitution: June 26, 1992 (referendum, 91% Yes)
- Membership: EU and NATO (2004)
- GNP/Capita: $3,360 (1999)
- Human Development Rank: 41
- I&R practice: nine nationwide referendums (since 1923), one citizen-initiated referendum (February 19, 1923) on reintroducing religious education. On March 3, 1991, 78.4% voted in favor of independence from the Soviet Union.

Types of Initiative and Referendum

Estonia is a parliamentary democracy with a president elected by parliament. The Constitution of 1992 establishes Estonia as a republic with separation of powers. Most formal powers are concentrated in the parliament and in the government that is dependent on parliamentary sanction. The presidency holds a mainly ceremonial role.

Estonia has several levels of government. Below the national level, it has 15 counties. There are 247 local governments: 42 cities and 205 rural municipalities. As it is a unitary state in which all/most taxes are raised at the national level.

According to the constitution, Estonia has one-tier local government, which delegates extensive powers to the municipalities. Nearly half of the budget of rural municipalities (including indirect support, this is as much as 75% in some areas) comes from the state. The budget funds are mainly used to preserve existing resources: to repair roads and buildings, fund the fire service, and pay the salaries of the people employed by the municipality. Local governments are mediators of state welfare rather than an economic and political power.

I. National Level

There are provisions in the constitution for the kind of direct democracy that includes referendums. In the Estonian Constitution, the referendum had been regarded as a complementary, but exceptional, feature of the traditional decision-making process. All citizens of Estonia have the right to elect the parliament (Riigikogu) and participate in referendums (Article 56).

a. Compulsory Referendum

Any change to the general provisions or any amendment to the constitution necessitates an obligatory referendum. The general provisions, which establish the legal basis of Estonia as a democratic independent state, are:

Article 1. (Sovereignty): Estonia is an independent and sovereign democratic republic in which the supreme power of the state is held by the people. Estonian independence and sovereignty are permanent and inalienable.

Article 3. (Rule of law and international law): Government power shall be exercised solely on the basis of this constitution and such laws which are in accordance with the constitution. Universally recognized principles and norms of international law shall be an inseparable part of the Estonian legal system. Laws shall be published in the prescribed manner. Only laws which have been published shall have obligatory force.

Article 161: The right to initiate amendments to the constitution shall rest with a minimum of one fifth of the members of Parliament and with the president of the republic. The constitution may be amended by law which has been adopted by 1) a referendum; 2) two successive complements of the parliament. A draft law to amend the constitution shall be debated in three readings in the parliament, whereof the interval between the first and second readings shall be at least three months, and the interval between the second and third readings shall be at least one month. The manner in which the constitution is to be amended shall be decided at the third reading; 3) the parliament, in matters of urgency (Article 163, Proceedings). However, in the Constitution of the Republic of Estonia Implementation Act (§8) it is stated that "the right to initiate an amendment of the Constitution during the three years following the adoption of the Constitution by a referendum also rests, by way of public initiative, with no less than ten thousand citizens with the right to vote. A proposal to amend the constitution made by public initiative shall be entered on the agenda of the Riigikogu as a matter of urgency and shall be resolved pursuant to the procedure provided by paragraph one of this section."

Article 162 of Chapter 1 (General Provisions) and Chapter 15 (Amendments to the Constitution) state that these may be amended only by referendum: The right to initiate laws shall rest with: 1) members of parliament; 2) factions of the parliament; 3) parliamentary committees; 4) the government of the republic; 5) the President of the Republic (Article 103).

To put a proposed amendment of the constitution to referendum, the approval of a three-fifths majority of the full membership of parliament is required. The referendum shall not be held earlier than three months after the resolution is adopted in the parliament (Article 164: Majority of Referendum). The law to amend the constitution shall be proclaimed by the President of the republic, and it shall enter into force on the date determined by the same law, but not earlier than three months after its proclamation (Article 167). An amendment to the constitution dealing with the same issue may not be re-introduced within one year of the rejection of the respective draft by referendum or by the parliament (Article 168).

b. Referendum Law

The referendum is regulated by a special law on referendums (1994), and according to this law it is up to the Riigikogu to decide whether or not a referendum will be held, the timing of such a referendum, and the questions to be posed.

Article 104 (Procedures, Qualified majority): Procedures for the adoption of laws shall be determined by the law on parliamentary bylaws. Techniques and procedures of popular votes are established by the law on referendums adopted in May 1994. The following laws can be adopted or amended only by a majority of the full house of the Parliament: law on citizenship, law on parliamentary elections, law on electing the president of the republic, referendum law (Article 104).

Article 105 and Referendum Law state clearly: 1) The parliament shall have a right to put draft legislation or other national issues to a referendum. Several drafts of legislation can be put to the referendum simultaneously. The questions to be put to popular vote should have a clear content understandable to every citizen. However, the State Court, if requested to intervene by the Chancellor of Justice, has a right to block the law by declaring the bill unconstitutional; 2) The decision of the people shall be determined by the majority of those participating in the referendum; 3) A law which has been adopted by referendum shall be immediately proclaimed by the president of the republic; 4) Should the draft law which has been put to referendum not receive a majority of "yes" votes, the president of the republic shall declare early elections for the parliament. (So far this has never happened.)

There are also some restrictions on the range of issues that may be referred to the citizens. Article 106 (Financial laws) of the Constitution states: 1) Issues related to the budget, taxes, the financial obligations of the state, the ratification of foreign treaties, and the enactment and ending of a state of emergency may not be put to referendum; 2) Procedures for referendums shall be determined by the referendum law.

A popular referendum can be held no sooner than three months and no later than six months after the parliamentary decision. (Article 15: Referendum Law). Voting is performed by secret ballot. The proposal submitted to the referendum will appear on the ballot paper along with the words "for" and "against." The central election commission and the county and district commissions are responsible for the practical arrangements for the popular vote. They count the signatures, ascertain the results, inform the president of the republic, and make the official public announcement about the outcome.

The law on referendums sharply limits the former right of popular initiative. The law states that only MPs, parliamentary factions, parliamentary committees, or the government can initiate referendums. In addition, no referendums can be held on questions concerning national defense, the financial obligations of the state, or the ratification of treaties with foreign countries.

II. Regional and Local Level

Other laws regulating direct democracy: Article 154 (Local Government Functions): 1) All local issues shall be decided and regulated by local government, which shall operate independently in accordance with the law. Obligations may be imposed upon local government in accordance with the law or in agreement with the local government. Expenses relating to the obligations imposed on the local government by law shall be covered by the national budget.

Local governments derive their powers largely, though not solely, through representative democracy: every three years people elect the council, and the council makes decisions on behalf of the people. To bring the local government closer to the interests of the people, it will be necessary to introduce additional elements of participatory democracy. Such elements already exist in the organization of local government in Estonia under certain circumstances: people have the right to initiate the adoption, repeal and amendment of council legislation, and the council may hold opinion polls on important issues.
(www.estonica.org)

III. Trends

The first constitution, in 1920, included the popular initiative. 25,000 votes were required to initiate or change any laws passed by the Estonian Riigikogu (Article 31). In practice, this happened only once, when the law that restored religious instruction in secondary schools was adopted by popular vote in 1923 ("yes" votes: 71.7%; turnout: 66.2%).

Between 1919 and 1933, the average term in office of national governments was only eight months. This political instability was greatly aggravated by the social effects of the great depression. Pressures for political reform mounted, particularly from the right—wing League of Freedom Fighters, an association of veterans of the war of independence. In October 1933, their proposal for constitutional reform won by 72.7% of the votes in a referendum (turnout 77%). The following March, the acting president, Konstantin Päts, used the new authoritarian constitution to declare a state of emergency, close Parliament, and disband the league of freedom fighters. A referendum on a new Constituent Assembly formally legalized his caretaker regime in 1936, and he ruled by presidential decree until 1938.

Soviet provocation against the Baltic States intensified at the beginning of 1991. Among other things, Soviet forces attacked and occupied strategic locations in some Baltic capitals, with the loss of several innocent lives. Estonia, Lithuania, Latvia, Georgia and Armenia now declared that they wanted full independence, and refused to take part in discussions on the new Union agreement.

Gorbachev attempted to apply pressure on these and other republics to sign a new Union treaty by holding a referendum on preserving the union. Talks with Moscow on independence stopped. The parliaments of six republics adopted decisions preventing a referendum in their territories. This in itself was a demonstration of the ability of the republics to go against the will of Moscow. As an alternative to the Soviet Union referendum, the Baltic republics of Georgia and Armenia held referendums on independence in their respective republics.

Two referendums were held during the transitional period in Estonia. The first—the referendum on independence—was held in March 1991, before Estonia regained independence. The second—the referendum on the draft constitution—was held in June 1992, when Estonia was already independent.

The conditions under which those two referendums were held were entirely different. The referendum on independence was held during an extremely critical and volatile period. In January 1991, coups had been attempted in Riga and Vilnius, and Estonia was expecting attacks from the Russian military special rapid deployment forces, Omon.

The referendum clearly demonstrated the opposition of pro-Estonia and pro-Russian empire forces. As aspirations toward independence had been strengthening among Estonians, a referendum became a topical issue.

The question in the referendum was "Do you want the restoration of the state sovereignty and independence of the Republic of Estonia?" A "yes" vote was cast by 77.8% and a "no" vote by 21.4% of those who answered the question. The percentage of "no" votes shows the strength of the devoted and active group of pro-Empire forces among the adult population of Estonia.

Three major decisions must be faced during a transitional period, and the thirty-three referendums in Eastern Europe and the former Soviet Union since 1987 can be placed into three categories based on them. The decisions are: What nation—state is this? What form of government shall it have? What policies shall it follow? Twelve of these referendums were concerned with sovereignty or independence, nine with constitutions or the form of governance, and twelve with policy issues including confidence in leaders, the economic system, and the disposition of armies and militia.[1]

---

1. Henry Brady and Cynthia Kaplan (1994): "Eastern Europe and the former Soviet Union," in Referendums around the World: The growing use of direct democracy, edited by D. Butler and A. Ranney, The AEI Press, p. 180.

a. The Constitutional Referendum, 1992

During the spring of 1992, the main issues of debate in the Supreme Council were the constitution, the power of the presidency, and citizenship laws.

A constitutional assembly composed of members of the Estonian Congress and the Estonian Supreme Council had prepared a draft constitution, and April 1992, it was decided that this constitution should be put to a public referendum. The question of whether people who had applied for citizenship should be allowed to vote in the coming parliamentary elections was also to be decided by the electorate. An essential question in the debate was whether a new constitution would mean the creation of a new state, which would make it difficult to regard the present Republic of Estonia as the legal successor of the Estonian Republic of 1918–1940. Some of the more nationalist political groups — the Estonian National Independence Party, Conservatives and Liberals — argued that the 1938 constitution should be re-established.

The main article of disagreement concerning the referendum, however, was who should have the right to vote. More moderate politicians — the Centre party, the Estonian Democratic Labour Party — wanted all the residents of Estonia to be included, and the more nationally — minded wanted only Estonian nationals to participate. The assembly's aim was to reinstate the republic as soon as possible, and it decided that the restoration of the republic of Estonia was a matter which primarily concerned Estonians.

The questions included in the referendum on the draft constitution were as follows. The main question was, "Are you in favor of the draft constitution of the republic of Estonia and of the draft law on the application of the Constitution? Answer 'Yes' or 'No.'" The additional question was, "Are you in favor of allowing applicants for Estonian citizenship who have applied before June 5, 1992, to take part in the first parliamentary and presidential elections after the constitution becomes effective? Answer 'Yes' or 'No.'"

In the referendum on independence, as we have seen, there was a clear-cut conflict between the supporters of independence and the supporters of the empire, and nearly every person knew how to answer.

However, the situation was much more complicated with regard to the Constitution. First, a serious conflict with the Russian community within Estonia was likely because they would not agree to being barred from voting; and there were also conflicts between two groups who supported independence. The more radical and left-centrist groups recommended that the constitution be accepted and a "yes" vote cast for the additional question. The right-centrist political forces — liberals and monarchists — had differences among themselves. The most radical politicians thought that the 1938 pre-war Constitution should be put into effect.

As to the additional question, the right-centrists were against it, the majority of centrists and left-centrists did not voice any opinion, and the communists, some of the left-centrists, and those supporting the restitution of the 1938 constitution were in favor of expanding the circle of electors. In general, the prevailing standpoint was that only Estonian citizens should have the right to make decisions concerning the Estonian state and that immigrants — non-citizens — should take no part. Moreover, the majority of non-citizens had voted against independence in the referendum on independence.

The new draft constitution was approved by 91.3% of those who went to the polls. The additional question was defeated by a vote of 53%.

b. Litmus Test for Democracy

All referendums tend to be litmus tests of democracy, although they are limited by the machinations of elites, who can decide if and when to hold them, what will be asked, what will be said through the media, how success will be defined, and whether the results are binding. In the Baltic States, referendums bestowed legitimacy on independence movements by allowing them to counter claims that their desire for independence was extremist or a minority opinion. In the best circumstances, elites took them seriously and tried to find a peaceful path to independence. In the worst circumstances, elites countered with force.

In the USSR, for example, the referendums in the Baltic States in February and March 1991 probably caused Gorbachev to rethink his strategy for the union treaty, but they also contributed to the reactionary coup attempt of August 1991. The failure of this coup then made it possible for the Baltic and other republics to leave the Soviet Union.

Referendums have been used in to break political stalemates and to resolve contested issues at the stage where constitutions are made. The fact that only two referendums have been held so far in post — communist Estonia emphasizes the fact that its political system is based very much on representative rather than direct democracy. Although the constitution sets limits to the use of direct democracy and strongly emphasizes the representative component, the political elite could have tried to involve the Estonian people more intensively in the decision-making process if they had so chosen.

Political parties in Estonia have not made any proposals concerning nationwide or local referendums since 1992. One reason for this reluctance might be that the majority parties have emphasized the role of parliament; also, perhaps, most parties have seen possibilities for more progressive politics within the framework of representative institutions. The only party which has started to support popular initiatives as binding decisions at the local level is the Center party (Post-Times, August 8, 2002).

In addition, the parties are in the process of modifying their programs and determining a firm ideological basis for their institutions. Their political positions have not yet stabilized and consolidated. So far there has been no serious interest in referendums, probably because the political situation is still too unstable: coalition governments are frequently changing, and the political parties lack stable membership and frequently merge or split.

A third reason could be a fear that referendums would undermine and reduce the significance of party politics.

Fourth, politicians realize that arranging referendums is very expensive.

Thus, the political culture of this small post-communist state has concentrated on the representative component, consciously neglecting the instruments of direct democracy. This is due in part to the fact that civil society is weak and people are only now learning that they may stand up for their interests. Estonia's constitutional provisions also make access to direct democracy rather difficult.

c. The EU Citizens' Decision

Like many western democracies, Estonia makes only occasional use of referendums. The referendum is used on an *ad hoc* basis when the parliamentary majority decides to hold a referendum. Popular initiatives are not widely accepted in Estonian democracy today.

However, the number of referendums may increase. Estonia is a country which has made a decisive break with its communist past, which is physically close to the European Union, which has civil traditions and a history of social self-organization, and which has already undertaken the basic steps of nation-building. There is a sense that the distance between routine political decision-making processes and the life of citizens has grown wider, and distrust of parties and politicians has increased. In this kind of atmosphere, referendums and other forms of direct democracy are often seen as means whereby such feelings of alienation might be countered and diminished because citizens are given a chance to participate actively in decision-making.

On September 14, 2003, the Estonians voted in favor of membership in the European Union. Most political parties, except the conservatives (ENC) and the leftist labour party (EDLP), agreed that this fundamental question should be decided only on the basis of a nationwide referendum.

Main author: Jüri Ruus

Constitutional Requirements for Legislation

Chapter XV: Amendments to the Constitution

Article 161 (Initiative): (1) The right to initiate amendments to the Constitution shall rest with at least one-fifth of the complement of the Parliament and with the President of the Republic. (2) Amendments to the Constitution may not be initiated, nor the Constitution amended, during a state of emergency or a state of war.

Article 162 (Referendum): Chapter I, "General Provisions," and Chapter XV, "Amendments to the Constitution," may be amended only by referendum.

Article 163 (Proceedings): (1) The Constitution may be amended by a law which is adopted by: 1) referendum; 2) two successive complements of the Parliament; 3) the Parliament, in matters of urgency. (2) A draft law to amend the Constitution shall be considered during three readings in the Parliament, whereby the interval between the first and second readings shall be at least three months, and the interval between the second and third readings shall be at least one month. The manner in which the Constitution is amended shall be decided at the third reading.

Article 164 (Majority for Referendum): In order to put a proposed amendment to the Constitution to referendum, the approval of a three-fifths majority of the complement of the Parliament shall be mandatory. The referendum shall not be held earlier than three months from the time that such a resolution is adopted in the Parliament.

Article 165 (Majority for Adoption by Parliament): (1) In order to amend the Constitution by two successive complements of the Parliament, the draft law to amend the Constitution must receive the support of the majority of the complement of the Parliament. (2) If the next complement of the Parliament adopts the draft which received the support of the majority of the previous complement, without amendment, on its first reading and with a three-fifths majority of its complement, the law to amend the Constitution shall be adopted.

Article 166 (Very Qualified Majority): A proposal to consider a proposed amendment to the Constitution as a matter of urgency shall be adopted by the Parliament by a four-fifths majority. In such a case the law to amend the Constitution shall be adopted by a two-thirds majority of the complement of the Parliament.

Article 167 (Proclamation): The law to amend the Constitution shall be proclaimed by the President of the Republic, and it shall enter into force on the date determined by the same law, but not earlier than three months after its proclamation.

Article 168 (Limit to Re-Introduction): An amendment to the Constitution dealing with the same issue may not be re-introduced within one year of the rejection of the respective draft by referendum or by the Parliament.

Finland

I&R plays a very weak role in this centralistic country, which has had even more centralistic Sweden as a model and an even less democratic Russia as a big neighbor to the east. European integration has, however, given it both the important experience of a well-designed referendum and the need to revitalize democracy.

There are no tools or devices which the citizens can use to trigger referendums. Moreover, the constitutional reform debate of the 1970s about the possible introduction of I&R was not repeated when the new constitution of 2000 was being prepared. At the local level, the popular initiative is more like a non-binding petition. The provision for local ballots has been "underused," with just 20 referendums in 448 municipalities.

- Population: 5,153,000 (2001)
- Area: 338,144 km²
- Capital: Helsinki (Helsingfors)
- Official languages: Finnish (93%), Swedish (6%), Sami
- Religion: Lutheran (85%), Finnish-Orthodox
- Political System: Republic (since 1919), with the autonomous region of Åland, which has its own parliament and right to decide on EU membership/reform
- Constitution: March 1, 2000 (without referendum)
- Membership: EU (1994)
- GNP/Capita: $24,430
- Human Development Rank: 14
- I&R practice: Two nationwide ballots (1931 on prohibition of alcohol, 1994 on joining the EU); two referendums on the Åland Islands; approximately 20 local referendums

Types of Initiative and Referendum

The current constitution dates from 2000 and is a general revision of the 1919 independence constitution.

Finland is a unitary state; however, the Åland Islands (population 25,000) enjoy a developed autonomy and have their own legislature, the Lagtinget. Levels of government include national, provinces (6), and municipalities (448). The municipalities have considerable competence.

Finland was at war against the Soviet Union in 1939–40 ("The Winter War") and again in 1941–44 ("The Continuation War"). It became a member of the United Nations in 1955, and of European Union in 1995.

At the national level, Finland has no popular initiative and only a non-binding advisory referendum, and it has no I&R instruments at the provincial level. At the local level it has non-binding referendums which may be initiated by the Council or the people.

I. National Level

There is no provision in Finland for the popular initiative at a national level, nor has the device been debated or analyzed very much in recent years. It is not to be expected that the popular initiative will be introduced in the foreseeable future.

Provision for national referendums, however, does exist. Such provision was not included in the 1919 Constitution, and the first national referendum in Finland in 1931 came about by means of special legislation initiated by the government. This advisory referendum concerned the continuation of a prohibition law that was passed in 1919, and a vast majority voted to repeal the law.

In 1987, through amendment, the referendum provision was incorporated into the constitution. The provision stipulates that advisory referendums can be called by Parliament by means of special laws that prescribe the date of voting and establish the alternatives to be presented to the voters. The second referendum in Finland in 1994 was called on the basis of this provision. This referendum was one in a series of European referendums on the matter of entering the European Union, and the voters decided by a majority of 57 per cent to approve Finland's entry into the Union.

In terms of institutional design, the parliament was given rather a free hand in shaping the use of the device, by which general matters of principle as well as detailed law proposals can be subjected to popular vote. Furthermore, besides "yes" and "no," other alternatives for answering can be added to the ballot by Parliament.

The Finnish Constitution was thoroughly amended in the year 2000; the purpose of the amendment was to revise and systematize the old constitution rather than to introduce a full new text. The 1987 provisions for organizing advisory referendums were included in the new constitution.

In Finland, therefore, the referendum device provides no tools of direct democracy and opens no channels for direct citizen participation. The device is operated and implemented from above, and its non-binding character adds to its weakness as an alternative political method.

II. Regional and Local Level

Finland has no I&R instruments at the provincial level, but it has them at the municipal level. The Municipal Law of 1917 stipulated that a certain proportion of the local population had the right to demand that decisions made by the Local Council be submitted to local referendums. The institution was applied only once, however, and in 1919 it was removed from Municipal Law because it was incompatible with the principles of representative government that were established that year on the national level.

The present Municipality Law of 1995 provides three separate devices for introducing I&R measures at the municipal level; however, none of these devices is in the category of a direct initiative. First, the Local Council may decide to hold non-binding referendums in municipal matters. Second, a popular initiative for the holding of a non-binding referendum in a municipal matter requires the signatures of at least 5 per cent of the electorate; when such an initiative is filed, the Local Council must decide without delay whether or not the referendum shall be held. Finally, individual citizens and groups of citizens may file an initiative on matters within the municipal sphere of competence, which is defined in the Municipal Law. The municipal authorities must report back to the signatories on measures taken, if any, on the basis of the initiative. If such an initiative is signed by more than 2 percent of the electorate, the Local Council is obliged to deal with the matter within two months.

There are no standard procedures prescribed by law for the management of citizens' initiatives in terms of review, drafting assistance, or the method of certifying signatures. Separate municipalities follow slightly differing procedures, which are laid down in administrative statutes. However, initiatives must be addressed to the Local Council, and are for registration purposes submitted to the local office, or in larger towns to the town registry.

Finland's I&R instruments have proven rather insignificant in their use and impact. One investigation (Sjöblom) of the use of the initiative device in the years of 1977–1979 in Finland's second largest town, Åbo (Turku), reports that a total of 387 initiatives were filed. One third of these resulted in decisions that were in accordance with the demands raised in the initiatives, and almost half were partly or totally rejected. Concerning outcome biases, it is evident from the study that established organizations which act on matters within their specific fields of interest have had the best prospects for success, while politically weak proponents have had only a limited opportunity to advance their goals through initiatives.

A later investigation (Sutela) shows that the municipal referendum is underused in Finland when compared to some other countries. Some twenty referendums have been held, dealing primarily with matters of municipal amalgamation (which are, in any case, finally decided by state authorities) and road construction.

These investigations, which are by far the most thorough studies in Finland of the initiative institution, unfortunately are published only in Swedish or Finnish. However, they provide useful English language summaries.

Bibliographical data: Stefan Sjöblom, Medborgarinitiativ i kommunalt beslutsfattande, Åbo: Åbo Academy Press, 1988. ISBN 951-9498-35-4; Marja Sutela, Suora kansanvalta kunnassa, Helsinki: Lakimiesliiton kustannus, 2000. ISBN 952-14-0287-3.

III. Trends

Representative democracy encounters difficulties throughout Europe and the world. Turnout falls, party membership declines, belief in government is eroded. All these problems are present in Finland; for instance, the turnout in the latest national election in 1999 was only 65 percent.

However, the possibility of revitalizing representative democracy by introducing direct democratic methods is not much debated in Finland by parties, politicians or the public. When in the early 1970s plans were made for a thorough reform of the Finnish Constitution, the introduction of the popular initiative was discussed in the committee that was appointed to prepare a proposed revision of the constitution. However, the vast majority of the committee members rejected the idea, which gained support only among small and peripheral political groups. When in the 1980s steps were taken for more modest constitutional reforms, the initiative device was no longer on the agenda.

There are probably two main reasons, both culture-bound, for the unresponsive attitude of the political establishment towards I&R. On the one hand, Sweden still forms in many respects a model for Finnish policy-making, and the restrictive attitude in Sweden towards direct democratic methods probably has a restraining effect in Finland. On the other hand, the necessity in post-war Finland of maintaining good relations with the neighboring Soviet Union created a political and mental climate that was suspicious of the power of public opinion. Although the impact of this factor has certainly declined in recent years, the suspicion of popular demands still has spillover effects in sectors of political life other than those directly related to foreign policy and international affairs. A recent and still quite preliminary debate on the method for deciding an eventual entry of Finland into NATO clearly indicates that the political authorities still take exception to the use of the referendum.

The near future looks more favorable for I&R. There is an indication that Prime Minister Matti Vanhanen is in favor of holding a referendum on the new EU constitution, and Justice Minister Johannes Koskinen has announced a debate on the introduction of I&R devices the next time the constitution is amended.

Main author: Dag Anckar

France

The initiative and referendum process is partly a French invention, with the first constitutional referendum having been held in France on August 8, 1793. The tradition since then has been to let the people decide on fundamental changes to the constitution and the law.

In a centralistic republic, it is the president and not the people or their representatives who has the right to initiate referendums. This trend has been strengthened during the Fifth Republic, which was founded — by referendum — by Charles de Gaulle in 1958.

Most citizens (65%) would like to have more participatory rights, including I&R. In his recent re-election campaign, President Chirac promised to introduce the popular initiative at both local and national levels. A local referendum bill, establishing a plebiscite tool in the municipalities, passed parliament in summer 2003.

- Population: 59,500,000
- Area: 547,030 km²
- Capital: Paris
- Official languages: French (93%), and regionally Basque, Breton, Corse.
- Religion: Roman Catholic 90%, Muslim 3%, Protestant 2%, Jewish 1%, unaffiliated 4%
- Political System: Republic (since 1875), with 4 overseas Provinces and 5 overseas territories
- Constitution: September 28, 1958 (referendum: 79% yes)
- Membership: EU, NATO
- GNP/Capita: $23,990
- Human Development Rank: 17
- I&R practice: 27 nationwide plebiscites (referendums) since 1793; nine since 1958 including the Maastricht-referendum (1992) and a referendum to shorten the presidential term from 7 to 5 years (2000).

Types of Initiative and Referendum

The executive branch consists of three parts: first, the President, as the chief of state directly elected by popular vote for a five-year term; second, the Prime Minister, as head of government nominated by a majority of the National Assembly and appointed by the President; and third, the Council of Ministers which is appointed by the President at the suggestion of the Prime Minister. This form of "divided government" can produce configurations in which the President and the Prime Minister are from opposing parties, also called "cohabitation."

The legislative branch consists of a bicameral Parliament composed of the National Assembly (Assemblée Nationale) and the Senate (Sénat). The National Assembly has 577 seats, and its members are elected by popular vote under a single-member majoritarian system to serve five-year terms. The Senate has 321 seats: 296 for metropolitan France, 13 for overseas departments and territories, and 12 for French nationals abroad. Its members are indirectly elected by an electoral college to serve nine-year terms.

Although a victor in World Wars I and II, France suffered extensive losses in its empire, wealth, power, and rank as a dominant nation-state. Nevertheless, France today is one of the most modern countries in the world and is a leader among European nations. Its reconciliation and cooperation with Germany have proved central to the economic and political integration of Europe. Universal suffrage at the age of 21 has existed since 1848 for men and since 1944 for women; the voting age was lowered to 18 in 1974.

Levels of government are: national; the regions (22); the departments (96); the communes (36,000); and the overseas territories (9). Political power is highly concentrated at the national level; thus, the influence of local units of government is limited. However, there is a trend towards decentralization.

I. National I & R

There is no provision in France for the popular initiative at a national level. The former Constitution of the Revolution in 1793, however, provided constitutional initiatives and optional legislative referendums. Due to high hurdles, referendums were used exclusively to decide on the constitutions of 1793, 1795 and 1799.

Later, the Napoleons misused plebiscites to increase personal power. This long tradition of plebiscites at the national level remained the only means of direct democracy until the present century.

French citizens voted on their current Constitution by referendum on September 28, 1958. Initial acceptance was widespread. In metropolitan France, 85 percent of the electorate voted, 79 percent in favor and 20 percent against, and among the overseas territories only Guinea rejected the new constitution and consequently withdrew from the French Community.

The constitution of the Fifth Republic of France came into effect on October 4, 1958, and is based on the principles of Western democracy. Article 3.1 clearly states: "National sovereignty belongs to the people, who exercise it through their representatives and by means of referendums." Significant provisions for referendums are made in Article 89 and Article 11. Article 89 provides for a constitutional referendum.

The initiative for amending the Constitution belongs both to the President of the Republic on the proposal of the Prime Minister and to the members of Parliament. If the amendment has passed both houses of parliament, the amendment shall be submitted to a referendum. "The proposed amendment shall however not be submitted to a referendum when the President of the Republic decides to submit it to Parliament convened in Congress" (Article 89.3). The amendment is approved if it is accepted by a three-fifths majority of the votes cast. In other words, the referendum can be bypassed if there is agreement between the two houses of Parliament and the President.

The Constitution also provides for legislative referendums, by which the President of the Republic has the authority to submit to the people a proposed bill relating to the general organization of the state (Article 11). Furthermore, Article 53 provides: "No cession, exchange, or adjunction of territory shall be valid without the consent of the populations concerned." In practically all cases it is the President, not the people or their representatives, who has the right to initiate referendums.

The referendum was used twice in settling the Algerian problem: first on January 8, 1961, to approve self-determination (75% voted in favor), and again on April 8, 1962, to approve the Evian Agreement, which gave Algeria its independence from France (91% voted in favor).

The use of referendums to amend the constitution without going through the preliminary phase of obtaining parliamentary approval is unconstitutional, but it was practiced and led to a significant result when, on October 28, 1962, the direct election of the President of the Republic by universal suffrage was approved by 62.25% of those voting. The direct election of the French President strengthened his role considerably and transformed France from a parliamentary system into a semi-presidential system.

Usually, French Presidents use referendums in a very controlled way and only if they feel safe about the outcome. On April 27, 1969, however, in a referendum concerning the transformation of the Senate into an economic and social council and the reform of the regional structure of France, only 47.6% voted in favor, bringing about de Gaulle's resignation.

In the 1970s and '80s the procedure was used only twice: in 1972 for a decision on the enlargement of the European Economic Community (EEC) by the proposed addition of Denmark, Ireland, Norway, and the United Kingdom, and in 1988 for a decision on the proposed future status of the overseas territory of New Caledonia. The turnout was low in both cases, particularly the latter.

In the '90s, the referendum was used only once: in 1992, when only 51% voted in favor of the Maastricht Treaty. On September 24, 2000, Chirac held a referendum on the length of the French presidential term, in which France decided to elect its President for a five-year rather than a seven-year term. It was approved by about 73% of those who actually participated. However the abstention rate was 70%: a record for the nine referendums held during the Fifth Republic.

II. Trend

This does not mean that the French dislike referendums as such. On the contrary, when the issue is one that inspires passion, the turnout is high: about 70% of the electorate voted on the Maastricht treaty in 1992. Moreover, in an opinion poll published in Le Figaro (September 25, 2000), 67% of the respondents said they favored more referendums—but only on major political issues such as taxation or pension reform. When asked about the introduction of the "popular initiative as in Switzerland or Italy," 65% said they favored this idea, while 27% would reject it.

In polls carried out in 1988, only 52% had been in favor of the idea, while 39% rejected it. Evidently there is a growing demand for further institutional reform, including popular initiative and referendums.

On the day of the 2000 referendum, President Chirac said that the referendum should be used more frequently and that there should be more referendums at the local level. He also called for the introduction of referendums based on popular initiatives. Chirac also included this demand in his manifesto for the Presidential Elections in 2002 (Le Monde, March 15, 2002). However, expectations should remain modest, since over the last 15 years all parties have promised to reform direct-democratic elements in France.

In summer 2003, a bill by Prime Minister Raffarin, which introduced the local referendum, was accepted by both chambers of parliament. A regional referendum on autonomy in Corsica was defeated by a small margin, which left the elite in Paris little idea of how to proceed with both the autonomy and I&R issues. When this book went to press in early 2004, it was not clear whether France would hold a referendum on the new EU constitution.

Main author: Carsten Berg

Constitutional Requirements for Legislation

Title XVI: On the Amendment of the Constitution

Article 89: The President of the Republic, on a proposal by both the Prime Minister and the Members of Parliament, shall have the right to initiate amendment of the Constitution. A government's or Member's bill to amend the Constitution shall be passed by the two assemblies in an identical form. The amendment shall take effect after approval by referendum.

However, a government bill to amend the Constitution shall not be submitted to referendum if the President of the Republic decides to submit it to Parliament convened in Congress: the government bill to amend the Constitution shall then be approved only if it is adopted by a three-fifths majority of the votes cast... No amendment procedure shall be commenced or continued if the integrity of the territory is jeopardized. The republican form of government shall not be the object of an amendment.

Germany

Germany has seen a very strong trend towards more direct democracy since reunification in 1990. The most developed of the federal states is Bavaria, which has had more than a quarter (33) of the 145 popular initiatives in the 16 Länder and 5 of the 10 citizen-initiated referendums since 1990.

A major problem has been poor design of the I&R instruments, which are not very citizen-friendly; this has weakened the potential of citizen lawmaking.

An average of approximately 200 local referendums are held in Germany every year. In Bavaria alone, more than 1,360 initiatives have been launched and 640 referendums held since I&R was established there in 1995.

At the national level, the Christian Democrats have blocked the introduction of direct democracy, which is promoted by almost all the other parties.

- Population: 82,047,000
- Area: 357,022 km²
- Capital: Berlin
- Official languages: German (91%), and in certain regions also Danish, Sorbian, Friesian
- Religion: Protestant (34%), Roman Catholic (33%)
- Political System: Federal Republic (since 1949), with 16 autonomous States (own constitution, parliament)
- Constitution: 1949 (without referendum)
- Membership: EU, NATO
- GNP/Capita: $25,350
- Human Development Rank: 18
- I&R practice: six nationwide before WWII (three referendums, three Hitler plebiscites), growing regional (54) and local (1000s) referendum experience.

Types of Initiative and Referendum

The Bundesrepublik is a federal country. Re-unified Germany consists of 16 states (Länder), 323 districts (Landkreis) and 13,854 local authorities (Kommune), of which 2,047 are towns and cities.

The federal states have important powers that are primarily administrative, for example in the areas of transport, education, culture, policing, and the environment. The states participate in national legislation on matters which concern them via the Bundesrat (national parliament), which is composed of representatives from all the state governments. The local authorities have competence in certain areas of decision-making, such as local taxation, energy supply, refuse collection, roads and transport, infrastructure, and planning permission.

I. National Level

Germany is one of the few EU countries which so far have no experience of national referendums. The constitution provides for national referendums only on changes to administrative boundaries. In the Weimar Republic, there were three popular initiatives and two national referendums (in 1926 and 1929); during the National Socialist period, three plebiscites were held, with biased questions and blatant manipulation of results.

II. Regional Level

Six of the 11 states of the former Federal Republic (the "old" Bundesländer) — Bavaria, Berlin, Bremen, Hesse, Nordrhein-Westfalen and Rheinland-Pfalz — incorporated both initiative and referendum into their new constitutions immediately after 1945. Baden-Württemberg and the Saarland followed suit in the 1970s. After 1990, the peaceful revolution in the former GDR unleashed a wave of reform which meant that by 1994, all 16 "old" and "new" federal states had introduced elements of direct legislation.

In all states, popular participation in the formulation and passing of laws is divided into three stages, but since the specific procedures have been elaborated by the individual states themselves, they vary considerably in detail. The following gives a broad outline of the most important provisions:

a. First Stage: Petition ("Popular Initiative," an application for the commencement of a process which may ultimately lead to a referendum)

- The first stage is when citizens present a formal application/request to initiate the process. This application can be called a popular initiative. In Brandenburg and Schleswig-Holstein, the state parliament is already involved at this stage, advising and deciding on the application.
- The legality of the application is checked at this stage.
- The quorum, or minimum required number of signatures to launch the initiative, varies from 3,000 (Nordrhein-Westfalen) to about 120,000 (Hesse). The quorum is usually expressed as a percentage of the electorate.
- Initiatives on both legislative and constitutional matters are allowable in principle in most parts of Germany, although in Berlin, Hesse and the Saarland, constitutional issues are excluded.
- In practice, only legislative proposals (draft laws) are allowed, although in principle "other political issues" can be raised in Brandenburg, Hamburg and Schleswig-Holstein.
- Initiatives dealing directly or indirectly with the economy (the so-called "finance tabu"), including taxation and the salaries of politicians and officials, are excluded.

b. Second Stage: Initiative ("Popular Demand," Volksbegehren)

- The second stage involves the collection of signatures supporting the initiative.
- Signature quorums usually vary between 8% and 20% of the state electorate. Only Brandenburg, Hamburg and Schleswig-Holstein have low, "citizen-friendly" quorums of 4% and 5%.
- Registration procedures vary. Nine states permit the free collection of signatures within time limits of between three and 12 months. In the seven remaining states, signatures have to be recorded in designated official places, and time limits vary between two weeks and two months.
- A "Volksbegehren" which achieves the required number of signatures must be debated in the state parliament (Landtag). If the latter accepts the proposal as it stands, no referendum need be held. If the proposal is not accepted and the issue is taken to referendum, the parliament has the right to make a competing, alternative legislative proposal.

c. Third Stage: Citizens' Decision ("Referendum," Volksentscheid)

- A referendum result is legally binding. However, in most states — in contrast to the rule in elections — a simple majority of votes cast does not automatically win.
- In referendums on straightforward laws, most states demand a minimal approval of either 20%, 25%, or 33% of the electorate. Nordrhein-Westfalen demands a participation quorum of 15%; Rheinland-Pfalz, of 30%. Only Bavaria, Hesse, Nordrhein-Westfalen and Saxony do not require such a threshold.
- In constitutional referendums, all states have a minimum approval quorum of 50%, with the exemption of Bavaria, where the approval quorum is 25%. Moreover, this quorum is further linked to a supermajority of two-thirds in favor of the reform, which makes any changes virtually impossible.

In practice, about one fourth of all citizens' initiatives are declared invalid on legal grounds. By 2003, 145 popular initiatives/petitions ("Volksinitiativen") had been started. 41 of them reached the second stage, the popular demand ("Volksbegehren"), and ten eventually went to referendum. The largest proportion of popular initiatives (31 out of 131) and referendums (5 out of 10) were in Bavaria, the only state which can claim any regular and active use of the instruments of direct democracy in Germany.

The overall view is somewhat sobering: in only four of the 16 federal states has there been a citizen-initiated referendum. As a statistical average, a referendum takes place in each federal state only once in 43 years. The direct success rate of all initiatives launched is around 20%.

In addition to legislative referendums, other types of referendums exist. 14 state constitutions were accepted by popular referendum. In Bavaria and Hesse, there is also the statutory constitutional referendum, which has been invoked on five occasions in each of these states. Seven referendums have been held on boundary changes. In all, there have been 34 referendums since 1946 in all the federal states combined.

III. Local Level

The wave of reform which spread after 1989 affected the local authority level as well as the state level. Before this reform, the right of popular involvement in decision-making by local referendum (Bürgerentscheid) was known only in Baden-Württemberg, but today direct democracy has been introduced at the local level in 15 of the 16 states. Only in Berlin is there still no direct democracy at the district level within the city.

Bavaria and Hamburg are special cases. Here the right to local referendum was introduced by the people themselves in statewide referendums, even though in both cases the state government was opposed to it. It is no surprise, therefore, that these two states have by far the most liberal procedures.

In all the states, the popular decision-making process is in two stages:

a. Popular Initiative (Bürgerbegehren)

- In the majority of states, certain important local issues are excluded from the process (these are listed in a so-called "negative catalogue"). Only Bavaria, Hamburg, Hesse and Saxony generally forego such exclusions.
- In half of the states there is a sliding scale of signature quota depending on the size of the community: in Hamburg it is from 2% to 3%; in Sachsen-Anhalt, from 6% to 15%. In the remaining states there is a uniform threshold, varying from 10% to 20% between states.
- Time limits for signature collection apply only when the initiative is directed against some decision taken by the local authority. The period of time allowed varies from four weeks to three months.
- Normally, the local authority decides on the admissibility of an initiative. The initiative group can appeal a negative decision.
- The local council can accept the initiative, in which case the issue does not go to referendum.

b. Citizens' Decision (Bürgerentscheid)

- In almost all the federal states there is a participation quorum of between 20% and 30%. Initially, Bavaria had no quorum, but the state government (Landtag) introduced a sliding scale of between 10% and 20% depending on the size of the community. Only in Hamburg is a simple majority of the votes accepted without further qualifications or restrictions.
- When a local referendum has been successful, the majority of states impose an exclusion period of one to three years, during which the referendum result can be repealed, or allowed to lapse, only by a new referendum.

An average of about 200 local referendums are held in Germany every year. The most by far are in Bavaria, where there were more than 1,260 initiatives and 578 referendums in the first six years after I&R was instituted. This still means that each community in Bavaria has a referendum only, on average, once every 24 years. In the other federal states, where the hurdles are higher, local referendums are used less frequently. For example, in Lower Saxony there have been only 54 initiatives and 18 referendums, giving an average of only one referendum per community every 344 years.

IV. Trends

There is a clear trend in Germany towards more direct democracy. However, the path towards a workable popular right to direct participation in decision-making is still long and arduous.

The ruling SPD/Green coalition presented a bill on citizens' initiative and referendum to the Bundestag in the summer of 2002. However, the proposal did not obtain the required supermajority of two-thirds of votes in the parliament.

The federal government elected in 1998—a coalition of the SPD, the citizens' rights party *Bündnis 90* and the Greens—had promised to introduce a national right to citizen participation in legislation. Three of the five parties represented in the Bundestag supported this intention, but without the support of the CDU, it could not obtain the two-thirds majority required in the Bundestag for constitutional change.

There is still a chance that the initiative element of I&R—the right to force parliament to debate a topic chosen by the people—might be introduced. All parties in the Bundestag promised that there would be a new attempt after the national elections in autumn 2002. This could be the first stage of a gradual introduction of direct democracy at the national level.

During the debate about a referendum on the new EU constitution, the Liberals and the Bavarian Christian Democrats proposed a single referendum law. However, the government coalition of Social democrats and Greens tried again to introduce the full right of initiative and referendum into the German constitution, and the Christian Democrats blocked everything.

a. Polls — Opinion polls show that between 70% and 85% of the public supports the idea of national referendum.

In September 2001, Mehr Demokratie launched a national campaign under the slogan "Menschen für Volksabstimmung" ("People for Popular Referendum"). The campaign is supported by an alliance of 80 different organizations representing the environment, citizens' rights, trade unions, employers, churches, and social groups.

At the state and local authority levels—in particular as a result of the wave of reform beginning in the early '90s—there has been a dramatic increase in the number of popular initiatives. However, for the majority of initiatives at the federal state level, the experience has been sobering. Despite wide popular support, they have typically failed to reach the high quorums required by current law. As a result, some states have already seen a decrease in the numbers of initiatives.

b. Wave of Reforms — There is an urgent need to reform institutions for direct democracy in the federal states.

After the initial successes of Mehr Demokratie in Bavaria and Hamburg, state governments and constitutional courts have blocked all subsequent popular initiatives to extend citizens' direct-democratic rights.

The justification for blocking them is the usual, highly questionable assertion that extending the right of citizens to be directly involved in decision-making—including the drafting, passing and repealing of laws—would violate the norms of German democracy. Opponents of direct democracy claim that the current, unsatisfactory state of German direct democracy represents the maximum that can be legally achieved. Such judgments reflect the enormous distrust of the people which still characterizes many in positions of power in Germany, especially within the political and legal elites.

Despite this, state parliaments in Bremen, Hamburg, Nordrhein-Westfalen and Rheinland-Pfalz recently decided to lower the hurdles for direct democracy at the state and local levels, although their reforms have been fairly minor. Other states are also debating whether to simplify the rules for popular initiatives.

Main author: Ralph Kampwirth, with additional remarks by Otmar Jung

Constitutional Requirements for Legislation

Chapter VII: Federal Legislative Power
Article 79 (Amendment of the Constitution):
(1) This Constitution can be amended only by statutes which expressly amend or supplement the text thereof. In respect of international treaties, when the subject of a treaty is a peace settlement, the preparation of a peace settlement, or the phasing out of an occupation regime, or when it is intended to serve the defense of the Federal Republic, it is sufficient, for the purpose of clarifying that the provisions of this Constitution do not preclude the conclusion and entry into force of such a treaty, to supplement the text of this Constitution confined to such clarification.

(2) Any such statute requires the consent of two thirds of the members of the House of Representatives [Bundestag] and two thirds of the votes of the Senate [Bundesrat].
(3) Amendments of this Constitution affecting the division of the Federation into States [Länder], the participation on principle of the States [Länder] in legislation, or the basic principles laid down in Articles 1 and 20 are inadmissible.

Hungary

At first glance, the Hungarians seem to have good opportunities for citizen-initiated referendums. But these opportunities are almost unused, and the few attempts to create a new law by initiative have all been unsuccessful.

The reason for this defeat of I&R are the excessive restrictions: 1) Many important issues are excluded from the process; 2) The Constitutional Court is free in many respects to restrict and change the rules of I&R; 3) The participation threshold was 50% until 1997, and was then reduced to 25%+1 identical answers.

- Population: 10,175,000
- Area: 93,030 km²
- Capital: Budapest
- Official language: Hungarian (98.5%)
- Religion: Roman-Catholic (62%), Calvinist (20%).
- Political System: Republic (since 1989)
- Constitution: 1949, basic changes: 1989/90 (both without referendum)
- Membership: EU and NATO member by referendum
- Per capita GDP: $12,340
- Human Development Rank: 38
- I&R practice: Seven nationwide referendums since 1989. 1989: four decisions about ending communism. 1991: direct election of president (turnout 12%). 1997: referendum on NATO. 2003: referendum on EU.

Types of Initiative and Referendum

I. National Level

The existing instruments for I&R are Paragraph 28 of the Constitution and the Third Law of 1998 on national referendums and initiatives. Everyone who is eligible to vote in the national elections can participate in referendums and initiatives. According to the constitution, a referendum can be either consultative or binding.

There are cases in which a referendum is obligatory; otherwise Parliament can choose whether or not to hold one. A referendum is obligatory if 200,000 eligible voters initiate it; if the referendum is valid, the outcome is binding on Parliament. Parliament can decide whether or not to hold a referendum if the referendum is initiated by the president of the republic, the government, one third of the Members of Parliament, or 100,000 voters.

Issues excluded from national referendums are: the budget; central government taxes; duties; the central regulation of local taxes; international treaties; paragraphs of the constitution dealing with I&R; personal and organizational issues in the jurisdiction of the Parliament; dissolution of the Parliament or local government; the Government's program; declaration of war or state of emergency; use of the military inside and outside the country; general amnesty.

Before the collection of signatures can begin, a copy of the signature forms must be presented to the National Election Committee (NEC) for verification. The NEC can deny verification only if the question is not in the jurisdiction of Parliament, if it is not eligible for a national referendum, and/or if the formulation of the question and/or the form for collecting signatures does not comply with the law.

The initiative can be presented to the chairman of the NEC within 4 months after verification, but only once: additional signatures presented later are invalid.

An obligatory referendum is automatically binding. Also binding is a referendum on a law adopted by parliament but not yet signed by the president of the republic. A referendum initiated by the president, the government or one third of the members of parliament can be either consultative or binding, depending on the decision of the parliament.

A binding referendum is successful if more than 50% of the valid votes cast are in favor and if these represent more than 25% of the electorate.

A national initiative can be presented by a minimum of 50,000 voters. Two months are allowed for collecting the signatures. If an initiative is presented with at least 50,000 signatures, Parliament must put the question in the initiative on its agenda.

The jurisdiction of national referendums is still not clear, because of changing rules and CC (Constitutional Court) decisions. Initiatives have come mostly from opposition political parties.

II. Local Level

The local council has to hold a referendum on the amalgamation or splitting-up of communities, setting up a new community, or other issues defined by local decrees. The local council may order a referendum on any issue within its jurisdiction except the budget, local taxes, personal and organizational issues, and the dissolution of the council.

A referendum can be presented to the mayor by a minimum of 25% of the councilors, a committee of the council, the governing body of a local civic organization, or 10% to 25% of the voters (defined in a local decree). In the latter case, the council is obliged to order a referendum.

A local referendum is valid if more than 50% of the eligible voters have cast their ballots and successful if more than half of the valid votes are in favor. The result is binding.

In practice, the local referendum is used most often for the amalgamation or secession of villages and for communities wishing to join a different county. In most cases the referendums initiated by civic organizations have been both valid and successful, although local referendums on environmental issues have been less successful.

III. Trends

Law XVII of 1989 on the referendum was adopted in May 1989 by the last communist parliament, just before the National Roundtable Negotiations started. Later that year, the institution of the referendum was also incorporated into constitutional law. After the free elections in 1990, the local referendum became part of local government law. In 1998, a new law on referendum and popular initiative was adopted.

The Constitutional Court's decisions, like this legislation, had a significant impact on the institution of referendums. The Constitutional Court had declared in 1990 that a decision by the people in a referendum is binding for legislation. Three years later—in answer to the question of whether it is possible to hold a referendum on the dissolution of Parliament—the Constitutional Court limited the possible jurisdiction of a referendum, saying that the question put to referendum may not contain a hidden modification of the constitution.

According to the Constitutional Court, the primary form of popular sovereignty is representation; the referendum is only an additional means of influencing it. This point was reinforced by a CC decision in 1999, which banned a referendum on the direct election of the president of the republic (according to the Hungarian constitution, Parliament elects the president of the republic). Incidentally, this was the fourth unsuccessful initiative since 1989 on the direct election of the president, which according to several opinion polls is supported by 70% to 80% of the population.

Although the CC defined the referendum as a secondary tool compared to representation, it also said that in those rare cases when direct democracy is used, it has primacy over parliament's decisions.

There is no broad political debate on I&R. There are some publications in professional journals, noting the fact that the CC and legislation are gradually restricting the range of I&R, which was very broadly but simply defined (partly unregulated) in 1989. A retired constitutional judge in his recent study (Kilényi Géza: A képviseleti és a közvetlen demokrácia viszonya a magyar államszervezetben—The relationship between representative and direct democracy in the Hungarian state; Magyar Közigazgatás, December 1999) came to the conclusion that "the legal institution of the referendum in its present form is hardly more than a silver button on the coat of the nation."

There have been three national referendums in the 13-year history of modern Hungarian democracy. The first one, in November 1989—the so-called "four-yes" referendum—was valid (51% participation). The people voted that the president of the republic should be elected only after the first free parliamentary elections, which in practice diminished the chances of directly electing a reform communist as president for a 5-year term just before the final move to democracy.

In July 1991, another referendum was held on direct election of the president, but the turnout was only 12%. The third national referendum was held in 1997 about NATO membership, with a participation of 49%. 108 days before the referendum, parliament reduced the success threshold from 50% of the electorate + 1 person to 25% + 1 valid votes in favor.

The Hungarian EU accession referendum took place on April 12, 2003, and was the third referendum (after Malta and Slovenia) on accession among the 10 new lands of Eastern Enlargement. The referendum was actually announced in October 2002, but only after the constitutional amendment of December 17, 2002, was it given a green light. The precise formulation of the question of the referendum, namely "Do you agree to Hungary becoming a member of the European Union?" was based on the consensus of the four parties of the Parliament.

The 2002 amendment to the constitution, initiated by the government and accepted by the parliament, made the referendum on accession obligatory; thus, the legal basis of the referendum is the Hungarian constitution. According to Article 28/C. (6) of the constitution, the decisive referendum is lawful if more than half of the electorate with valid votes, and more than one quarter of the entire electorate, has given the same answer to the question. Therefore, the referendum is valid only when 25% + 1 of the electorate has cast the same vote.

In the domestic context, the campaign was not influenced by any other parallel vote or election. The law defines the length of the campaign, which begins when the referendum is announced and ends at 12 pm on the day before the election (Art.40 I/ 1997. C). From this time until the end of the election, the campaign is banned (Art.40.II /1997.C).

The campaign's financing began with the establishment of the EU Communication Foundation on November 29, 2002 (with a possible 550 million HUF in 2002 and 1.5 billion HUF in 2003, from the parties and the central budget). The media campaign began on February 15, 2003.

Strong opposition to EU accession came from the far-right political groups and the MIEP, and from the negative campaign of FIDESZ-MPP, which is now in opposition.

The participation quota clearly highlights the deficiency of the campaign: only 45.62% of the electorate (3,669,252) actually took part, of whom 83.76% (3,056,027) voted for joining the EU and only 16.24% (592,690) against it. A reason for this could be "too good a campaign," meaning that the accession was represented as a highly positive act and as more an established fact than a choice.

Participation was higher in the west because the people living there have been able to take advantage of the approaching accession for years: future Schengen borders with Austria would reinforce today's practice of commuting to Austria, and a greater portion of PHARE aid was directed to this area. However, the proportion of "yes" ballots was higher in the east.

Main author: Pal Reti, with comments by Kristina Fabian

Constitutional Requirements for Legislation

Chapter XII: Fundamental Rights and Duties
Article 64 (Appeal):
In the Republic of Hungary everyone has the right to present, individually or together with others, written petitions or complaints to the relevant public authority.
Chapter II: The Parliament
Article 19:
(5) The Parliament shall have the right to call a national referendum. A majority of two thirds of the votes of the Members of Parliament present is required to pass the law on national referendums.
Article 28B:
(1) The subject of national referendums or popular initiatives may fall under the jurisdiction of the Parliament.
(2) A majority of two-thirds of the votes of the Members of Parliament present shall be required for the Parliament to pass the law on national referendums and popular initiatives.
Article 28C:
(1) A national referendum may be held to reach a decision or to express an opinion. Carrying out a national referendum may be mandatory or may be the result of the consideration of a matter.
(2) A national referendum shall be held if so initiated by at least 200,000 voting citizens.
(3) If a national referendum is mandatory, the result of the successfully held national referendum shall be binding on Parliament.
(4) After considering the issue, Parliament may order a national referendum on an initiative by the President of the Republic, by the Government, by one-third of Members of the Parliament or by 100,000 voting citizens.
(5) National referendums may not be held on the following subjects: a) laws on the central budget, the execution of the central budget, taxes to the central government and duties, customs tariffs, and the central government conditions for local taxes, b) obligations set forth in valid international treaties and the contents of laws prescribing such obligations, c) the provisions of the Constitution on national referendums and popular initiatives, d) personnel and restructuring (reorganization, termination) matters falling under parliamentary jurisdiction, e) dissolution of Parliament, f) the Government's program, g) declaration of a state of war, a state of emergency or a state of national crisis, h) use of the Armed Forces abroad or within the country, i) dissolution of the representative body of local governments, j) amnesty.

(6) A national referendum shall be considered successful if more than half of the voting citizens cast valid votes and a minimum of 25% + 1 of all voting citizens give the same answer to the referendum question.

Article 28D:

At least 50,000 voting citizens are required for a national popular initiative. A national popular initiative may be for the purpose of forcing the Parliament to place a subject under its jurisdiction on the agenda. The Parliament shall debate the subject defined by the national popular initiative.

Ireland

Ireland can be described as a referendum-friendly country. The citizens have a say on quite a large number of issues, ranging from technical matters to institutional changes, moral issues, and votes on European integration. The compulsory binding referendum is a basic standard.

On the other hand, there are no provisions for citizen-initiated referendums in the Irish Constitution. A recent proposal to introduce the initiative has been rejected by all mainstream political parties.

In connection with the Irish referendum on the Nice Treaty, the role of the so-called Referendum Commission has been debated. This Commission has to provide basic information and arguments for both the "yes" and "no" sides before a vote. The Supreme Court plays a rather positive role in protecting I&R.

- Population: 3,744,700
- Area: 84,421 km^2
- Capital: Dublin (Baile Atha Cliath)
- Official languages: Irish and English
- Religion: Roman Catholic (88%)
- Political System: Republic (since 1937)
- Constitution: July 1, 1937 (Referendum, 56% Yes)
- Membership: EU
- GNP/Capita: $32,410
- Human Development Rank: 12
- I&R practice: 28 nationwide referendums (since 1937). EU Membership, 1973, 83% yes. Nice Treaty, 2001, 53% no. Pro-life, 2002, 50.4% no. Nice Treaty II, autumn 2002, 62.9% yes.

Types of Initiative and Referendum

Under the terms of the Anglo-Irish Treaty signed in December 1921, twenty-six counties gained independence from Britain as the Irish Free State, while six Ulster counties remained within the United Kingdom. In 1948 the Republic of Ireland Act severed the remaining constitutional links between Britain and the twenty-six counties. Universal suffrage was granted in 1923, and the current constitution was drafted in 1937 and approved by the electorate in a referendum.

Ireland may be described as a centralized parliamentary democracy, with rather weak local government. Although significant reform of local government structures has taken place in recent years, Irish local authorities still enjoy little autonomy, carry out a limited range of functions, and remain largely dependent on the central government for financial resources. The Department of the Environment and Local Government oversees the operation of the local government system and implements policy in relation to local government structures, functions, human resources and financing.

Local government in Ireland consists of a number of local and regional authorities at different levels:

- At county/city level: 34 local authorities are the providers of local government services: 29 county councils and five city councils.
- At sub-county level: 80 town authorities.
- At regional level: eight regional authorities.
- Two additional regional Assemblies were established in 1999 under new structures for regionalization. Ireland's parliament consists of two houses: the lower, directly elected, Dáil consisting of 166 members elected from 41 constituencies; and the upper house, the indirectly elected Seanad, which has 60 members.

I. National Level

The Irish Constitution of 1937 includes the use of the referendum but not the initiative. The 1922 Constitution provided for the initiative, but because of the political climate of the time, it was not activated. The passage of the Constitution (Amendment No. 10) Act in 1928 removed the Initiative from the Constitution of the Irish Free State.

The 1922 constitution was based on parliamentary acts implementing the Anglo-Irish Treaty, while the present 1937 constitution was adopted by referendum of the people. It states that sovereignty rests with the people, and it may be amended only by popular referendum.

a. Referendum Law

The law relating to the referendum is contained in Articles 27, 46 and 47 of the Constitution of Ireland and in the Electoral Act, 1992; the Referendum Act, 1994; the Electoral (Amendment) Act, 1996; the Referendum Act, 1998; and the Referendum Act, 2001.

Two types of referendum are provided in the Irish Constitution: a referendum to amend the Constitution (Article 46) and a referendum on a proposal other than a proposal to amend the Constitution (Articles 27 and 47). All referendums held in the Irish State since the 1937 constitution was adopted have been of the former kind: that is, they have been on proposals to amend the constitution put before the people under Article 46.

Irish referendums are a form of direct legislation, in which citizens vote on a bill that is put before them by a majority in parliament, whether it is a bill to amend the constitution or to enact some other law. Articles 27 and 47 of the Constitution provide for a referendum on a proposal other than a proposal to amend the Constitution—referred to in law as an "ordinary referendum." This may take place when the President, on receipt of a joint petition from a majority of the members of the Seanad and not less than one third of the members of the Dáil and following consultation with the Council of State, decides that a Bill contains a proposal of such national importance that the will of the people should be ascertained before the measure becomes law.

In this instance, the President must decline to sign the Bill unless it is approved either by the people in a referendum within 18 months of the President's decision or by a resolution of the Dáil within the 18-month period after a general election. The procedure is similar to that for a constitutional referendum, except that the proposal is regarded as vetoed by the people if a majority of votes are cast against the proposal and if these votes represent at least one third of the presidential electors in the register of electors.

No such ordinary referendum has been held to date. Since it needs to be triggered by a majority of the Seanad, the likelihood of such a vote is slight due to the nomination procedure for the Seanad. This procedure allows the Taoiseach (prime minister) to nominate eleven of its sixty members, so the government of the day almost always commands a majority in the house.

b. Conduct of Referendums

In recent years there has been increasing cross-party support for referendum proposals, particularly in referendums on European integration. This has led to intensified activity by pressure groups. There has also been an increase in the involvement of the courts in regulating campaigns in recent years.

Most of Ireland's European referendums derive from the 1987 Crotty case. Ireland's accession to the European Community in 1973 required a constitutional referendum to permit European law to override Irish law in case of conflict in matters covered by the European treaties. Thirteen years later, when the Single European Act treaty was being ratified, the government proposed to do this by parliamentary majority, which is the normal mode of ratifying treaties. An Irish citizen, Mr. Raymond Crotty, contended that because the Single European Act contained amendments to the original Community treaties which transferred further legislative, executive and judicial powers to European institutions, it could be ratified only by the people themselves as the ultimate repository of sovereignty.

The Supreme Court upheld this view, and the Government had to get the approval of citizens in a referendum before it could ratify the treaty. The people voted on an amendment to the constitution allowing the state to ratify the Single European Act. The Crotty case delayed the introduction of the S.E.A. by six months. Later Irish referendums on Community and Union treaties—the Treaty of Maastricht of 1992, the Treaty of Amsterdam of 1998, and the Treaty of Nice of 2001—have stemmed from the Supreme Court's judgment in the Crotty case, since these treaties all required the surrender of further portions of sovereignty to the EC/EU and so required popular consent.

In the 11 constitutional referendums held between the 1937 adoption of the Irish constitution and the 1987 referendum on the Single European Act, the political parties and other organized interests on each side financed their campaigns out of their own resources. Irish law did not provide any public funding for referendum or election campaigns.

In 1987, when the government of the day had a to hold a referendum on the S.E.A. treaty before it could be ratified, it amended the Referendum Act to permit a substantial sum of public money to be spent on advertising urging voters to vote "yes." This practice of using public funds, which come from citizens holding both "yes" and "no" viewpoints, to advance the position of the government side alone, was repeated in the 1992 Maastricht referendum and in three other constitutional referendums between 1987 and 1995.

Two judgments in constitutional cases brought by individual citizens since then have had a profound influence on the operation of Irish referendum campaigns. In 1995, in a case brought by Green Party MEP Patricia McKenna, the Supreme Court declared that in expending monies in the promotion of a particular vote, the government was in breach of the Constitution and the rights of citizens to equality, democracy, and fairness in constitutional referendums. In the use of public funding, there had to be equality between the "yes" and "no" propositions: either no funding at all, which had been the case in referendums between 1937 and 1987, or else some 50–50 arrangement.

In 2000, in a case brought by Anthony Coughlan, the Supreme Court applied the principle of equality in the use of public resources to the allocation of free broadcasts to political parties and other interests in referendums. Either there should be no free broadcasts, or broadcasts should be allocated on a 50–50 basis to both opposing camps in a referendum campaign.

The government responded to the McKenna judgment by introducing the 1998 Referendum Act. This provided for the establishment of an independent statutory Referendum Commission whose primary role was to explain the subject matter of the referendum to the voters, and who must ensure that the arguments of those who oppose the proposal and of those who defend it are presented in a way that is fair to all the interests concerned. The Act also provided for the allocation of public funds to the Commission for this purpose, to be spent on advertising in the print and broadcast media and on other means of promoting public debate and discussion on a referendum proposal.

Four Referendum Commissions have been established to date under the 1998 Referendum Act, although they have all had the same individual members. They interpreted their statutory obligation to be "fair to all interests concerned" as requiring a 50–50 allocation of advertising funds to arguments of the "yes" side and "no" side, taking the view that every citizen had an interest in a referendum and that the Commission was bound by the equality principles laid down by the Supreme Court.

Considerable controversy has surrounded the Referendum Commission's efforts. The Commission was criticized for the mechanical character of its radio and TV advertisements, in which "yes" and "no" arguments were rather artificially propounded by supposed husband-and-wife pairs or by disputing friends. Critics of the Commission accused it of being responsible for a lack of campaigning vigor by the political parties, especially in the 1998 Treaty of Amsterdam and the 2001 Treaty of Nice referendums.

Its defenders have pointed out that in these two referendums the Commission had an inherently difficult job to do, because it had to publicize more than one referendum at the same time. Thus, in 1998, the Commission's plans to sponsor televised public debates between proponents of both sides on the Amsterdam Treaty had to be cancelled when it had to publicize the referendum on the Northern Ireland Agreement on the same day. In the 2001 Nice referendum, the government gave the Commission three unrelated referendum issues to publicize, and the Commission's chairman, a former Chief Justice, complained of having insufficient time.

Supporters of the Referendum Commission pointed out that whatever criticism might be made of its yes/no advertisements, these had to be relevant to the referendum proposition. They could not be spin-doctored or contain irrelevancies, in contrast to ads placed by political parties or private interests, and were the only assured way that citizens could have the pros and cons of a referendum proposition put adequately before them.

On the issue of how to encourage vigorous political debate on referendums, it probably is true that when the key yes/no arguments were being publicized impartially by a public body, political parties and other interests may have spent less of their own money even if they were concerned about an issue, and that in that sense they were less involved. It should be noted that in some Irish referendums, political parties are the initiators of the referendum issue and are much involved with it, while in others, their role is marginal compared with that of private lobby groups.

In December 2001, following the refusal of Irish voters to change the Constitution to permit the ratification of the Treaty of Nice—a referendum in which the sum of 2.5 million Irish pounds had been spent to publicize the Treaty and the arguments for and against it—the government pushed a new Referendum Act through the Irish Parliament, going through all its stages in less than two days. This Act removes from the Referendum Commission its functions, under section 3 of the 1998 Act, of preparing a statement or statements concerning the referendum proposal, setting out the arguments for and against, and fostering, promoting, and facilitating debate or discussion on the proposal. The new Act also gives the Commission two new functions: to promote awareness of the referendum and to encourage citizens to vote.

II. Regional and Local Level

There are no formal regulations to allow for regional or local referendums and initiatives.

III. Trends

Ireland can be described as a referendum-friendly country. Despite the narrow basis for holding referendums as outlined in Article 46, in reality the people have been consulted on quite a large number of issues, ranging from technical matters to institutional changes, to moral issues, to votes on European integration. All decisions by the people are binding.

The people have been consulted on 25 occasions since they first accepted the Constitution by referendum in 1937. Eighteen of the proposals were accepted, while six were rejected. The most recent rejections have been those of the Treaty of Nice, referred to above, and of the pro-life (anti-abortion) referendum.

There has been very little debate about direct democracy in Ireland. The public is largely unaware of the possibilities inherent in the initiative process.

In 1996 the Constitutional Review Group, which was set up to advise the government on possible changes to the Constitution, briefly explored the possibility of introducing the initiative. Their report (May 1996) considered whether provision should be made for a popular initiative to amend the Constitution other than the existing provision of Articles 46 and 47. The consensus in the Group was that there should be no provision to allow constitutional change to be proposed either directly or indirectly by means of an initiative, concluding that it would be inappropriate to a representative democracy. The Review Group did recommend that the possibility of introducing a pre-referendum system be kept under review.

The mainstream political parties—the centre-right Fianna Fail, Fine Gael and Progressive Democratic parties, and the centre-left Labour Party—show very little interest in promoting the involvement the people in areas outside those provided in the Constitution. There is greater support for referendums on a wider range of issues from smaller parties, such as the Greens.

Voters rarely express an opinion on the question of whether there should be more referendums, although there have been exceptions. In 2001, opinion polls showed there was strong support (70%) for another referendum on abortion, despite the contentious nature of previous referendums on this issue. Later polls, however, showed less support for it.

Significantly, there was a strong expectation that Fianna Fail, the main governing party in the Fianna Fail/Progressive Democrat government, would keep an election promise to hold a referendum before joining NATO's Partnership for Peace. Its failure to do so left a residue of resentment amongst voters, of whom 70% had expressed support in polls for a referendum on the issue.

Main author: Dolores Taaffe, with additional remarks by Anthony Coughlan

Constitutional Requirements for Legislation

Chapter XIV: Amendment of the Constitution
Article 46 (Amendment):
(1) Any provision of this Constitution may be amended, whether by way of variation, addition, or repeal, in the manner provided by this article.
(2) Every proposal for an amendment of this Constitution shall be initiated in the House of Representatives as a Bill, and shall, upon having been passed or deemed to have been passed by both Houses of Parliament, be submitted by Referendum to the decision of the people in accordance with the law for the time being in force relating to the Referendum.
(3) Every such Bill shall be expressed to be "An Act to amend the Constitution."
(4) A Bill containing a proposal or proposals for the amendment of this Constitution shall not contain any other proposal.
(5) A Bill containing a proposal for the amendment of this Constitution shall be signed by the President forthwith upon his being satisfied that the provisions of this article have been complied with in respect thereof and that such proposal has been duly approved by the people in accordance with the provisions of Article 47 (1) and shall be duly promulgated by the President as a law.

———————

Italy

Italy has, after Switzerland and Liechtenstein, the most extensive I&R experience in Europe. After the delayed legal implementation of the citizen-initiated "abrogative referendum" in 1970, the Italian people were frequently called to the ballot box.

Several of these referendums have played a significant role in the democratization of Italian society and party politics. However, the particular Italian I&R procedures and the almost complete monopoly which Prime Minister and media magnate Silvio Berlusconi has over TV channels raise some doubts about the quality of Italian I&R practice.

- Population: 57,646,000
- Area: 301,336 km²
- Capital: Rome (Roma)
- Official languages: Italian (90%), German, French, Slovenian.
- Religion: Roman Catholic (90%)
- Political System: Republic (referendum 2/6/1946), federal structure with 20 autonomous regions.
- Constitution: January 1, 1948 (without referendum)
- Membership: EU, NATO
- GNP/capita: $24,670
- Human Development Rank: 21
- I&R Practice: 54 nationwide referendums (since 1929)

Types of Initiative and Referendum

In the 1990s, the functioning of the Italian political system changed considerably. The center-right Christian Democratic Party, which had governed the county without interruption since 1946, and most of its smaller coalition partners collapsed as prosecutors discovered the involvement of several leading politicians in a dense web of political corruption.

Subsequently, several abrogative referendums led to a new electoral system based on majoritarian representation, which compelled the Italian political classes to organize themselves into two new major political alliances: the conservative "house of freedom," led by the media magnate Silvio Berlusconi, and the "olive tree" alliance, a coalition of socialists, centre-left Christian democrats, liberals, Greens, and Italian communists.

The "olive tree" coalition governed the country from 1996 to 2001, but Silvio Berlusconi became Prime Minister in May 2001. Berlusconi's victorious coalition includes his own "political club," *Forza Italia*; the *National Alliance*, a party with political roots in fascism; the *Northern League*, a xenophobic regional party of Northern Italy; and two small centre-right Christian democratic parties.

I. National/Federal Level

On June 2, 1946, the Italian people voted in an ad-hoc institutional referendum, which was initiated by the anti-fascist provisional government, against monarchy and in favor of a new Italian republic. Subsequently, the constituent assembly approved a new Constitution that includes two types of national referendums and two articles on regional referendums.

Moreover, in 1989, the Italian Parliament adopted an ad-hoc "constitutional law" (a constitutional amendment that is not formally incorporated in the body of the Constitution) in order to enable an ad-hoc referendum on a European Constitution-making mandate for the European Parliament.

Finally, Italian legal dictionaries also mention the "trade union referendum" as a noteworthy feature of Italian I&R practice.

a. The "abrogative referendum" (*referendum abrogativo*) to repeal a law (or parts of it) at the national level

Article 75 of the Italian Constitution states that a popular referendum shall be held to decide on the total or partial repeal of a law or of an act having force of law whenever it is requested by 500,000 voters or by five regional councils. This means that only 1% of the electorate is able to initiate a popular vote about the complete or partial abrogation of a particular law.

The electorate does not only play a negative role, because it can change the meaning of a law by repealing some of its articles. This use of the "abrogative referendum" compensates for the lack of a law proposing popular initiatives, but only partially, since issues that are not already covered by existing laws cannot be made the subject of a popular vote.

Some matters are constitutionally excluded from the scope of abrogative referendums, namely tax or budget laws, amnesties or pardons, or laws authorizing the ratification of international treaties.

Finally, the result of an Italian "abrogative referendum" is valid only if it fulfils the following participation quorum: to be legally binding, a particular proposition must receive not only a majority of the valid votes cast, but a majority of those eligible to vote (i.e. more than 50% of the total electorate).

Law No. 352 of May 25, 1970 practically implements Article 75 of the Constitution. It states that the 500,000 signatures can be collected freely on the streets and must be gathered within a period of 90 days before September 30 each year. Moreover, it regulates the procedure of judicial review and defines the rather marginal roles of the Italian executives (president and government) and the parliament in the referendum process.

The constitutional court reviews the legal conformity of the abrogative referendum before the actual vote takes place. Since the procedural provisions concerning Law No. 352 are open to conflicting interpretations, the constitutional court has acquired wide discretionary powers in this matter.

Finally, Law No. 352 indicates that abrogative referendums must normally take place on a Sunday between April 15 and June 15 in the year following the collection of signatures.

Despite its constitutional recognition, the first abrogative referendum took place many years after the adoption of the Constitution in 1948. Parliament did not transform the constitutional principle into practice until the adoption of Law No. 352 of May 25, 1970, since the governing political parties never displayed any great interest in enabling the "abrogative referendum." This is hardly surprising, since this instrument might counterbalance and limit the power of the government.

In 1969/70 this situation accidentally changed, when the major governmental party, the Christian democrats, made a deal with its coalition partners whereby they would support the adoption of Law No. 352 in exchange for Christian democrat support for a law that allowed civic divorce.

Whereas enabling civic divorce was a high priority of the secular coalition partners, most Christian democrats were, in principle, against the legalization of divorce, but at the same time feared that a veto could alienate their coalition partners. Given this dilemma, many Christian democrats mistakenly hoped that the introduction of the "abrogative referendum" would eventually enable the abrogation of the civic divorce law without risking the ruling coalition.

However, its attempted abrogation failed when almost 60% of the votes backed civic divorce in the first Italian abrogative referendum on May 12, 1974. Hence, the introduction of the citizen-initiated "abrogative referendum" is not merely a result of a democratization of Italian society in the late 1960s, but the unintended consequence of an instrumental miscalculation of the major governmental party.

b. The "constitutional referendum" (*referendum costituzionale or referendum*) over a constitutional amendment which has been passed but not yet implemented

Article 138 of the Constitution states that a constitutional amendment must be approved by an absolute majority of both chambers of parliament and submitted to a popular vote when, within three months of their publication, a request is made by one fifth of the members of either chamber, by 500,000 electors, or by five regional councils. A law thus submitted to vote may not be promulgated unless approved by a majority of the valid votes cast. The result of the vote is legally binding regardless of the turnout, in contrast to the vote on "abrogative referendums." However, no vote will be held if the amendment has been approved by both chambers, with a two-thirds majority in each.

The first constitutional referendum took place on October 7, 2001, when more than one fifth of the Italian parliament had called for a constitutional referendum on the spring 2001 "federalism reform" of the "Olive tree" majority. This constitutional amendment was endorsed by referendum (64.2% "yes" votes), despite its low turnout of 35.8%.

Given the commitment of the current Berlusconi government to fundamental modification of the Italian constitution, in particular of its federal structure and functioning and Italy's judicial system, it is likely that additional "constitutional referendums" will take place in the near future.

c. The 1989 ad-hoc Referendum on a European Constitution

Article 71 of the Italian Constitution states that the legislative initiative belongs not only to the Government and to each Member of Parliament, but also to 50,000 voters. Generally such "popular law initiatives" are not successful, because parliament is not obliged to put them either on its own agenda or to a popular vote.

In one case, however, such an initiative was very successful. In June 1988, the Italian section of the European federalist movement sent a proposition with 114,000 signatures to the Italian Parliament. The proposition called for a referendum on conferring a mandate on the European Parliament to create a European Constitution. In November 1989 the two chambers of Parliament backed this proposition by means of an ad-hoc constitutional amendment. The referendum took place in parallel with the European elections on June 18, 1989, and attained a high turnout (81%) and an 88% yes-vote.

d. The Labour Union's Referendum (*referendum sindacale*)

In Italy, political decision-making does not only take place in Parliament. In contrast to the Anglo-Saxon liberal-democratic tradition of "territorial democracy," economic and social policy can also be made through collective bargaining and "social pacts" between the trade unions, the employers' organizations, and the government. Therefore, it is helpful to refer also to the I&R procedures in this arena of so-called "functional democracy."

On May 20, 1970, the Italian Parliament adopted Law No. 300, the so-called "workers statute," whose Article 21 introduced the "trade union referendum." According to this provision, the unions can initiate referendums on "trade union questions" involving the workforce of a single enterprise, an economic sector, or even the whole national economy.

After an initially negligible use of the instrument, this expression of direct democracy gained importance in 1988, when the three Italian metalworkers' unions began to jointly submit their bargaining agendas and demands to a workers' referendum. In 1995, the three Italian trade union confederations even initiated a national inter-professional "trade union referendum" in which Italian workers approved an essential pension of the Dini-government.

Conversely, in autumn 2001, a trade union referendum over a national wage agreement in the metal industry was successfully barred by the two smaller, centrist unions—the Catholic CISL and the secular UIL—even though the largest, left-wing CGIL union had collected 350,000 signatures of metal industry employees (approximately 50% of the whole constituency) in favor of it. This situation reflects the failure of Italian labour law to regulate the right of Initiative for the "trade union referendum" in cases where the three representative unions disagree among themselves.

II. Regional and Local Levels

a. The Regional Referendum (*referendum regionale*)

Article 123 of the Italian Constitution states that every region shall have a statute which determines its form of government and the fundamental principles of its organization and function, in accordance with the Constitution. This statute shall also regulate the exercise of "consultative" or "abrogative referendums" on regional laws and regional administrative decisions, and the publication of regional laws and regulations.

Despite these constitutional provisions, the regional referendum still does not have practical significance. It is likely that this will change because of the increased competence and importance that the Italian regions gained with the adoption of the 2001 federalism reform.

b. The Territorial Referendum on Regional Boundaries (*referendum territoriale*)

Article 132 of the Italian Constitution states that existing regions may be merged or new regions created, provided that the population of any new region is at least one million, the change is requested by municipal Councils which represent at least one third of the population involved, and the proposal has been approved by the majority of the involved population in a referendum.

By means of a referendum, provinces and municipalities that request it may also be detached from one region and attached to another. Territorial boundaries have never been a political issue in modern Italy.

c. Local I&R (*instruments and requirements*)

"Consultative referendums" can take place at a local level, according to the national "Bassanini" Law No. 142 on local government (June 8, 1990). However, the municipalities and provinces are not obliged to introduce the referendum into their local statutes. Moreover, the results of these popular consultations are not legally binding.

Similar provisions already existed in the Kingdom of Italy in 1903, but the increasing introduction of "consultative referendums" in many local statutes is a recent development.

The specific requirements governing local referendums differ considerably from place to place. In most municipalities, the mayor, a qualified or simple majority of the municipal council, or a qualified minority of the municipal council can initiate a "consultative referendum." However, in many municipalities, including Rome, Turin, Florence, and Genoa, popular consultations can also be initiated by a number of citizens; the number of required signatures varies.

In contrast to national I&R practice, citizens can not only abrogate but also propose bylaws. However, the instrument of local consultative referendums is not yet frequently used.

III. Trends

Despite its institutional roots in party politics, the abrogative referendum became in the late 1970's an important tool of political forces that were closer to civil society than to the political system, such as civil liberty, women's, and environmental groups. Later, the major opposition parties also made increasing use of the abrogative referendum.

At the beginning of the 1990s, two referendums about the electoral system (1991 and 1993) played an important role in the transformation of Italy's "blocked democracy" into a new bipolar party system. Today, the abrogative referendum is an established institution in Italy.

Nevertheless, some of its limitations have also become visible. In 1995, Italians had to vote on 12 initiatives on the same day, which made a proper public debate about each subject impossible. Moreover, three of the 12 abrogative referendums were aimed at breaking up Berlusconi's almost complete private monopoly of TV channels in order to guarantee fair political and economic competition. These attempts were not successful, probably due precisely to Berlusconi's use of his private TV-channel monopoly: his TV commentators persistently "informed" the public that no good movies or TV shows could be broadcast any longer if the Italian people accepted the anti-trust propositions of the 1995 referendum.

Since the 2001 elections, the conflict of interest between Berlusconi's private role as media magnate and richest man in Italy and his public role as politician has become even more evident. Fair political competition seems to be very much in danger, because he now also controls the public broadcasting system in addition to his own private media empire. Silvio Berlusconi has also used his immense political, media and economic power to gain control of the judicial system and to stop, in summer 2003, a "corruption" trial against himself by Italian attorneys and prosecutors. This could lead to a constitutional referendum in the near future that would put fundamental legal and democratic principles to a decisive test.

The turnout threshold of 50% is also a problem, at least from the point of view of a deliberative democracy. Since approximately 20% of the Italian electorate never votes, the opponents of an abrogative referendum can win even if they represent a minority of politically active citizens.

In 1990, the opponents of an anti-hunting proposition successfully used a boycott of the vote and of the prior public debate in place of a "no" campaign. Subsequently, boycotting the ballot has become a frequent strategy. This has led to the paradoxical result that referendums which secured more than 90% "yes" votes were rejected because they narrowly missed the 50% turnout threshold. Of 53 countrywide referendums, 18 have failed because they failed to meet the threshold requirements. The consequence has been a decline in political discussion favoring the use of the referendum process.

Finally, the manipulation of laws by abrogating particular articles has often led not only to a change in their meanings—as desired by the initiators of the respective referendum—but also to awkward laws that have made it necessary for parliament to subsequently revise them. The revisions, in turn, have caused heated discussion and disappointments, because parliamentarians have frequently interpreted the results of a popular consultation in a different way from its initiators.

Because of these weaknesses in the abrogative referendum, the idea of introducing the right of popular Initiative (*referendum propositivo*) has gained some exposure in constitutional debates, without becoming a major political issue so far.

Main author: Roland Erne with comments by Bruno Kaufmann

Constitutional Requirements for Legislation

Section II Amendments to the Constitution. Constitutional Laws
Article 138 [Procedure for Constitutional Amendment]
(1) Amendments to the Constitution and other constitutional acts shall be adopted by each of the two Chambers twice with an interval of not less than three months between the votes, and shall be approved by a majority of the members of each Chamber in the second voting.
(2) Such laws shall be submitted to popular referendum when, within three months of their publication, a request is made by one fifth of the members of either Chamber or by 500,000 electors or by five regional Councils. The law submitted to referendum shall not be promulgated unless approved by a majority of valid votes.
(3) No referendum may be held if the law has been approved by each Chamber, in the second vote, with a majority of two thirds of its members.
Article 139 [Limit to Constitutional Amendments]
The Republican form of the State may not be changed by constitutional amendment.

Latvia

Latvia is one of the few countries in Europe in which the citizens have a full range of I&R rights which enable them to launch initiatives to amend the constitution, create a new law, or veto a decision by parliament.

However, the restrictions and framework are rather complicated and not very citizen-friendly. The biggest hurdle is the acceptance quorum, which makes it very difficult to get valid referendum decisions. With a special law for the EU accession referendum in late 2003, the government could avoid risking the referendum decision by changing the acceptance quorum.

- Population: 2,336,818
- Area: 64,589 km²
- Capital: Riga
- Official language: Latvian (55%), other languages: Russian (37%)
- Religion: Lutheran (55%), Roman Catholic (24%).
- Political System: Republic (since 1991)
- Constitution: 1922 (without referendum)
- Membership: EU and NATO (2004)
- GNP/Capita: $7,730
- I&R practice: Eight nationwide ballots (since 1923). Two citizen-initiated ballots (referendums): October 3, 1998 on naturalization and November 13, 1999 on the pension system. EU accession referendum on September 20, 2003.

Types of initiative and referendum

Latvia is a republic; its 100-member Saeima (parliament) is elected through proportional elections in five districts, using the Saint-Lague formula with a nationwide 5% threshold. The President, who is elected by the Saeima, is head of state, and the Cabinet of Ministers, led by the Prime Minister, is responsible to the Saeima.

Latvia is a centralized state dominated by the capital city, Riga, which has more than one third of the population. It has no constitutional guarantee for local government; the reform of the latter is currently under discussion.

I. National Level

The Latvian constitution provides for three kinds of initiative and four kinds of referendum. Procedural details are dealt with in the 1994 law "On Public Referendums and Legislative Initiative"5 and in two instructions issued by the Central Electoral Commission: "On the procedure in which the Central Electoral Commission accepts a draft law or a draft constitutional amendment" and "On the collection of signatures for the initiation of a referendum on a law whose publication has been postponed."[2]

a. Popular Initiative

1) **Constitutional:** Article 78 provides for the right of not less than one tenth of the electorate7 to submit a fully elaborated draft of an amendment of the constitution to the President, who then presents it to the Saeima. Consideration of the draft constitutional amendment is mandatory, and if the Saeima does not adopt it without change to its content, a referendum is held on the draft as originally submitted.

2) **Legislative:** Article 78 contains identical provisions in relation to a fully elaborated draft law: one tenth of the electorate may submit it to the President, who then forwards it to the Saeima. The failure of the Saeima to adopt the draft law without change to its content triggers a referendum on the initial version of the draft.

Both the legislative and the constitutional initiative have two stages. During the first stage, the signatures of at least 10,000 citizens entitled to vote must be collected; their collection is entirely up to the proponents of the initiative. The initiative does not have to be registered, and the period of time for collecting the required signatures is not limited. The initiative group does not have any formal status.

The signatures have to be certified either by a notary public or by the competent local government authority, which involves expenses by the signatories or the initiators. When the required 10,000 signatures have been collected, the initiators submit the draft to the Central Election Commission, which reviews the signatures and may require certification by the citizenship and immigration authorities that the persons who have signed the initiative have the right to vote.

If the number of signatures is still at least 10,000 after the invalidation of the signatures of persons who do not meet this requirement, the second stage of the initiative begins: the official collection of signatures. Local electoral commissions must ensure the opportunity to support the initiative, and at least one place for signing has to be provided for every 10,000 electors. This stage is financed by the state, and there is no requirement for the signatures to be officially certified.

2. Published in Latvijas Vestnesis (Official Gazette), April 20 4,1994; amendments published August 2, 1995, and September 8, 1998. Both instructions were published in Latvijas Vestnesis (Official Gazette), July 10,1998.

Unlike the referendum, in which the vote is secret, the initiation of a law or a constitutional amendment is open, and in the second stage a stamp is put in the passports of those sign to express their support for the initiative.[3]

The second stage of the initiative is limited to 30 days, excluding the days when elections—general or local—are held: no signatures can be collected on these days. If within this 30-day period the initiative is signed by at least one tenth of the citizens who voted in the last general election, the president submits the draft to the Saeima. The Saeima has to consider the draft during the same session in which it was submitted or, if it is submitted between sessions, in the next ordinary session or in an extraordinary session convened specifically for the consideration of the draft.

3) Popular veto initiative: According to Article 72 of the constitution, the President may suspend for two months the publication of a law adopted by the Saeima, either on his own initiative or if requested by at least one third of the members of the Saeima within seven days after the adoption of the law. The Central Electoral Commission has to ensure 30 days during these two months for the collection of signatures, and if at least one tenth of the electorate supports the initiative, a referendum is held on the repeal of the law. There is one exception to this rule: if the Saeima votes on the law a second time and it receives a favorable vote of at least three fourths of all members of the Saeima, no referendum takes place and the law is promulgated.

b. Referendum

1) Mandatory constitutional referendum: Article 77 of the constitution provides that if the Saeima has amended Article 1, 2, 3, 4, 6, or 77 of the constitution, the amendment must be confirmed by a referendum in order to come into force. The referendum has to be held not earlier than one month and not later than two months after the adoption of the amendments by the Saeima, and, according to Article 79 of the constitution, the constitutional amendment submitted to a referendum is deemed adopted if at least half of the electorate has voted in its favor.

c. Citizens' Decision (ballot vote)

1) Initiative ballot vote: According to Article 78 of the constitution, if the Saeima does not adopt a draft law or constitutional amendment initiated by the people without changing its content, a referendum is held on the original draft between one and two months after the Saeima rejects the draft law or constitutional amendment or adopts it with changes. A constitutional amendment is adopted if at least half of the electorate votes in its favor, while the adoption of a draft law requires the turnout of at least half of the citizens who voted in the last election to the Saeima, with the majority of the votes cast favoring the adoption of the law (Article 79 of the constitution).

This type of referendum has been called "automatic," but it could also be called "conditional," since it automatically takes place if the condition of non-adoption of the original version of the draft is satisfied.

2) Referendum or popular veto ballot vote: According to Article 72 of the constitution, if the popular veto initiative has collected the required number of signatures and if the Saeima has not overridden the referendum request by re-adopting the law with a three-fourths majority of its total membership, a referendum is held on the repeal of the law. It is held not earlier than one month and not later than two months after the Central Electoral Commission has verified the signatures and announced that the referendum will be held. The repeal of the law or constitutional amendment requires the turnout of at least half of the citizens who voted in the last election to the Saeima, with the majority of the votes cast favoring the repeal (Article 74 of the constitution).

It must be noted that the possibility of a legislative initiative, which can result in an automatic referendum to amend or repeal the law, remains available even if the popular veto referendum does not succeed in repealing the law. The legislative initiative is still possible even if the promulgation of the law has not been postponed and therefore there is no opportunity for a popular veto initiative and referendum.

3) Constitutionally defined Presidential Plebiscite: Article 48 of the constitution gives the president the right to propose the dissolution of the Saeima. A referendum is held following this proposal, not earlier than one month and not later than two months after the President has announced the proposal to the Central Electoral Commission.

This is the only referendum in the Latvian constitution that takes place on an issue rather than on the text of a law, the only one for whose initiation the will of a single actor—the President—is sufficient, and also the only one that does not contain a built-in quorum requirement.

---

3. It must be explained that stamps in passports are nothing unusual in Latvia, since in the general elections (which are proportional), an individual may vote in any district of his choice; thus, there are no electoral rolls and a stamp is put in the passport to exclude the possibility of multiple voting. A submission has been made to the National Human Rights Office challenging the requirement of stamping the passport during the process of popular initiative, and despite the opinion of the National Human Rights Office that what matters is secrecy when the vote is actually cast, one may hope that computerization will soon make it possible to abolish this requirement.

If the majority of the votes cast favor the dissolution of the Saeima, the Saeima is dissolved. If the majority of the votes cast oppose the dissolution, the President himself loses his office: a construction that has, at least so far, forestalled any legal efforts to dissolve the parliament.

Several things have to be noted concerning the first three types of referendum (namely, the mandatory constitutional referendum, initiative ballot vote and popular veto ballot vote or referendum) which were mentioned before; the Presidential Plebiscite referendum is, in several respects, an exceptional one.

First, a referendum is only possible on the text of a draft law; no generally worded questions can find their way to a referendum.

Second, no referendum can be brought about by the will of a single individual. The mandatory constitutional referendum takes place pursuant to a constitutional requirement. The initiative ballot vote or automatic referendum on the adoption of a law takes place only if the Saeima has not, without substantial changes, adopted the popularly initiated draft law, but the Saeima is first given the opportunity to adopt the draft, and no law can be taken directly to a referendum because the object of this initiative is the law, not the referendum. The popular veto referendum requires joint action of either the President or one third of the members of the Saeima and one tenth of the electorate.

Third, a quorum requirement is built into all referendums except the referendum on the dissolution of the Saeima. If less than half of the electorate participates in the referendum, it produces no legal result, however overwhelming the majority of the votes cast.

Fourth, there is no such thing as a consultative referendum: the results of any type of referendum are legally binding. Although there are no legal obstacles to prevent parliament from re-adopting of a law that has been repealed by referendum or amending a law adopted by a referendum, good reasons would be required for such an action.

Finally, Article 73 of the constitution lists exempted issues, stating that the budget and laws concerning loans, taxes, customs duties, railroad tariffs, military conscription, declaration and commencement of war, peace treaties, declaration and termination of a state of emergency, mobilization and demobilization, and agreements with other nations may not be submitted to national referendum. This also means that the promulgation of the laws related to these areas cannot be postponed pursuant to Article 72, since the purpose of such postponement is a referendum. However, the constitution not exclude legislative initiative on these issues, although in these cases the failure of the Saeima to adopt the draft without change to its content would not bring about an automatic referendum.

Another category of laws that cannot be submitted to a referendum—which obviously concerns only the popular veto referendum—is laws that the Saeima has declared urgent by a two-thirds majority (Article 75).

Several practical issues have to be mentioned. First, one of the easiest situations to imagine is when the Saeima adopts a popular legislative or constitutional initiative with changes. How are editorial changes dictated by the requirements of legal drafting to be distinguished from changes to its content? No rule specifies who is to determine which changes are acceptable, although it might seem that this task falls to the Central Electoral Commission, which organizes the referendum if the draft has been rejected by the Saeima or adopted with changes to its content. It is hard to speculate whether the issue would be regarded as adjudicable by courts if the decision of the Central Electoral Commission were challenged.

Second, the formulation of the issue in a popular veto referendum may be confusing. If the question in the referendum is "Are you in favor of the repeal of law X?" the supporters of the law need to vote in the negative, while those against it have to vote in the affirmative. There is no requirement for an official summary of the law or for mailing it to voters, but the text of the law has to be made available at the places where signatures are collected.

II. Regional and Local Level

There is no division of Latvia into regions except a historical one, which is used for the purpose of dividing the country into electoral districts. These regions have no competencies, and consequently there is no rule providing for I&R at the regional level. There are currently no legal rules providing for local I&R.

III. Practical Guide

As already noted, there are three types of initiative: constitutional and legislative, for which identical rules apply, and the popular veto initiative. The object of the first two is the initiation of a draft law or constitutional amendment, and they do not necessarily entail a referendum. The object of the popular veto initiative is to bring about a popular veto referendum, which can take place only if the precondition for it—namely, the postponement of the promulgation of the law—has been fulfilled.

Legislative and constitutional initiatives are governed by Article 2, §65 and §78 of the constitution and the popular veto initiative by Article 72, and all three types of initiative are covered in more detail in the already mentioned law "On Public Referendums and Legislative Initiative"16 and in the instructions issued by the Central Electoral Commission: "On the procedure in which the Central Electoral Commission accepts a draft law or a draft constitutional amendment" and "On the collection of signatures for the initiation of a referendum on a law whose publication has been postponed."

For constitutional and legislative initiatives, the basic steps are as follows. The initiators of the draft must collect the signatures of at least 10,000 electors; there are no official forms and no time limits, but each sheet of paper or set of sheets on which signatures are collected must contain the full text of the draft. The signatures have to be certified by a notary public or a local government authority; in both cases the name and personal ID code of the signatory must be indicated, since they will be used by the Central Electoral Commission to verify that the person who signed is a Latvian citizen with the right to vote.

Three of the signatories submit the collected signatures to the Central Electoral Commission, and if their number still exceeds the required 10,000 after the verification of signatures and removal of the invalid ones, the Central Electoral Commission announces the official collection of signatures that will last 30 days and can take place only in specifically designated places. The designation of these places is up to each municipality, but there must be at least one such place for every 10,000 electors. If the total number of signatures collected is at least one tenth of the citizens who had the right to vote in the last election to the Saeima, the initiative has been successful and the Saeima must consider the draft.

The popular veto initiative does not go through the initiating stage: if the promulgation of the law is postponed, the Central Electoral Commission announces the official collection of signatures after the President informs it of the postponement. Thus, there is no initiative group, although campaigning is still desirable for the timely collection of the required number of signatures. This is even more important for popular veto initiatives than for other initiatives: while in the latter case the signatures collected at the initiation stage of the initiative also count as part of the required one-tenth of the electorate, there are no previously collected signatures when the popular veto referendum is being initiated, and hence the deadline is more pressing.

The website of the Central Electoral Commission at www.cvk.lv (currently only in Latvian) contains the official information of the Commission and can be used to verify whether there are any referendums announced or there is any initiative in its official stage; unfortunately, there is no information on the website about previous initiatives and referendums.

IV. Trends

The provisions for direct democracy as part of the renewed 1922 constitution have been accepted as given: there has been no debate on their desirability or acceptability. Nor was the issue regarded as a contentious one by the drafters of the constitution, who found their ideological inspiration in the Swiss constitution and their model for the actual construction of the instruments of direct democracy in the constitution of the Weimar Republic.

In the interwar period or, more precisely, until the 1934 coup d'état, there have been six popular veto initiatives: two initiated by the people and four by the legislature. The first popular veto referendum took place in 1923, aiming to repeal the law that gave the Lutheran church of St. James to the Roman Catholic Church to serve as the archbishop's cathedral; despite overwhelming support for the repeal, it failed for the lack of quorum. In the autumn of the same year, a legislative initiative succeeded in getting the Saeima to adopt a law dealing with land reform.

Another popular veto initiative to repeal amendments to the citizenship law was successful in 1927. However, the Saeima overrode the referendum by readopting the law with the required three-fourths majority of its membership. In the same year a legislative initiative dealing with the repeal of certain privileges in acquiring land succeeded, and no referendum followed.

In 1931, the Saeima refused to adopt a popularly initiated law to hand over the largest church in Riga—the Doma church—to the Lutheran parish, and a referendum followed. This is an interesting case, because it illustrates the persuasive element of referendum: although the automatic referendum failed for lack of quorum, the fact that more than 30% of the electorate favored the draft persuaded the Saeima to reconsider its view and adopt the draft it had initially rejected (or, more precisely, to adopt an analogous law).

The last referendum in pre-war Latvia took place in 1933, and again failed for the lack of a quorum; this time the Saeima was not persuaded by the popular support for the draft and did not reconsider its view. Thus, while there were successful initiatives, all referendums prior to World War II failed due to the quorum requirement.

Direct democracy has resurged since the restoration of independence, and thanks to the decision of the Central Electoral Commission to schedule the popular veto referendum on the same day as the general elections on October 3, 1998, Latvia can even boast a referendum in which the quorum requirement was satisfied. Another referendum on independence took place in 1991 prior to the re-entry into force of the 1922 constitution.

In 1995, an initiative aimed at introducing the recall of individual members of the Saeima was on the agenda; although it reportedly collected the required initial 10,000 signatures, it was never submitted to the Central Electoral Commission.

Given the unofficial character of the initial stage of the initiative, it is impossible to ascertain whether there are any other initiatives that have failed to receive the 10,000 signatures or whose initiators have decided not to proceed with them despite the evidence of initial support.

In 1996, a legislative initiative to make the citizenship law more stringent failed to receive the support of one tenth of the electorate. However, in 1999 an initiative to repeal amendments to the state's pension law failed at the referendum stage: although 94% of the votes cast favored the repeal, the turnout equaled only 35.25% of the electors voting at the previous general election.

So far, the 1998 popular veto initiative on the repeal of amendments to the citizenship law has been the only one to satisfy both the initiative requirements and the turnout requirement at the referendum. Because the referendum was held on election day, which prevented the use of the obstructive tactic of inviting opponents not to participate, the turnout equaled 97% of the electors who had voted at the previous general elections; 52.54% of the votes were cast against repeal of the amendments.

The June 2000 initiative obtained the signatures of 22.9% of the electorate for a draft law to prohibit the privatization of the state-owned energy enterprise "Latvenergo"; the law was adopted by the Saeima and hence no referendum followed. There are currently two constitutional initiatives at the initial stage: a draft of a new Constitution sponsored by the Social Democratic party and a constitutional amendment to introduce the direct election of the President.

The constitution did not permit a government-initiated referendum on the issue of joining the EU: Latvia's membership in it required constitutional amendment because of the entrenched Article 2, which can be modified only by a compulsory constitutional referendum requiring the consent of half the electorate. A working group under the auspices of the Ministry of Justice produced a draft constitutional amendment specifically providing for a compulsory "membership of the EU" referendum to take place after the conclusion of the membership treaty with the EU in 2003. The "membership of the EU" formulation specifies that withdrawal from the EU would also be subject to compulsory referendum.

A turnout of at least half of the citizens who voted in the last elections to the Saeima, with the majority of the votes cast favoring membership, would ordinarily have been required. But the authors of the draft adhered to the view that the notion of sovereignty referred to in Article 2 of the constitution had already undergone significant changes in view of the development of international law and thus would not be further affected by Latvia's membership. This position implied that there was no need for a compulsory constitutional referendum, and made it possible to avoid the requirement of the support of one half of the electorate. On September 20, 2003, Latvians voted in favor of EU membership by a margin of 67% to 32.3%, with a 72.5% turnout.

Main author: Gita Feldhune

Constitutional Requirements for Legislation

Chapter IV: The Government

Article 69 (Promulgation): The President shall proclaim laws passed by the Parliament not earlier than the seventh day and not later than the twenty-first day after the law has been adopted. A law shall come into force fourteen days after its proclamation unless a different term has been specified in the law.

Article 70 (Formula of Promulgation): The President shall proclaim adopted laws in the following manner: *"The Parliament (that is, the People) has adopted and the President has proclaimed the following law: (text of the law)."*

Article 71 (Request for Revision): Within seven days of the adoption of a law by the Parliament, the President, by means of a written and reasoned request to the Chairperson of the Parliament, may require that a law be reconsidered. If the Parliament does not amend the law, the President may not raise objections a second time.

Article 72 (Withholding Promulgation): The President has the right to suspend the proclamation of a law for a period of two months. The President shall suspend the proclamation of a law if so requested by not less than one third of the members of the Parliament. This right may be exercised by the President, or by one third of the members of the Parliament, within seven days of the adoption of the law by the Parliament. The law thus suspended shall be put to a national referendum if so requested by not less than one tenth of the electorate. If no such request is received during the aforementioned two-month period, the law shall then be proclaimed after the expiration of such period. A national referendum shall not take place, however, if the Parliament votes again on the law and not less than three quarters of all members of the Parliament vote for the adoption of the law.

Article 73 (Matters Excluded from Referendum): The Budget and laws concerning loans, taxes, customs duties, railroad tariffs, military conscription, declaration and commencement of war, peace treaties, declaration of a state of emergency and its termination, mobilization and demobilization, and agreements with other nations may not be submitted to national referendum.

Article 74 (Annulment by Referendum): A law adopted by the Parliament and suspended pursuant to the procedures specified in Article 72 shall be repealed by national referendum if the number of voters is at least half the number of electors who participated in the previous parliamentary election and if the majority has voted for repeal of the law.

Article 75 (Urgency): Should the Parliament, by not less than a two-thirds majority vote, determine a law to be urgent, the President may not request reconsideration of such a law, it may not be submitted to national referendum, and the adopted law shall be proclaimed no later than the third day after the President has received it.

Article 76 (Amendment of the Constitution): The Parliament may amend the Constitution in sittings at which at least two-thirds of the members of Parliament participate. The amendments shall be passed in three readings by a majority of not less than two-thirds of the members present.

Article 77 (Referendum About Amendment): If Parliament has amended Articles 1, 2, 3, 4, 6, or 77 of the Constitution, such amendments, in order to come into force as law, shall be submitted to a national referendum. Article 78 (Amendment by Popular Initiative): Electors, in number comprising not less than one tenth of the electorate, have the right to submit a fully-elaborated draft of an amendment to the Constitution or of a law to the President, who shall present it to the Parliament. If the Parliament does not adopt it without change as to its content, it shall then be submitted to national referendum.

Article 79 (Referendum After Popular Initiative): An amendment to the Constitution submitted for national referendum shall be deemed adopted if at least half of the electorate has voted in favor. A draft law submitted for national referendum shall be deemed adopted if the number of voters is at least half the number of electors who participated in the previous parliamentary election and if the majority has voted in favor of the draft law.

Article 80 (Right to Vote in Referendum): All citizens of Latvia who have the right to vote in elections of the Parliament may participate in national referendums.

Liechtenstein

Like Switzerland, the Principality of Liechtenstein belongs to the small group of countries with well-developed, direct-democratic citizens' rights. This honour is marred, however, by the absolute right of veto of the head of state, the Prince Regnant of Liechtenstein, who can block an initiative which has been popularly approved.

No law can enter into force in Liechtenstein without the signature of the Prince Regnant. During the last 10 years, Prince Hans-Adam has brought about alterations to laws by threatening not to approve them (education law; law on adult education) or has blocked laws by refusing to sign them (law on the constitutional court).

Citizens' rights are fully developed—including initiative and referendum rights—at the level of the eleven political districts. The head of state has no right of veto at the communal level.

Because of its small size, Liechtenstein has no intermediate political level (region, canton, federal state).

- Population: 33,500 (34.4% foreigners)
- Surface area: 160 km²
- Capital: Vaduz
- Official language: German
- Religion: 80% Catholic, 7% Protestant, 13% other or no affiliation.
- Form of state: Constitutional hereditary monarchy on a democratic and parliamentary basis
- Constitution (new): March 16, 2003, approved by referendum on constitutional proposals put forward by the Prince Regnant (65.3% Yes)
- Membership of: UN, EFTA, EEA, European Council, OSCE
- GDP:[4] 4,000,000,000 Swiss Francs (Liechtenstein has a currency and customs union with Switzerland)
- I&R practice: since 1918, an average of one national referendum per year resulting from a citizens' initiative or a legislative or constitutional referendum. At the communal level, referendums and initiatives on local legislation.

---

4. A peculiarity of Liechtenstein's GDP is that it is based to a considerable extent on the earnings of workers from other countries. In 1999, 38.5% of those employed in Liechtenstein (around 9,700 people) were cross-border commuters. For this reason, the per capita GDP cannot be calculated solely by dividing overall GDP by the average population figure. Calculating GDP per resident would produce misleading results in an international comparison.

Types of Initiative and Referendum

I. National Level

In 1699, the Liechtenstein family, which belonged to the higher nobility and resided in Vienna, acquired the fief of Schellenberg, and in 1712, it acquired another fief, Vadeuz. In 1719, Emperor Charles VI granted the title of principality to these lands.

In 1806, Liechtenstein became part of the Rhenish Confederation and a sovereign state. In 1852, Liechtenstein and the Austrian Empire entered into a customs union.

Liechtenstein was not drawn into either WWI or WWII (Liechtenstein did not even have an army). WWI saw the collapse of the Austro-Hungarian Empire. At the same time, democratic forces began to make themselves heard in Liechtenstein, questioning the absolute rule of the princely house. This resulted in the 1921 Constitution, which allotted state power jointly to two supreme organs: the Prince and the people.

The constitutions of 1818 and 1862 had been imposed and had given no rights of co-determination, or at best highly marginal rights, to the people.

The 1921 Constitution gave adult male citizens of Liechtenstein unrestricted rights to elect their members of parliament; women finally secured both active and passive voting rights at the national level on July 1, 1984. The 1921 Constitution provided direct-democratic citizens' rights similar to those in Switzerland: constitutional and legislative initiatives, referendums to challenge parliamentary decrees, consultative referendums, and initiatives to dissolve or convene parliament.

In legislative and constitutional initiatives—the two most powerful instruments—any amendment voted by the people must be submitted to the Prince for his approval before it can enter into force. A popular initiative launched in August 2002 to contest proposed changes to the constitution was unsuccessful: the Prince had launched an initiative for a major revision of the constitution, and the referendum of March 16, 2003[5] on the two initiatives resulted in a confirmation of the Prince's right of veto, with 65.4% of voters accepting the Prince's initiative.

The legal bases for the people's direct-democratic rights are to be found in the (revised) 1921 constitution and in the 1973 law on citizens' rights.

A popular initiative for a total or partial revision of the law requires a minimum 1500 signatures of registered voters for a constitutional initiative, or 1000 signatures for a legislative initiative or referendum.

Referendums are decided by a simple majority of the valid votes cast nationally. There is no minimum turnout requirement.

a. Constitutional and Legislative Initiative

Article 64 of the 1921 constitution:

1) The right of initiative with regard to legislation, that is to say, the right of introducing bills, shall appertain to:

a) the Prince Regnant, in the form of Government bills;

b) the Diet itself;

c) citizens with the right to vote, subject to the following provisions.

2) If not less than 1,000 citizens entitled to vote, whose signatures and qualification to vote are duly certified by the authorities of the commune in which they reside, submit a petition in writing, or if at least three communes do so in the form of resolutions of the communal assembly in similar terms requesting the enactment, amendment or revocation of a law, such petition must he debated at the next session of the Diet. (1)

3) If a petition from one of the organs referred to under a) to c) above concerns the enactment of a law which has not already been provided for in the present Constitution and the adoption of which would involve public expenditure, whether in a single sum not provided for in the Finance Bill or in payments extending over a longer period, such petition shall be discussed by the Diet only if it is accompanied by proposals for providing the necessary funds.

4) A petition submitted under the right of initiative and concerning the Constitution may only be brought by not less than 1,500 citizens entitled to vote or by at least four communes. (2)

5) Further detailed regulations regarding this popular initiative shall be laid down in a law:

(1) Art. 64 Para. 2 amended by LGBl. 1947 No. 55 and LGBl. 1984 No. 27. (2) Art. 64 Para. 4 amended by LGBl. 1947 No. 55 and LGBl. 1984 No. 27.

---

5. The Prince's initiative for a revision of the 1921 Constitution had not entered into force by copy deadline (August 20, 2003). Publication of the amended constitution has been delayed due to the extensive changes required to the organisation of the judiciary and of the constitutional court.

The government must be advised of popular initiatives before any signatures are collected. The government checks the initiative to ensure that it is consistent with the constitution and international treaties and submits a report to parliament for further consideration.

Parliament can declare the initiative invalid if it contravenes the constitution or international treaties, but its proponents can appeal this declaration to the constitutional court. So far, no initiative has been declared invalid.

After parliament has considered the initiative, commencement of the collection of signatures is announced by the Interior Minister. The period allowed for collection is six weeks. The initiative committee has to have all the signatures validated by the communal authorities within this period. When the required number of signatures has been reached, the initiative is officially launched. The initiative is debated in the next session of parliament, and the government then has two weeks to choose and announce a date for the referendum, which must take place within three months of the announcement.

In 1987, the possibility of a "double yes" vote was introduced for cases where there is more than one proposal (e.g. original initiative, counter-initiative, counter-proposal by parliament). The voter can either reject all the proposals or vote for one or more of them. In such cases there is also a "tie-break" question, which asks the voter to choose which of the proposals he or she would prefer in the event that each of two or more proposals secures an absolute majority. In this case, the result of the tie-break question is used to decide which of the proposals has gained the most votes.

b. Referendum

A request for a referendum to overturn legislative or fiscal decisions by parliament or decisions by parliament to enter into international agreements will be accepted if the required number of validated signatures is submitted within 30 days of the official announcement of the parliamentary decisions. The government then has 14 days to declare a date for a referendum, which must be held within 3 months.

1. General referendum

Article 66 of the 1921 constitution:

1) Every law passed by the Diet which it does not declare to be urgent or any financial resolution which it does not declare urgent, if it involves a new non-recurrent expenditure of not less than 300,000 francs or a new annual expenditure of 150,000 francs, shall be submitted to a referendum if the Diet so decides or if not less than 1,000 citizens with the right to vote or not less than three communes submit a petition requesting it, according to the procedure prescribed in Article 64, within 30 days of the official publication of the resolution of the Diet. (1)

2) If the issue affects the Constitution as a whole or in part, the demand for a referendum must be made by not less than 1,500 citizens with the right to vote or by not less than four communes. (2)

3) The Diet is authorized to call for a referendum on the adoption of any of the principles embodied in a proposed law.

4) The referendum shall be held by the communes; the acceptance or rejection of the resolution on the enactment of the law shall be decided by an absolute majority of the valid votes recorded in the whole of the country.

5) Resolutions on the enactment of laws subject to a referendum shall not be submitted to the Prince Regnant for sanction until the referendum has been held or until the statutory period of thirty days within which a petition for a referendum may be submitted has expired without any such action. (3)

6) If the Diet rejects a bill drawn up in due form and accompanied if necessary by proposals for providing the necessary funds and which has been submitted to it through the procedure of the popular initiative (Art. 64 Para. 1 lit. c), the said bill shall be submitted to a referendum. The acceptance of the bill by the citizens entitled to vote shall then have the same force as a resolution of the Diet otherwise necessary for the adoption of a law.

7) Further detailed regulations regarding the referendum shall be issued in the form of a law.

(1) Art. 66 Para. 1 amended by LGBl. 1996 No. 85.

(2) Art. 66 Para. 2 amended by LGBl. 1947 No. 55 and LGBl. 1984 No. 27.

(3) The words "...nach fruchtlosem Ablauf der für die Stellung des Begehrens..." (...expired without any such action...) are not contained in the original but were added by Mr. Ferdinand Nigg, Government Secretary from 1923 to 1945.

2. Referendum on state treaties

1) Any resolution of the Diet concerning assent to a treaty (Art. 8) must be submitted to a referendum if the Diet so decides or if not less than 1,500 citizens with the right to vote or not less than four communes submit a petition to that effect, according to the procedure prescribed in Art. 64, within 30 days of the official publication of the resolution of the Diet.

2) In the referendum, the acceptance or rejection of the resolution by the Diet shall be decided by an absolute majority of the valid votes recorded in the whole of the country.

3) Further detailed regulations regarding the referendum shall be issued in the form of a law.

(1) Art. 66bis inserted by LGBl. 1992 No. 27.

c. Popular Request to Dissolve or Convene Parliament

1) The Prince Regnant has the right, subject to the exception laid down in the following paragraph, to convene the Diet, to close it, and, on warrantable grounds, which must on each occasion be communicated to the assembled Diet, to prorogue it for three months or to dissolve it. The prorogation, closing or dissolution of the Diet may only be proclaimed before the assembled Diet. (1)

2) In pursuance of a substantiated written request submitted by not less than 1,000 citizens entitled to vote or of a resolution adopted by the communal assemblies of not less than three communes, the Diet must be convened. (2)

3) Subject to the same conditions as in the preceding paragraph, 1,500 citizens entitled to vote or four communes which have adopted resolutions to that effect at their communal assemblies may demand a referendum with regard to the dissolution of the Diet. (3)

(1) Art. 48 Para. 1 of the Constitution is to be understood in such a manner that in the event of the dissolution of the Diet by the Prince Regnant a four-year mandate of the Diet resulting from the new election shall commence. (LGBl. 1929 No. 5.)

(2) Art. 48 Para. 2 amended by LGBl. 1947 No. 55 and LGBl. 1984 No. 27. (3) Art. 48 Para. 3 amended by LGBl. 1947 No. 55 and LGBl. 1984 No. 27.

II. Local Level

Voters enjoy the same direct-democratic rights of initiative and referendum at the communal level.

III. Trend

In the last decade, eleven national referendums have been held in addition to the general elections held every four years.

On four occasions, parliament presented a proposal for approval in a referendum. In two cases (accession to the EEA in 1995; amendment to law on citizenship in 2000), the proposals were accepted. In the other two cases, they were rejected (finance for a new parliament building in 1993; law on town and country planning in 2002).

On three occasions, the referendum right was used to challenge bills adopted by parliament. In one case, voters supported the bill (introduction of an engine-size-related heavy goods vehicle tax in 2000). In the other two cases, the electorate voted down the bills (change to housing construction law, 2000; financing of the "Little Big One" Open Air Festival, 2002).

In the last decade, Liechtenstein's electorate has voted four times on citizens' initiatives. Three of the initiatives were constitutional initiatives (traffic initiative, 2002; constitutional reform initiative of the Prince Regnant, 2003; popular initiative "for constitutional peace" as a counter-proposal to the Prince's initiative); one initiative was a legislative initiative (health insurance, 1999). All the initiatives, with the exception of the Prince's initiative for a large-scale revision of the 1921 constitution (voted on in the referendum of March 16, 2003), were rejected in the resulting referendums.

Main author: Sigward Wohlwend

Lithuania

During a period of only five years (1991–1996), Lithuanians had a direct say on ten different issues, from independence to privatizations and institutional questions. But before and since this five-year period, no referendum decisions have taken place.

In Soviet times, and even before—during the first period of independence—there were no provisions for I&R, and since 1996 the current design with very high hurdles and thresholds does not seem citizen-friendly enough. However, there was a successful EU accession referendum in May 2003, which brought the idea of citizen lawmaking back on stage.

- Population: 3,490,000
- Area: 65,301 km²
- Capital: Vilnius
- Official language: Lithuanian (82%), other languages: Polish (6.7%), Russian (6.3%)
- Religion: Roman Catholic (85%)
- Political System: Republic (since 1991)
- Constitution: October 25, 1992 (referendum, 78% yes, turnout 75%)
- Membership: EU and NATO (2004)

- GNP/Capita: $8,470
- Human Development Rank: 45
- I&R practice: 11 countrywide ballots (since 1991); of 10 legislative and constitutional citizen initiatives, only one reached the 50% participation threshold.

Types of Initiative and Referendum

Lithuania is a centralist unitary state: regional institutions are strongly subordinated to central government. Heads of regional authorities are appointed by central government. Local self-government has considerable competencies in housing, urban planning, healthcare, local transport systems, police and public safety, education, and environment. Local government is elected according to a proportional electoral formula.

I. National Level

According to Article 68 of Lithuania's Constitution, legislative initiative is vested in the Seimas, the Government, the President, and groups of at least 50,000 citizens. The Supreme Soviet of the Lithuanian Soviet Socialist Republic passed the law on referendums on November 3, 1989. This law was amended by the Seimas of the Republic of Lithuania in 1990, 1992, 1994, 1995, 1996, 1997, 1999 and 2000. A new referendum law was passed by the Lithuanian Seimas in June 2002.

a. Popular Initiative

Article 1 of the 1989 referendum law stated that "the most urgent issues relating to the life of the State and the Nation shall be resolved and the provisions of laws of the Republic of Lithuania may be adopted by a referendum." This means that all politically, economically, and socially relevant issues can be the subjects of referendums.

The President of Lithuania must within five days sign and officially promulgate laws and other acts adopted by referendum.

The 2002 referendum law introduced two different types: compulsory and consultative referendum. Compulsory referendum is designed to deal primarily with constitutional issues, including Lithuania's membership in international organizations, if such membership requires the delegation of certain functions of the Lithuanian state to supranational bodies of these international organizations (for example, the EU). Compulsory and consultative referendums can be called on all other major issues of the life of the state and society as a result of a citizens' or Seimas initiative.

The right of initiative to call a referendum belongs to parliament and to the citizens. This right is implemented at the request of no less than one fourth of the members of the Seimas, whereas the citizens' initiative has to be expressed by a request of at least 300,000 citizens who have the right to vote.

Before the 1996 amendments, the proposal of a referendum required more than half of the members of the Seimas. After 1996, the procedure was made easier for the members of parliament in that a minimum of only one third of the Seimas members was required to initiate a referendum.

The 2002 referendum law further decreased the threshold for the members of the Seimas. The referendum law guarantees citizens and various organized groups the right to campaign freely in the process of petitioning for a referendum. Both supporters and opponents of the specific issue in a referendum have a guarantee of seven hours of debates on national TV and radio.

b. Requirements

Procedures for the organization and execution of all compulsory and consultative referendums are the same.

Time-frame and procedure for referendum petitions: A term of three months is set for the implementation of the citizens' right to initiate a referendum on a specific issue. This term is counted from the day of a referendum petition is registered with the Central Electoral Commission by the initiating group of citizens, which must consist of at least fifteen persons. The act of registration must be recorded at the time of the registration, and one copy of the record must be sent to the Speaker of the Seimas no later than on the day following the registration.

Collection of signatures: Citizens' signatures are collected on special signature collection lists, and a citizen who signs the referendum petition must indicate his/her name, date of birth, permanent place of residence, and passport number. The Central Electoral Commission counts the signatures and judges their validity.

c. Citizens' Decision

Calling a ballot vote: After receiving the documents for the calling of a ballot vote, the Central Electoral Commission must check them within fifteen days. After the signatures have been checked, the concluding statement of the citizens' initiative group is submitted to the Seimas, along with the citizens' requests and the conclusion of the Central Electoral Commission that the documents are in conformity with the law.

The parliament considers the issue of calling the referendum at its next sitting, which representatives of the referendum initiative must be invited to attend. The referendum must be held no earlier than two months and no later than three months after the day the Seimas resolution is adopted.

Organization and execution of the referendum vote: The Central Electoral Commission prepares and conducts the referendum, and all costs of organizing the referendum are covered by the state.

Establishment of the referendum results: A law or any other decision is adopted by referendum if more than half of all registered electors have approved the referendum issue. If participation is less than 50% of the total electorate, the referendum is deemed invalid.

Constitutional decisions which have been adopted by referendum can be amended or repealed only by referendum. The decisions of a consultative referendum must be presented and discussed in the Seimas no later than one month after the declaration of the official referendum results, in order to implement the referendum decisions.

d. Petition

The right to initiate legislation belongs not only to members of the Seimas, the President of the Republic, and the government, but also to citizens: "A draft law may be submitted to the Seimas by 50,000 citizens of the Republic of Lithuania who have the right to vote. The Seimas must consider this draft law."

The procedure for the submission of a draft law by citizens is regulated by the law on legislative initiatives passed by the Seimas on October 22, 1998. The requirements for initiating a law or changes to an existing law are simpler than those for a referendum petition in that a final legislative proposal needs to be signed by only 50,000 voters.

II. Regional and Local I&R

Because the initial Lithuanian referendum Law was passed in the last days of the Communist regime, during a period of political upheaval, it was designed only for decisions on nationwide issues. The referendum law does not apply at regional and local levels.

The new law of 2002 still has no provisions which might make it possible to organize regional and local referendums. Municipalities have made no attempts to introduce their own referendum bylaws or to allow the popular initiative. In theory, it is possible to use the right of legislative initiative at regional and local levels, but it has never been employed since 1998, i.e. since the adoption of the law on the legislative initiative.

III. Trend

In June 2002, a new referendum law was passed which introduced two different types of referendum: compulsory and consultative. Compulsory referendum was designed to deal primarily with constitutional issues, including Lithuania's membership in international organizations, if such membership requires delegating certain functions of Lithuanian state to supranational bodies of these international organizations.

As Article 7 of the Law of the Republic of Lithuania on the Referendum says, a mandatory referendum is considered to have taken place if over one half of the citizens who have the right to vote and are registered in voter lists have taken part in it. If participation is less than 50% of the total electorate, the binding referendum is deemed invalid.

When constitutional decisions have been adopted by referendum, they can only be amended or repealed by referendum.

On the eve of the euro referendum, the Lithuanian Seimas passed an amendment to the referendum law easing the requirements for a referendum on participation by the Republic of Lithuania in international organizations when this participation involves the partial transfer of the competence of Government bodies to the institutions of international organizations. Under the new amendment, the measure is passed if it is approved by more than one half of the voters who have participated in the referendum, rather than the previously required 50% of the total electorate.

The final referendum results must be officially published by the Central Electoral Committee in the "State Gazette," no later than 4 days after the referendum vote.

If the referendum had failed because of a lack of voters, the government could have held another one later in 2003. The parliament itself could also have chosen to approve EU membership, although that would probably have been viewed as less than democratic.

As a rule, all victorious political campaigns are evaluated as successful and efficient, while all political campaigns which lead to the defeat of a candidate or an issue are viewed critically. The euro referendum campaign was intense and quite innovative. New elements of the campaign included visits by EU officials, a referendum in Lithuanian high schools on EU, and the successful mobilization of opinion leaders including the Catholic Church, the mass media, and most authoritative social institutions which had enjoyed a high level of voter confidence since 1990.

In general, the informational campaign was evaluated positively. In a poll about the information campaign, 76.6% of the respondents said they had received enough information during the campaign, 6.9% said they had received too much information, and 11.5% said they had received too little. 47.6% approved the information on Lithuanian-EU relations provided by Committee of European Affairs to the Lithuanian government, and only 8.0% disapproved it. The way the issue was advertised in the mass media was seen positively by 60.5% of the respondents and negatively by 21.8%. Generally, the euro referendum campaign was seen as free and fair by most domestic and external observers.

On the other hand, certain weaknesses of the campaign were noted. These included the limited funding of the campaign (only 3.5 million Lt. or ~1 million Euro, in comparison to 15.9 million Euro in Malta), attempts to change the Referendum Law to allow the parliament to make the final decision on the Lithuania's entry into the EU, the failure of initial forecasts that a majority of voters would come to vote on Saturday, and a lack of confidence in the voters expressed by political leaders in the mass media.

Looking on the euro referendum results in Lithuania from a comparative perspective, these conclusions might be drawn:

- Voter turnout was the second highest among the EU candidate-countries which held a referendum in or before June 2003.
- In its proportion of "yes" votes, Lithuania was the second highest after Slovakia.
- Lithuania had the highest percentage of the total electorate voting "yes": 57.76%.

Main author: Algis Krupavicius

Constitutional Requirements for Legislation

Chapter 14 (Amending the Constitution):
Article 147:
(1) In order to amend or append the Constitution of the Republic of Lithuania, a proposal must be submitted to the Parliament either by no less than one fourth of the members of the Parliament or by at least 300,000 voters.
(2) The Constitution may not be amended during a state of emergency or martial law.
Article 148:
(1) The provision of Article 1 that the State of Lithuania is an independent democratic republic may be amended only by a referendum in which at least three fourths of the electorate of Lithuania vote in favor of the amendment.
(2) The provisions of Chapter 1 and Chapter 14 may be amended only by referendum.
(3) Amendments of other chapters of the Constitution must be considered and voted on twice in the Parliament. There must be a lapse of at least three months between each vote. Bills for constitutional amendments shall be deemed adopted by the Parliament if, in each of the votes, at least two thirds of all the members of the Parliament vote in favor of the Bill.
(4) An amendment to the Constitution which is rejected by the Parliament may not be submitted to the Parliament for reconsideration for the period of one year.
Article 149:
(1) An adopted law on an amendment to the Constitution shall be signed by the President of the Republic of Lithuania and officially promulgated within 5 days.
(2) If the President of the Republic of Lithuania does not sign and promulgate such a law in due time, this law shall become effective when the Chairperson of the Parliament signs and promulgates it.
(3) The law on an amendment to the Constitution shall become effective no earlier than one month after the adoption thereof.
Chapter 15 (Final Provisions):
Article 150:
(1) The constituent parts of the Constitution of the Republic of Lithuania shall be:
(2) The February 11, 1991 Constitutional Law *"On the State of Lithuania"*;
(3) The June 8, 1992 Constitutional Act *"On the Non-Alignment of the Republic of Lithuania with Post-Soviet Eastern Alliances."*
Article 151:
This Constitution of the Republic of Lithuania shall become effective the day following the official promulgation of the results of the Referendum, provided that in the Referendum more than half of the electorate of Lithuania voted in favor thereof.

Article 152:

The procedure for the enforcement of this Constitution and separate provisions thereof shall be regulated by the Law of the Republic of Lithuania *"On the Procedure for the Enforcement of the Constitution of the Republic of Lithuania,"* which, together with this Constitution of the Republic of Lithuania, shall be adopted by referendum.

Article 153:

Upon the adoption of this Constitution in the Referendum, the Parliament of the Republic of Lithuania may, by October 25, 1993, amend by three-fifths majority vote of all the Parliament members the provisions of the Constitution of the Republic of Lithuania set forth in Articles 47, 55, 56, 58 (2) No. 2, 65, 68, 69, 84 No. 11 & 12, 87 (1), 96, 103, 118 and 119.

Article 154:

Upon their adoption by referendum, the Constitution of the Republic of Lithuania and the Law of the Republic of Lithuania *"On the Procedure for the Enforcement of the Constitution of the Republic of Lithuania"* shall be signed and promulgated within 15 days by the President of the Supreme Council of the Republic of Lithuania.

Luxembourg

Luxembourg has a very weak experience of referendums. There is no provision for a citizens' initiative at the national level, and there are no binding referendums: they are all purely consultative. The constitution provides for voters to be asked to express their opinion by means of referendum in certain cases and under such conditions as are to be determined by law. However, no such law currently exists.

- Population: 448,569 (July 2002) (1/3 non-Luxembourg citizens)
- Surface area: 2,586 km²
- Capital: Luxembourg City
- Official languages: Lëtzebuergesch (Luxembourgish), German, French
- Religion: predominantly Catholic
- Political system: parliamentary democracy, with a Grand Duke as head of state
- Constitution: 1868 (with revisions)
- Membership: EU, NATO, EMU
- GNP/cap. : $53,780
- Human Development Rank : 15
- I&R practice: two national referendums (1919, 1937) and five local referendums (since 1988)

The Grand Duchy of Luxembourg is a democratic, free, independent and indivisible State (Article 1 of constitution). Sovereign power resides in the Nation. The Grand Duke exercises this power in accordance with the constitution and the laws of the country (Article 32). The Grand Duchy is ruled by a system of parliamentary democracy (Article 51.1). The electors may be requested to express their view by way of referendum in cases and under conditions to be determined by law (Article 51.7).

I. National Level

Luxembourg, which has a surface area of 2586 km² and a population of 448,569 (July 2002), has existed as a neutral and independent state since 1867. In 1870, a popular petition in the form of a spontaneous referendum confirmed the citizens' desire for independence, which became an issue from that moment on. General voting rights were introduced in 1919, and Article 52.7 (now 51.7) of the new constitution of May 8, 1919, provided for referendums. The law provided for in this article of the constitution has still not been adopted by parliament; nonetheless, there have been two national referendums in Luxembourg's history.

The first referendum was authorized by a simple law on March 18, 1919, and was held on September 18, 1919. The first question concerned the form of the state : monarchy or republic. The second asked Luxembourgers to decide on the question of economic cooperation. The vote was purely consultative, but in view of the particular circumstances and the political crisis at the time, it had considerable significance.

Against the background of the threat from national socialism, a bill to determine the form of referendums was introduced by H. Clement in 1935, but it did not provide for a popular initiative with decision-making powers. The bill was not implemented.

In May 1935, a bill was presented by J. Bech (labeled the "muzzling" law), aimed at banning the Communist party and similar organisations. The ruling politicians wanted to have their plan ratified by a popular plebiscite. Despite the fact that the proposed bill had the support of a large parliamentary majority which was confident that the public would back them in the referendum, the people rejected the bill on June 6, 1937. There have been no more referendums since then in Luxembourg.

The next attempt to introduce a bill regulating future referendums was made by the Socialist Party in 1948. The bill was rejected.

Since 1987, there has been a new quality to the debate on referendums following the launching that year of the "Iwweparteilech Biergeraktioun fir direkt Demokratie" (Non-partisan Citizens' Direct Democracy Campaign). This initiative proposed the introduction of participative democracy in three stages (citizens' initiative; citizens' submission; referendum) at both the national and local levels, as well as a number of constitutional changes providing for more direct democracy. The effects of this initiative and the emergence of a number of other popular initiatives have resulted in the introduction of a "popular consultation" at the local level as part of a review of communal law.

A national opinion poll showed that 76% of citizens support the introduction of national referendums, but a bill proposed by R. Mehlen of ADR (Action Committee for Democracy and Justice) in 1993 to institute a citizens' initiative referendum was not adopted.

II. Local Level

Communal referendums were instituted by Article 35 of communal law on December 13, 1988 : "The local council can ask the voters to decide by referendum on local issues under conditions determined by the council. A referendum must be held when requested by 20% of the voters in communities with a population of more than 3,000, or by 25% of the voters in the remaining communities. In such cases, the local council must arrange a referendum within three months of the request." Voting is obligatory, and in all cases the referendums are purely consultative. The details of the referendum were determined by a ruling of the Grand Duke on October 18, 1989.

There have been very few referendums to date: only five since 1988. The issues were: industrial discharge; sporting and cultural centre; hostel for immigrants (withdrawn); discharge of non-reactive substances; development of a public square. In addition, there was one simple public consultation (Article 36 of communal law; voting not obligatory) regarding a proposed building development.

III. Trends

Since 2001, the "Initiative for Direct Democracy" (MTK-IDEE) has been trying to revive the debate about I&R with its own proposal, which it presented at the first Luxembourg Social Forum in May 2003. Following on from the Forum, a platform for democracy has been created in order to unite members of civil society around the issue of promoting democracy, and an Internet forum (www.demokratie.lu) has also been created.

What is new in this is the alliance between the Initiative for Direct Democracy and similar groups in other member states of the European Community. Together, the groups form the Democracy International network, which is campaigning for pan-European referendum rights.

There has already been some progress at two levels. On the first level, several member states of the EU, including Luxembourg, have decided to organise referendums in 2004 on the new European Constitution.

On the second level, the government of Luxembourg put forward a bill on May 20, 2003, relating to popular initiatives on legislative matters and referendums. It provides for three areas of use:

1) A popular initiative referendum on legislative matters, which refers legislation to a vote when:
- a citizens' law initiative has been voted on by the Chamber of Deputies and has not been adopted in its original form, or
- a citizens' law initiative in its original draft has been rejected by a negative vote in the Chamber of Deputies.
In both cases the referendum will be purely consultative.

2) A consultative referendum on any planned or draft law or on any other issue of general interest if two thirds of the members of the Chamber of Deputies request it (referendum provided for in Article 51.7 of the Constitution).

3) A consultative referendum on a bill to revise the constitution which has been adopted in a first vote by the Chamber of Deputies. The referendum takes place if it is requested by more than a quarter of the deputies of the Chamber or by 25,000 voters within two months of that first vote (Article 114 of the constitution).

Unfortunately, all these referendums are purely consultative : a binding result would be appropriate when there is a clear majority of votes. It would also be more desirable if voting were non-obligatory, there were no restriction on issues, and there were no participation or turnout thresholds.

The number of signatures required for the citizens' initiative referendums is much higher than it is, for example, in Switzerland or in some U.S. states. The time allowed for the collection of signatures is much too short and favours only the powerful lobby groups.

The provision of information and public debate is left to each commune, which is required to do no more than put up a few public notices. There is no requirement either for a leaflet presenting the pros and cons of the issues, or for any official publication of the arguments in the press. But at least the debate has been re-opened.

Main author: Alfred Groff

Malta

Malta is a melting pot of cultures at the crossroads between Europe and North Africa, situated right at the centre of the Mediterranean.

The Maltese were granted self-government in 1921 and independence in 1964. The country became a republic in 1974, and the last British forces left in 1979. The country enjoys a rather stable democratic bi-polar system with the Roman Catholic Church having considerable, although slowly waning, influence. The electorate has been called to vote in only three national referendums in the country's modern history.

Timing and Question

A referendum on European Union membership was promised by the Nationalist Party in its electoral programme for the 1998 general election. The referendum was held on Saturday, March 8, 2003, five weeks after it was announced.

The question was formulated by the prime minister at his own discretion and was as follows:

> "Do you agree that Malta should become a member of the European Union in the enlargement that is to take place on 1st May, 2004?"

The question was placed on the ballot in Maltese and English, the two official languages of the country.

Legal Framework

Maltese legislation does not provide for propositive referendums. On the other hand, there are well-defined rules regarding abrogative referendums, which can be requested by a petition signed by 10% of the country's registered voters. The voters can ask for a referendum on the abrogation of any law except the constitution and laws governing human rights and taxes. Such abrogative referendums require a 50%+1 quorum to be binding.

The EU referendum was of a consultative type, for which no quorum was specified and which was not binding. Furthermore, there is no specific timeframe and no moratorium on subsequent referendums on the same subject.

The length of a referendum campaign is not defined by law, which only specifies that voters should be allowed a day of reflection before referendum day. Even though the official campaign lasted five weeks, the actual campaign had started at least 24 months earlier.

Context

The EU referendum took place on the same day as local council elections in one third of Maltese localities. It was also well known that a general election would almost immediately follow the referendum.

The Labour Party, which is in opposition, made it clear that it considered the referendum as non-binding and that the decision on EU membership would be made in a general election. Before the referendum was announced, Labour proposed a compromise to the Nationalist government: an election would be held, and the party that won the election would promise to hold a referendum immediately after. Government did not accept this proposal.

Conflicts

The main conflict was between capitalists and working people, with the former in favour and the latter against EU membership. Nevertheless, there were notable defections on both sides, especially the latter. Another very visible conflict was between openness and isolation, with the advocates of EU membership claiming that the country would be isolated unless it becomes an EU member state. The opposing camp claimed that being open and belonging to the international community depended not on membership in the European Union but on national leadership.

The division was very clear when it came to political parties. The centre-right Christian democrat Nationalist Party drove the "yes" campaign, with the help of the Green Party, which is not represented in parliament. The centre-left Labour Party was against membership and suggested to its supporters that they should either vote "no," invalidate the vote, or abstain from voting altogether. This is a very important aspect that should be noted because of the impact of this vote on other countries. It was the first of its kind in accession countries, and an adverse vote could possibly have led to similar results in other countries.

The state-owned media, the Nationalist Party media, and the so-called independent English language media all supported a "yes" vote, while only Labour and General Workers' Union media opposed it.

Finance

There was no public financing of political parties or referendum committees and no mandatory requirement for political parties to disclose their source of funding. In fact, only Labour and the Greens publish their financial statements in a regular manner.

The two main political parties got considerable funding from fundraising telethons which they organised on their respectively-owned television stations. A large part of the business community backed the Nationalist Party.

There was no control over funding from foreign sources, and the disproportion in finance is very evident. A rough estimate is as follows:

"Yes":
Government: € 9.6 million
European Commission: € 4.8 million
Nationalist Party: € 1.2 million
Green Party: € 0.05 million
Others: € 0.25 million
Total: € 15.9 million

"No / Invalidate / Abstain":
Labour: € 0.25 million
General Workers' Union: € 0.15 million
Others: € 0.15 million
Total: € 0.55 million

Result and Interpretation

91% of the electorate turned out to vote. This is a very high turnout by European standards but slightly below the normal turnout in Maltese national elections, which is generally around 96%.

Of the electors who voted, 53.6% voted in favour of European Union membership. Nevertheless, this represented only 48% of all eligible voters. The latter interpretation must be given weight because Labour had from the beginning promoted a "No/Invalidate/Abstain" vote, and the number of abstentions and invalidations was higher than is usual in Maltese general elections.

The Nationalist Party did not concur with Labour's interpretation, even though it had given a similar interpretation to a 1956 referendum on integration with the United Kingdom promoted by the Labour government. On that occasion, 75% of the 59% of electors who turned out to vote were in favour of such integration; nevertheless, the Nationalist Party, which had ordered a boycott of the ballot, said that these represented only 44% of the electorate.

Labour and the smaller parties had also adopted this stand in the 1964 referendum on independence where, with a turnout of 83%, 50.7% voted in favour. These represented 42% of the electorate eligible to vote.

Future Prospects

It is still too early to state whether more referendums will be held in Malta in the near future. There seems to be a campaign in the offing in favour of a referendum on the EU Constitutional Treaty. The only way such a referendum can take place by public initiative is through the process of the abrogative referendum. It is unlikely that government will call a consultative referendum on the issue.

The author of this article thinks that rather than embarking on ad hoc referendum campaigns, the promoters of public initiative should encourage the European Parliament and the European Commission to formulate basic rules for initiative and referendum. This is a prerequisite for the effective establishment of I&R in Europe.

Main author: Joseph Muscat

Netherlands

The Netherlands is one of the only four countries worldwide that have never held a nationwide referendum.

At the local level, some hundred referendums have been held since 1912, most of them plebiscites. In the 1990s, many municipal constitutions were amended to allow for citizen-initiated referendums. The first was held in 1995 in the City of Leiden. However, high participation and approval quorums made it very difficult to get successful results.

At the national level, one party (D66) has made I&R a priority: the issue became part of the "lilac" coalition agreement in 1994, triggered a government crisis in 1999, and led to the Temporary Referendum Law in 2002. Under the current government, a two-thirds majority in parliament is necessary to introduce a binding referendum. But the rightist-populist government has announced its intention to abolish all citizen-initiated referendums.

- Population: 16,000,000
- Area: 41,526 km²
- Capital: Amsterdam
- Official languages: Dutch, Friesian (regional)
- Religion: Roman Catholic (36%), Protestant (26%)
- Political System: Parliamentary monarchy (since 1848), with the overseas territories of Dutch Antilles and Aruba.
- Constitution: February 17, 1983 (without referendum)
- Membership: EU, NATO
- GNP/Capita: $227,190
- Human Development Rank: 5
- I&R practice: No practice at national level, six regional referendums in the Antilles (1994–2000), 100 local referendums since 1912.

Types of Initiative and Referendum

The Netherlands is a centralist unitary state (93% of all taxes are raised at the national level). The provinces and especially the municipalities have considerable responsibilities and competences (provinces: environment, spatial planning, water, public utilities; municipalities: housing, health care, spatial planning, welfare, social and city renewal, traffic, police) but these are in the spirit of "co-rule" generally carried out within the framework of national rules. Some large municipalities (cities) have municipal governments with separate elected bodies.

The Kingdom of the Netherlands is composed of the Netherlands, the Dutch Antilles and Aruba (islands in the Caribbean).

I. National Level

On January 1, 2002, the *Tijdelijke Referendumwet* (Temporary Referendum Law; TRW) entered into force and introduced a citizen-initiated "consultative corrective referendum" (non-binding rejective referendum) at the national, provincial and municipal levels. It was intended to exist until the introduction of a binding version in the Constitution, but the new rightist-populist government announced that it would break with the I&R policy of the last two "lilac" governments and abolish all citizen-initiated referendums.

At the national level, laws are subject to referendum, as are treaties which are, within the Kingdom, only valid in the Netherlands, including revisions of laws and treaties. Excluded are constitutional changes, laws on the monarchy, the royal house, the budget (but not taxes), laws which are valid in the entire Kingdom, and laws which only serve to implement international decisions.

After the monarch signs a law which has been adopted by the parliament, or a treaty has been accepted, the Home Secretary announces within a week—in the state newspaper (*Staatscourant*)—whether the law can be the subject of a referendum. If it can be, a three-week period starts in which citizens can make an "initial request" for a referendum by delivering 40,000 signatures. When the Central Voting Bureau publicly announces that enough valid signatures have been delivered, a 6-week period begins in which citizens can make a "definitive request" by delivering 600,000 signatures.

Signatures must be entered on official forms by citizens in person at the municipal office of their municipality. (The mayor may indicate other places within his municipality.) During the definitive phase, citizens can also send their signatures on an official form by mail to their municipal office. The government may decide by executive measure that citizens can also give signatures electronically, but there is no sign that this will happen soon.

Signatures are counted and considered valid or invalid by the voting bureaus, of which each municipality has at least one. They send the results to the provincial voting bureaus, which total the numbers in their provinces and send them to the national central voting bureau (the Election Council), which checks and totals the numbers given by the local and provincial voting bureaus.

If the prime voting bureau announces that enough valid signatures have been delivered, a date for the referendum is chosen no earlier than 50 days and no later than four months after the bureau's announcement. If an election takes place within this period, the referendum is held on the same day as the election. It is possible to hold more than one referendum on the same day.

The TRW does not say who will draft the question, although the context suggests the government, or which rules should be applied. The Prime Minister is responsible for writing a summary of the law or treaty, which will be mailed by the mayor to the address of each voter no later than two weeks before the referendum. The text of the law or treaty is freely available at each municipal office four weeks before the referendum.

There is an approval quorum: the outcome is only valid when a majority votes against the law, and when this majority comprises at least 30% of the electorate.

Citizens can challenge before the administrative court (*Raad van State*) the decision on whether a law or decision can be the subject of a referendum and decisions of the prime voting bureau of a political unit about the initial request, the definitive request, and the outcome of the vote. Citizens cannot challenge decisions of lower voting bureaus or the decision on the date of the referendum.

The freedom of lower government levels is greatly restricted: according to the rules of the TRW, provinces and municipalities can hold only rejective referendums on decisions of the provincial and municipal councils. Municipalities and provinces can hold referendums with their own specific requirements only on topics which are not dealt with by the TRW (either explicitly allowed or excluded) and on decisions of governmental institutions other than the provincial and municipal councils.

Municipalities and provinces which had their own referendum bylaws on February 15, 2001, can keep them until the introduction of a binding rejective referendum in the constitution (planned for 2005). However, municipalities and provinces are entirely free to introduce (through a municipal or provincial bylaw) popular initiatives with self-made requirements, as well as government-initiated referendums (plebiscites). There is one exception: the Constitution prohibits binding referendums.

Municipalities and provinces can adopt bylaws which prohibit referendums about municipal and provincial taxes or the salaries of elected officials.

The TRW is valid until January 1, 2005, when, according to plan, a rejective referendum with the same requirements but with legally binding outcomes will have been adopted. However, the incoming rightist-populist government (July 2002) announced that it would break with the I&R policy of the last two "lilac" governments and dismantle all forms of citizen-initiated referendums. Since the TRW and the Constitutional amendment also provide I&R rights at the provincial and municipal levels, their abolition would also mean a blow to I&R at the local level, although it would increase the freedom of local governments to install their own I&R bylaws.

II. Regional Level

The same rules exist as at the national level, with the following exceptions. Referendums can be held on decisions of the provincial parliaments if they form a "generally binding regulation"; on provincial decisions to take part in private organizations; on changes to the name of the province; and on arrangements in which several provinces, municipalities or water authorities take part. Referendums cannot be held on decisions which serve to execute international treaties or decisions of international organizations (or laws which have this purpose); on subjects outside the competence of the province; or on zoning plans.

The provincial parliament can decide by bylaw that no referendum can be held on provincial taxes or on the salaries and compensations of politicians and officials. The Provincial Council acts on the same issues on the provincial level as the Administration does at the national level.

The signature quorum is 0.33 per cent of the electorate for the "initial request" and 5 per cent of the electorate for the "definitive request." The prime voting bureau of the province is responsible for checking the number of signatures and votes, and for determining the outcome of the vote.

Only the province of North Holland has had, since 1995, its own referendum bylaw, which provides a citizen-initiated rejective referendum with many excluded topics and a participation quorum of 50% of the turnout of the last provincial election.

III. Local Level

The same requirements exist as at the national level: the Council of Mayor and Aldermen act on issues where, at the national level, the Administration acts. The topics about which referendums can and cannot be held are the same as at the provincial level; furthermore, referendums can be held on readjustments of municipal borders when all municipalities involved agree on them. The municipal council can decide by bylaw that no referendums can be held on municipal taxes and salaries or on compensations of politicians and officials.

At the municipal level, the signature quorums of the "initial request" and "definitive request" are respectively:

a) in municipalities with fewer than 20,001 voters, 1 per cent of the voters (minimum of 50 and maximum of 125) and 10 per cent of the voters (minimum of 200 and maximum of 1250);

b) in municipalities with 20,001 to 40,000 voters, 0.7 per cent of the voters (maximum of 200) and 7 per cent of the voters (maximum of 2250);

c) in municipalities with 40,001 to 100,000 voters, 0.5 per cent of the voters (maximum of 300) and 6 per cent of the voters (maximum of 5000);

d) in municipalities with more than 100,000 voters, 0.33 per cent of the voters and 5 per cent of the voters.

The prime voting bureau of the municipality is responsible for checking the number of signatures and votes, and for determining the outcome of the vote.

Of 537 municipalities, at least 61 introduced their own referendum bylaws between 1990 and the beginning of 2001. These remain valid for now, as stated above. Most allow a government-initiated and/or citizen-initiated "consultative" referendum: a non-binding rejective referendum on a government decision which is held before the government formally makes the decision. Currently, only two municipalities (Nijmegen and Oosterhout) allow the popular initiative.

Requirements vary with each municipality, but most have a participation quorum — often lower than that specified in the Temporary Referendum Law — and most exclude topics on the budget, politicians' salaries, "vulnerable groups" (asylum seekers, prostitutes etc.), and "urgent decisions." Some cities (e.g. Amsterdam, Amersfoort) also allow referendums at the city district level.

IV. Practical Guide

Additional rules are set in various executive documents. A *General Executive Measure* (*Tijdelijke Referendumbesluit*, STB 2001 389) provides rules on many topics. A *Ministerial Arrangement* (*Tijdelijke Referendumregeling Modellen*, CW 2001/82245) sets, among other things, the form of a ballot question (the name of the law, followed by the options "for" and "against") and the form of signature-gathering petitions.

Several executive papers (*circulaires*) instruct municipal and provincial governments regarding the effects of the referendum process on their internal organization: CW 2001/82050 and 82554. There is *de facto* free signature-gathering for activists in the "definitive phase": they can obtain official forms from the municipal offices, copy them, ask citizens to sign, and send them in bulk back to the municipal offices. They cannot obtain forms from a provincial or national government.

There is no government support, financial or otherwise, for the citizen groups which request a referendum. The "referendum booklet," which is distributed to all households, consists solely of a formal summary of the law or decision. However, at the local level there is a tradition that governments subsidize the initiating citizen committees.

On the website www.referendumwet.nl, the Home Office keeps lists of laws on which a referendum can be held and information on all referendum rules and requirements.

The full text of all I&R legislation, including all executive papers, can be downloaded (in Dutch only) from the Referendum Platform's website www.referendumplatform.nl.

V. Trends

The Netherlands is one of only four countries worldwide that have never held a national referendum (cf. Butler & Ranney). Only at the municipal level have at least 101 rejective referendums been held from 1912 until December 2003. Most of them were plebiscites.

Only in the 1990s were municipal bylaws adopted which gave rights to citizens to enforce (mostly rejective) referendums through a prescribed number of signatures; the first citizen-initiated referendum was held in 1995 in the city of Leiden. Of these 101 referendums, 51 were held on restructuring municipal borders, i.e. abolishing small municipalities. Also popular were building plans (15 referendums), the reorganization of municipal government (11), and traffic and parking policy (6). Three referendums were held in the overseas territories on a change to their status within the Kingdom.

Because high participation quorums were often adopted, many important subjects were excluded, and the outcomes were not legally binding, many municipal referendums failed. This caused some cynicism among the political elite, which had falsely hoped that the widespread political malaise among the population would disappear once some referendums had been held.

The debate about direct democracy dates from the end of the 19th century, when the Social Democratic League (since 1882) and the Social Democratic Workers Party (since 1895) demanded the introduction of "direct citizen lawmaking." Since 1903, the Parliament has held seven debates on introducing the referendum or initiative, and five commissions have been set up to investigate I&R.

These efforts were generally blocked by the Christian democratic parties, which were at the centre of every government coalition from 1917 to 1994. In 1994, however, a coalition without the Christian democrats was formed with the pro-referendum party D66, which was able to make the inclusion of a binding rejective referendum part of their coalition agreement. Because of the binding outcome, a constitutional change (which needs a two-thirds majority) was deemed necessary.

Mainly because of resistance by the right-wing liberal coalition party VVD, the proposal was not far-reaching; nevertheless, during the final vote in the Senate in May 1999, a majority including one VVD senator voted against it. D66 caused a government crisis by angrily leaving the coalition. They returned after a promise by the VVD leaders that they would present the constitutional change to Parliament again and would support a non-binding version of this proposal by ordinary law in the meantime. This became the Temporary Referendum Law.

Under the original plan, the constitutional change would be adopted by 2005. But the new rightist-populist government that was formed after the turbulent elections of May 2002, in which maverick politician Pim Fortuyn was murdered, announced their intention to break with the I&R policy of the last two "lilac" governments and abolish all citizen-initiated referendums: a move which caused some cynicism among commentators and the public because the new government pays lip service to "political renewal" and "giving the country back to the citizens." Instead of referendums, then, the government may only hold an occasional plebiscite.

The Dutch public supports I&R: 80% are in favor of "deciding directly on important issues, the so-called referendum"; 15% are against it, and 5% are undecided (SCP poll, 1998). A poll taken by NIPO in October 1995 found, however, that only 49% were in favor of the government proposal for a rejective referendum (10% were against and 40% undecided).

We know of only one poll on the difference between the referendum and the initiative, conducted among the Amsterdam population in 1992: if they had to choose between the rejective referendum and the initiative, 60% preferred the initiative, 20% the referendum, and 20% were undecided.

Most Dutch politicians are against I&R. The most "moderate" poll, a 1994 poll of the University of Leiden among local politicians, showed 36% in favor and 52% against the rejective referendum.

The debate centers very much on the rejective referendum; lately, however, interest in the initiative has grown. Currently, the parties which are in favor of the referendum—PvdA, D66, GroenLinks, and SP (the VVD, CDA, Christen-Unie & SGP are all opposed)—also moderately favor the initiative. Since the TRW leaves this area unregulated, a beginning could be made with the introduction of popular initiatives at the municipal and provincial levels. This would require the support of political parties.

At the same time, experience with the referendum can be gained through the TRW. Because of criticism of the high quorums, parliament will evaluate the practical effects of the TRW in 2004. Advocates of I&R hope this evaluation will lead to more democratic provisions in the constitutional amendment.

Main author: Arjen Nijeboer

Constitutional Requirements for Legislation

Chapter 8 (Revision of the Constitution):

Article 137:

(1) An Act of Parliament shall be passed stating that an amendment to the Constitution shall be considered in the form proposed.

(2) The Second Chamber may divide a Bill presented for this purpose into a number of separate Bills, either upon a proposal presented by or on behalf of the King or otherwise.

(3) The two Chambers of the Parliament shall be dissolved after the Act referred to in the first paragraph has been published.

(4) The newly elected Chambers shall consider the Bill, and it shall be passed only if at least two thirds of the votes cast are in favor.

(5) The Second Chamber may divide a Bill for the amendment of the Constitution into a number of separate Bills, either upon a proposal presented by or on behalf of the King or otherwise, if at least two thirds of the votes cast are in favor.

Article 138:

(1) Before Bills to amend the Constitution which have been given a second reading have been ratified by the King, provisions may be introduced by Act of Parliament whereby: (a) the proposals adopted and the unchanged provisions of the Constitution are adjusted to each other as required; (b) the division into chapters, sections, and articles and the headings and numbering thereof are modified.

(2) A Bill containing provisions as referred to under Paragraph (1)(a) shall be passed by the two Chambers only if at least two thirds of the votes cast are in favor.

Article 139:

Amendments to the Constitution passed by the Parliament and ratified by the King shall enter into force immediately after they have been published.

Article 140: Existing Acts of Parliament and other regulations and decrees which are in conflict with an amendment to the Constitution shall remain in force until provisions are made in accordance with the Constitution. Article 141: The text of the revised Constitution shall be published by Royal Decree in which the chapters, sections and articles may be renumbered and references to them altered accordingly.

Article 142: The Constitution may be brought into line with the Charter for the Kingdom of the Netherlands by Act of Parliament. Articles 139, 140 and 141 shall apply by analogy.

———————

Norway

As early as 1891, the Labour party proposed that the popular legislative initiative should be incorporated into the Norwegian constitution. Since then, the national Parliament has debated I&R proposals 26 times, but has so far failed to implement any provisions. However, since a majority of the parliament (at the local as well as the national level) can trigger a non-binding referendum, important issues like monarchy, prohibition and European integration have been issues for referendums.

At the local level, a special initiative right gave 5% of the electorate the right to trigger a binding referendum on the sale of alcohol. But this institution, established in 1894, was abolished in 1989. A far less attractive initiative instrument still exists for language issues.

Nonetheless, more than 500 local referendums took place between 1970 and 2002, and there is a national discussion on how to strengthen I&R legislation.

- Population: 4,510,000
- Area: 323,759 km²
- Capital: Oslo
- Official languages: Norwegian (Bokmål, Nynorsk), Sami (regional)
- Religion: Lutheran (86%)
- Political System: Parliamentary monarchy (since 1905)
- Constitution: 1814 (without referendum)
- Membership: NATO, UN
- GNP/Capita: $29,620

- Human Development Rank: 1
- I&R practice: six nationwide referendums. 1905: union with Sweden and monarchy; 1919 & 1926: alcohol prohibition; 1972 & 1994: EU membership. More than 1000 local referendums in almost 450 municipalities.

Types of Initiative and Referendum

Referendums are not a part of the Norwegian constitution. The word "referendum" is not even mentioned, though many attempts to incorporate it have been made.

However, no one has questioned the right of Parliament (Storting) to ask the people for advice through voluntary referendums. A majority of representatives in the Storting can decide to submit an issue to the whole electorate.

Legally, the referendum can only be advisory, since the sovereignty of parliament cannot be undermined. Ultimate responsibility resides in parliament. Thus, nationwide referendums in Norway are by definition advisory referendums.

I. National Level

The referendum device has been discussed in the Storting on a number of occasions. Before the turn of the century, there were 26 debates in the Storting on proposals for a constitutional amendment to allow for referendums. Most of the proposals were for facultative referendums that would give a minority in the Storting the right to submit a bill that had already been passed to the electorate for approval or rejection. In such referendums, the people play the role of an appeal court and have the right to accept or reject a decision by parliament.

More generally, this type of referendum illustrates the role the referendum often plays in political debate: demands originate from the opposition, and the referendum is a tool in the hands of the minority. Political parties in an entrenched and seemingly everlasting opposition always seem to support the referendum as their last chance of exercising some power. However, once they themselves are elected, they lose interest in referendums.

The direct popular initiative, which gives voters themselves legislative authority and the right to decide an issue, has attracted little interest among Norwegian political parties. Labour's first party manifesto of 1891 mentioned the people's right to participate in the legislative process. The phrase was taken from the famous German Gotha-manifesto, but it disappeared from the party manifesto of 1903 and has never reappeared.

However, demands for initiatives and other types of referendums have been made since then by the Progress Party. No other party has so firmly defended direct democracy. That is not surprising, since the Progress Party is a right-wing populist party: populism and support for referendums tend to go together, given the populists' trust in the people and their mistrust of politicians and the establishment.

All proposals for a constitutional amendment to include referendums in the constitution have been rejected in the Storting. Amendments require a two-thirds majority, and most of these proposals have not come close to being passed. Usually, there has been only minority support for a referendum proposal; a proposal in 1968 was the only one to exceed 50 per cent support.

However, Norwegian reluctance to support referendums in principle has not stood in the way of six nationwide referendums in its history.

a. Foundations of a Kingdom

The first two referendums were held in 1905, and pressure from abroad played a central role in both. In 1905 the unpopular union with Sweden was unilaterally dissolved by Norway, which was declared a sovereign country. Sweden responded that it would accept the dissolution only if certain conditions were met, one of which was that the people themselves would agree in a referendum. The result of the referendum left no doubt: 99.9 per cent of the votes (only men were allowed to vote) favored the dissolution of the union.

The question then arose whether Norway was to be a republic or a monarchy. The government proposed that a Danish prince should be appointed King of Norway. Some republicans protested and demanded that the question of monarchy versus republic be decided in a referendum.

The Danish prince agreed to the demand for a referendum and declared that he would become King only if the people endorsed the idea. 78.9 percent of the voters (all men) voted in his favor.

b. Prohibition

The next two referendums, in 1919 and 1926, concerned the prohibition of alcohol. In the first one, a 61.6% majority supported the prohibition of all liquors containing more than 12% alcohol by volume. In 1926, prohibition was repealed with an even clearer majority of 64.8%.

In the inter-war period, the prohibition issue was a burning question. One reason for the political turbulence, as well as one reason why a referendum was held, was that some of the major political parties were split on the issue. That was especially true of the Liberals, who at that time were the most important party. As some voters became increasingly committed and personally involved in prohibition, the split in the party became highly visible. As the largest party, the Liberals had the power to decide whether or not a referendum should be held.

Suddenly, after a long period of resistance, the party leader became a proponent of a referendum. Because the Liberals were regarded as defenders of prohibition, the party had lost a lot of voters in the cities among those who disapproved of alcohol restrictions. The demand for a referendum seems partly to have been an attempt to disassociate the party from the issue: it implied that the voters should decide, not the political parties.

c. European Integration

Prohibition triggered many problems, but it was not possible to end prohibition without a new referendum. A decision made by the people can be nullified only by the people themselves.

The same logic can be applied to the referendums on Norway's membership of the European Union. The people have twice rejected membership, in 1972 and 1994. The results were almost identical: 53.5% against membership the first time and 52.4% the second time.

Referendums on membership in the European Union have been obligatory since 1972, but that was not the case in 1962, when the Storting decided in to hold a referendum on membership of the Common Market, the precursor of the European Union. At that time, no other country had yet held a referendum on its entry into the Common Market.

In many ways, the background of the 1962 referendum decision was similar to that of the 1919 prohibition referendum: the most important party in 1962 (Labour) was divided, and the minority, who opposed membership, asked for a popular vote on the issue.

By agreeing to the demand for a referendum, the Labour leadership separated the EU issue from ordinary party politics. Labour voters who disagreed with the pro-membership position of the party leaders could be mollified: the voters would decide. That made it possible to be a Labour voter and still oppose membership.

The political establishment was defeated in the two EU referendums, just as it had been in the 1919 prohibition referendum. The periphery won, and the centre lost.

II. Local Level

Norway has a long tradition of local referendums. At the local level there has also been access to the direct popular initiative, but this is restricted to only two issues: the sale and purchase of alcohol and the choice of language in the primary schools.

There are two official languages in Norway, "Nynorsk" and "Bokmål." "Nynorsk" is based on the dialects spoken in the countryside in Western Norway: it is a rural language. "Bokmål" is spoken in urban areas and is more similar to Danish than "Nynorsk" is. In fact, the differences between them are rather small, but they have symbolic significance.

The rules regarding popular initiative on the language issue have differed somewhat. For a long time, either the municipal council or 25 per cent of the electorate had the right to approve the use of referendums. The result was binding on the school board if the majority comprised at least 40 per cent of the electorate.

There has been some dispute about who is entitled to vote in a language referendum: should it be all the citizens living in the school district, or should it be restricted to the parents or caretakers of children under the age of 14? The first alternative has been defended by the proponents of "Nynorsk," who argue that language is a cultural question with far-reaching consequences and that, consequently, it involves the whole local community.

However, to understand this argument it is also necessary to understand a tactical aspect. The "Nynorsk" movement has traditionally had a stronger foothold in the local elites, among teachers and local politicians, than among the grassroots. In fact, spokesmen for "Nynorsk" have been suspicious of I&R, so they have supported the position that in order to accept the people's voice as the last word, various requirements have to be met.

In spite of these requirements, in recent decades "Nynorsk" has been in retreat. The use of initiative has been a weapon against "Nynorsk," and this weapon is easier to use when the right to demand a referendum or to vote is limited to parents only. In 2000, they again changed the definition of who is entitled to vote—from parents only, to all the citizens in the school district—after a mushrooming of initiatives with the aim of replacing "Nynorsk" with "Bokmål"; the change was intended as a rescue operation for "Nynorsk."

In contrast to the "Nynorsk" movement, the temperance movement has been one of the strongest grassroots movements in Norwegian history. The main strategy of the temperance movement was to ban the sale of alcoholic beverages step by step, using local referendums, with the ultimate aim of making the whole country dry.

The history of local alcohol referendums started in 1894 and ended nearly a hundred years later. In 1989, the rules on decisive referendums and people's initiatives were abandoned; times had changed, and the fight against alcohol was lost, which put an end to a long history of referendums and initiatives.

Prior to 1989, five percent of the voters had the right to approve a referendum to establish a new license for selling alcohol or to ban an old one. Both men and women were included in the electorate: nearly 20 years before women were given the general franchise, they had the right to vote in these referendums. The municipal council also had the right to demand a referendum.

Until 1989, a referendum was required in order to authorize a license to sell alcohol in a municipality. Over a period of nearly a hundred years, the popular initiative changed its political role: at the start, it was a weapon in the hands of those who wanted to ban alcohol; at the end, it was a weapon for those who wanted the right to purchase alcohol.

In municipal law the words "referendum" and "initiative" are absent, but that does not prevent the various municipal councils from organizing advisory referendums. There usually is at least one referendum every year on the merging of municipalities, even though there are no laws requiring referendums in these cases. Inhabitants are usually opposed to being "swallowed up" by neighboring municipalities, and leading politicians have argued that no municipality should be dissolved and become a part of a larger one without the consent of its inhabitants.

A survey among all Norwegian municipalities indicates that at least 514 local referendums were held between 1970 and 2000: an average of 16 per year. About half of these ballot votes involved the whole local electorate, while the other half took place in larger or smaller parts of the municipality. The issues of alcohol and language were by far the most frequent, representing 75% of the total. Other issues were "local territorial"—mainly merging of municipalities (58), "school district regulation" (63), "environmental issues" (4), and "identity"—name of city or status of township or city—(2). Average participation was 52.4% of the electorate, or 58.3% of the total number of voters.

In 2001–2003, at least three local referendums were held on three different issues: alcohol, identity, and environment. In the past three decades, almost half of Norway's 435 municipalities have had experience in local referendums. Further investigation revealed that the use of local referendums does not depend on the number of citizens in the municipality, so there has been a fairly even use of the instrument.

III. Trends

Norway is a country which has almost no statutory rules on I&R but which enjoys a long historical tradition of referendums. The two issue areas with special laws demanding local referendums reflect a past time; the procedure for deciding the language question is still used, but the reduced status of "Nynorsk" makes it less relevant.

Although there is less demand today for the use of the referendum, proposals have been submitted for popular initiatives at the local level in order to revitalize democracy. In the second half of the 1990s, an organization (Kommunenes Sentralforbund) started a campaign to improve local democracy. The background was concern about the decline in turnout for local elections from 81.0 per cent in 1963 to 60.4 per cent in 1999. One of their proposals was for all municipalities to adopt the rule that five per cent of the citizens could urge the municipal council to arrange advisory referendums.

The decline in voter turnout at the local level has been accompanied by a pronounced increase in participation in single-issue actions over recent decades. It is easy to draw a parallel to referendums, which are also linked to single issues, but this indication of improved conditions for I&R has not yet led to a rise in direct democracy.

Main author: Tor Björklund with additional remarks by Aimée Lind Adamiak

Constitutional Requirements for Legislation

Article 112 (General provisions):

If experience shows that any part of this Constitution of the Kingdom of Norway ought to be amended, the proposal to this effect shall be submitted to the first, second or third Storting after a new General Election and be publicly announced in print. It shall be left to the first, second or third Storting after the following General Election to decide whether or not the proposed amendment shall be adopted.

Such amendment must never, however, contradict the principles embodied in this Constitution, but solely relate to modifications of particular provisions which do not alter the spirit of the Constitution, and such amendment requires that two thirds of the Storting agree thereto. An amendment to the Constitution adopted in the manner aforesaid shall be signed by the President and the Secretary of the Storting, and shall be sent to the King for public announcement in print, as an applicable provision of the Constitution of the Kingdom of Norway.

Portugal

The right of petition, falsely called a citizens' referendum initiative, is very weak, with crucial issues like the constitution, taxation and the legislative competence of Parliament excluded from referendum. In 1998, for the first time, Portugal tried out this restricted set of I&R institutions. The experiment was not successful: none of the referendums received the required 50% turnout, so the ballots were merely non-binding exercises.

A vote on European integration would have greatly furthered the cause of I&R in Portugal, but the Constitutional court ruled that it could not be held because the Amsterdam referendum did not respect "the requirements of objectivity, clarity and accuracy" demanded in the Constitution. However, plans have been made for a referendum on the new EU constitution.

- Population: 10,355,824
- Area: 92,345 km²
- Capital: Lisbon (Lisboa)
- Official language: Portuguese
- Religion: Roman Catholic (90%)
- Political System: Republic (since 1910)
- Constitution: April 2, 1976 (without referendum)
- Membership: EU and NATO
- GNP/Capita: $18,150
- Human Development Rank: 23
- I&R practice: three nationwide referendums since 1933. The first ballot was a de-facto fascist plebiscite on the constitution. The second (on legalizing abortion, June 26, 1998) and the third (on regionalization, November 8, 1998) did not achieve the 50% turnout quorum, making the "no" results (abortion 50.2%; regionalization 63%) non-binding

Types of Initiative and Referendum

Portugal is a parliamentary republic, with a President elected by direct, universal and secret vote by Portuguese citizens above the age of 18. His term is for five years, and he cannot be re-elected for a third consecutive term.

The Government is formed by the Council of Ministers, headed by the Prime Minister. The Prime Minister is politically responsible to the President and Parliament.

Legislative power is exercised by Parliament, the representative assembly of the people. It is made up of a single house of deputies, with a minimum of 180 and a maximum of 230 parliamentary seats. Members of Parliament are elected for four years by the universal, direct, and secret vote of Portuguese citizens above the age of eighteen according to the system of proportional representation and the Hondt method of the highest average.

Within the limitations prescribed by the Constitution, the President has powers to dissolve Parliament,[6] appoint a Prime Minister, and dismiss the Government. The present Constitution was approved in 1976, and marked the end of the process of replacing the dictatorship, which was ended in 1974. The Constitution has been revised several times.

I. National Level

Portugal does not have the citizens' legislative initiative, only the citizens' referendum initiative. Article 52, No. 2 of the constitutional revision of 1989 added the principle by which certain collective petitions presented to Parliament would be given consideration in plenary sessions.

Article 178, No. 3 states that petitions presented to Parliament will be considered by its committees, or by a committee specifically appointed for that purpose. The committee can consult other relevant committees on the matter and request evidence from citizens. These petitions may have the practical effect of a citizens' legislative initiative.

---

6. The President of the Republic, after consultation with the Parliament and the Council of Ministers and according to Article 133, line e) of the Constitution, has decided to dissolve Parliament, following the result of the last elections held on December 16, 2001. A new Parliament was elected on March 17, 2002.

a. Referendum (ballot)

Under Article 115 of the Constitution, law No. 15-A/98 regulates the procedures for national referendums.

A referendum can deal only with questions which relate to national interest and which are decided by Parliament or the Government, including pieces of legislation and the approval of international conventions. The following issues are excluded from referendums: changes to the constitution; issues or procedures relating to taxation and to annual state budget matters; and matters within the absolute legislative competence of the parliament, with the exception of general laws about the educational system.

Each referendum can deal only with a single issue. A maximum of three questions are allowed in each referendum, with simple answers of either "yes" or "no."

The President of the Republic makes the final decision to call a referendum. The referendum can be proposed to the President by either the government (on matters within its own competence) or parliament (on matters within its specific competence). Initiatives addressed to parliament may come from the deputies, the government, or the citizens.

b. Petition ("citizens' referendum initiative")

The citizens' petition is presented in written form and is addressed to parliament. The petition must includes the names of 25 sponsors and be signed by at least 75,000 citizens, who normally must be registered electors residing on national territory, although Portuguese citizens living abroad are asked to participate if their specific interests are affected.

The referendum request must include the full name and identity card number of each person signing it. Parliament may verify the authenticity of the signatures and the identities of the signatories through public administration services and by sampling,

The petition, which takes the form of a resolution proposal to be discussed and voted on in parliament, states the questions to be decided in the referendum. If appropriate, the petition will refer to the specific acts passed by, or under consideration by, parliament; otherwise, the petition will be presented as a proposal for legislation. After being accepted by parliament, the citizens' petition is published in the Parliament's newspaper, *Diário da Assembleia da República*.

Within two days after receiving the petition, the President of the Parliament consults the relevant committee(s) about it. After considering the committee's advice, the President of the Parliament can either accept the petition proposal as it stands or return it within 20 days to the citizens' representatives for them to modify the text.

Once accepted, the petition is referred to the relevant committee. The committee can question the citizens' representatives in order to clarify any details necessary to the understanding and formulation of the petition, after which the committee has 20 days to formulate the resolution proposal, which includes the text of the referendum petition.

The President of the Parliament must schedule the consideration of the resolution proposal for one of the next ten parliamentary plenary sessions. After debate and a vote, the proposal embodying the citizens' petition is either approved or rejected. A rejected petition cannot be re-presented within the same legislative session.[7]

In the 8 days following publication of the Parliament's decision, the President of the Republic submits the referendum proposal to the constitutional court for an assessment of its constitutionality and legality. If the court finds it unconstitutional or illegal, the President of the Republic cannot promote it. Following the final decision of the constitutional court, the President of the Republic has 20 days to call the referendum. If the President decides not to call it, he must notify Parliament and the citizens' representatives.

The referendum is binding only if participation is greater than 50% of the registered electorate. If the voting results in a positive binding answer to the question(s) referred to referendum, the Parliament or the Government will approve the international convention or piece of legislation concerned (within 90 days for the former, or 60 days for the latter). The President of the Republic cannot refuse to ratify an international treaty or to sign an act that approves an international agreement or the promulgation of a legislative act if he disagrees with the result of a binding referendum.

If the voters reject the referendum, neither Parliament nor Government can approve any international convention or piece of legislation relating to the question which was rejected unless there is either an election for a new Parliament or a new referendum with a positive result. Referendum proposals which the voters have rejected cannot be presented again in the same legislative session unless there is an election for a new Parliament or, in the case of a governmental petition, until the establishment of a new Government.

II. Regional Level

The referendum process does not exist at this level because, at present, there is no regional division of administration.

---

7. Each legislature has 4 legislative sessions. In other words, one legislative session amounts to one year's parliamentary work.

Future administrative regions are considered in Article 255-262 of the Constitution; their establishment would require a special referendum envisaged in Article 256 of the Constitution and Article 245-251 of Law No. 15-A/98, which approves the specific "Organic Law of the Referendum Regime."

The specific rules are as follows. The decision to call the referendum is made by the President of the Republic after being proposed by Parliament; a direct proposal by the Government is not allowed. The referendum has two questions: a national question and a question relating to each region. Only the voters within a region vote on the question relating to that region; outside the regional areas to be established, the referendum includes only the national question.

On November 8, 1998, a national referendum was held on establishing administrative regions for mainland Portugal; the result was negative. The constitutional revision of 1997 introduced the possibility for a referendum in the Autonomous Regions of Madeira and Azores by adding No. 2 to Article 232: "The regional Parliament has the power to propose referendums through which the President of the Republic will call on the electorate of the region to vote on matters of regional interest, whereupon Article 151 will be applied with the necessary changes." So far, there has been no referendum in the Autonomous Regions.

III. Local Level

The local referendum directly consults the voters of a local parish or municipality on issues that are the responsibility of the local authority. Tax issues or other matters already subject to an irrevocable decision are excluded from local referendums. Only voters registered in the parish or municipality are allowed to vote, and the result is binding.

Proposals for a local referendum can be made by the councils or executive boards of the local authorities, and the parish council or municipal council makes the decision to call the referendum. Within eight days after a referendum is proposed, the president of the local assembly forwards the application to the constitutional court for an assessment of its constitutionality and legality. If the court confirms its constitutionality and legality, the referendum must be held within not less than 70 and not more than 90 days.

Since 1998, there have been several local referendums on matters including the creation of a new parish, the demolition of an old water reservoir, a road layout, and the designation of an environmental area.

IV. Trend

It was only after the revolution of 1974 that a decentralized state became a reality in Portugal. The 1976 constitution established three tiers of local democratic government to replace the centrally controlled administration of the former regime. The three tiers were parishes, municipalities, and regional government; the first two were put in place in 1976, but the regional tier of government has not yet been established.

Local government has been autonomous and democratically elected since 1976. Although accountable to central government, it can undertake any actions that are for the benefit of the inhabitants of the locality. The failure to create any form of regional government has ensured the continuing importance of local authorities and their pivotal role in the creation of new forms of governance.

Local authorities are grouped into districts, each run by a Civil Governor appointed by the Government. There have been important changes in the relationships among the levels of government (supranational, national, regional, and local), in the relationships between locally based institutions (business organizations, community groups, and educational and training institutions), and in the roles of different sectors (public, private, voluntary, and community). There have been changes in the nature of local government, the influence of supranational resources and policy agendas, and national state policy. There is now more local variation, a greater decentralization of the state, and a broader base of participating actors.

The rejection, in the national referendum of 1998, of the proposal to create regional administrations means that existing regional institutions, such as the centrally-controlled regional planning authorities (CCRs), retain a central role; it also encouraged the development of new forms of governance on the regional level, most notably the creation of the Regional Development Agencies (RDAs).

The EU has played a central role in the development of sub-national governments in terms of both finance and organization. Financially, regional and local levels have benefited from EU resources in almost all fields of activity. Besides the Regional Operational Programs, which are mainly for the construction of basic infrastructure, municipalities have also benefited from the EU Initiatives and from the Cohesion Fund. Organizationally, the administration of EU funds has encouraged the significant development of the five CCRs.

Since 1974, there have been two referendums in Portugal:

June 28, 1998: "Do you agree that the voluntary interruption of pregnancy should not be penalized, when decided by the woman during the first 10 weeks [and carried out] in a legally authorized health centre?" Only 31.94% of registered voters participated, of whom 50.91% answered no and 49.09% answered yes. The referendum was not binding.

November 8, 1998: Question one: "Do you agree with the practical establishment of administrative regions?" 48.29% of the registered voters participated, of whom 63.51% answered no and 36.49% answered yes. Question two: "Do you agree with the practical establishment of an administrative region in your electoral area?" (This question was asked only of the citizens registered in the regions which the new law would have created.) 48.29% of the registered voters participated, of whom 63.93% answered no and 36.07% answered yes. The referendum was not binding, but the negative response led to the revocation of Law No. 19/98.

On June 29, 1998, the Parliament proposed to the President of the Republic a referendum on the question: "Do you agree that Portugal should continue to participate in the construction of the European Union within the Amsterdam Treaty?" On July 29, 1998, the Constitutional Court judged the referendum unconstitutional because the treaty did not respect "the requirements of objectivity, clarity and accuracy" demanded in Article 115, 262, No. 6 of the Constitution.

Main authors: Elisabete Cidre and Manuel Malheiros

Constitutional Requirements for Legislation

Section II: Revision of the Constitution

Article 284 (Competence and Time of Revision): (1) The Assembly of the Republic may revise the Constitution when five years have elapsed after the publication of any revision law. (2) The Assembly of the Republic may, by a majority of four-fifths of its members entitled to vote, assume powers of constitutional reform at any time after revision provided for in the foregoing article.

Article 285 (Power to Initiate Constitutional Reform): (1) Members of the Assembly are competent to initiate constitutional reform. (2) When a plan for constitutional reform has been tabled, any further such plans must be tabled within 30 days.

Article 286 (Approval and Promulgation): (1) Amendments to the Constitution are approved by a two-thirds majority of the members of the Assembly entitled to vote. (2) Changes in the Constitution which are approved are incorporated in a single revision law. (3) The President of the Republic may not refuse to promulgate the revision law.

Article 287 (New Text of the Constitution): (1) Amendments to the Constitution are inserted in their proper place with the necessary substitutions, deletions, and additions. (2) The new text of the Constitution is published together with the revision law.

Article 288 (Limits to the Revision on the Substance): The laws revising the Constitution safeguard: a) National independence and the unity of the State; b) The republican form of government; c) The separation of the Churches from the State; d) The rights, freedoms, and safeguards of the citizens; e) The rights of the workers, workers' committees, and trade unions; f) The co-existence of the public, the private, and the cooperative and social sectors, with respect to the property of the means of production; g) The existence of economic plans within the framework of a mixed economy; h) Universal, direct, secret, and periodical suffrage for the appointment of the elected members of the organs of supreme authority, the autonomous regions, and the organs of local government, as well as the system of proportional representation; i) Plurality of expression and political organization, including political parties and the right to a democratic opposition; j) Separation and interdependence of the organs of supreme authority; l) The scrutiny of legal provisions for active unconstitutionality and unconstitutionality by omission; m) The independence of the courts; n) The autonomy of local authorities; o) The political and administrative autonomy of the archipelagos of the Azores and Madeira.

Article 289 (Circumstantial Limits to Revision): No act may be undertaken to revise the Constitution while a state of siege or emergency is in force.

Romania

A few instruments of I&R are provided in the Romanian Constitution, but they are saddled with such quorums and requirements that their practical use is almost non-existent. The country's totalitarian heritage is hindering its movement towards democracy, for the structure of the state is still very centralistic and based on the powers of the president.

In 1986, the dictator Ceausescu organized a plebiscite to reduce the size of the army, which officially had a turnout of 99.99% and a 100% "yes" vote. However, since 1864 there has been the tradition of letting the citizens decide on the constitution. The upcoming decision on EU accession will probably lead to a positive referendum experience; it is hoped that this new experience will also encourage I&R on the local level, where a new law gives more autonomy and greater freedom.

- Population: 22,458,000
- Area: 238,391 km²
- Capital: Bucharest (Bucuresti)
- Official languages: Romanian
- Religion: Romanian Orthodox (86%)
- Political System: Republic (since 1991)
- Constitution: December 8, 1991 (referendum; 79.11% yes).
- Membership: NATO, EU applicant
- GNP/Capita: $5,830
- Human Development Rank: 72
- I&R practice: seven nationwide referendums since 1864. Only one since 1991: on December 8, 67% of the electorate participated in a constitutional referendum. No local experience at all.

I. National Level

a. National Referendum

The law (No. 3/2000) on national and local referendums was adopted on February 22, 2000. There are three possible subjects of a national referendum: modifying the Constitution, dismissing the President of Romania, and issues of national interest. The constitutional articles concerning the character of the state and the fundamental rights and liberties of the people, which cannot be modified, cannot be the subject of a referendum.

Several referendums on separate issues may take place on the same day, but they must be on separate referendum forms. At least 50% + 1 of the electorate must participate for a referendum to be valid.

A referendum is compulsory within 30 days after parliament has voted either to modify the constitution or to dismiss the president. In the case of modifying the constitution or removing the president, the date and purpose of the referendum must be determined by parliament by means of a special law.

The president may request a national referendum on issues of national interest after consulting parliament. He issues a decree setting the date and specifying the issue, and the date and the issue must be publicized in the media. The campaign has to start at least 20 days before the date determined for the referendum.

Issues of national interest are considered to be:

A. Decisions about economic reform and national strategy.

B. Special political decisions concerning:

    1. rules on private and public property,

    2. the organization of local administration and rules about local autonomy,

    3. the organization of the educational system,

    4. the structure of the national defense system, the organization of the army, and the participation of the army in certain international actions,

    5. international actions committing Romania for an undetermined period or a period longer than 10 years, and

    6. the integration of Romania into the European and Euro-Atlantic structures.

There are no provisions by which citizens, acting on their own, can legally require a referendum.

b. The Legislative Initiative of the Citizens

In the Romanian legal system, there are three kinds and levels of laws: simple, organic, and constitutional. The Constitution includes the civic legislative initiative for all three kinds of laws except laws concerning taxes, international issues, amnesty, and the commutation of penal sentences.

For simple and organic laws, at least 250,000 signatures must be gathered from at least one fourth of Romania's 41 counties, including at least 10,000 from each county. To modify the constitution through the citizens' initiative, at least 500,000 signatures must be gathered from at least half of Romania's counties, with at least 20,000 coming from each county.

According to law No. 189/1999, an initiative committee must be formed through a legally registered declaration, and headed by a president elected by its members. The committee must be comprised of at least ten citizens having the right to vote; the president of the country, members of the government, and people who are not allowed to be members of political parties (judges, military personnel, or policemen), may not be members. The names of the executive committee, along with their legislative proposal, must be published in Romania's Official Monitor.

The proposal must be formally presented to Parliament, along with the collected signatures, within three months after the signature collection is begun. The list of signatures must contain: the name of the legislative proposal and the number of the country's Official Monitor which published it, the full names and addresses of the citizens, their ID numbers, their personal numbers and, of course, their signatures. The mayors or the police must verify the signatures. The lists are public, and any challenge to a signature means that the person whose signature has been contested must provide evidence for it.

The Constitutional Court must confirm the proposal within a maximum of 30 days for normal and organic laws and 60 days for modifications to the constitution. The Legislative Council of Parliament also has to approve the proposal, within a maximum of 30 days before it is published.

It is important to note that after this phase the legislative proposal does not become law and does not automatically become the subject of a national referendum; the initiative only becomes a legislative proposal after it has been discussed and approved in parliament. Parliament makes the final decision on whether a referendum will be held by approving or rejecting the legislative proposal through a simple majority vote.

There have been a number of attempts, but so far no initiative has cleared all the hurdles. The most recent one is currently in the process of being published: a civic coalition which brings together many NGOs under the title of "The Civic Initiative for the Responsibility of the Political Act" is promoting a project to replace the current electoral laws with a unique "Electoral Code." The proposed Electoral Code would substantively change the whole Romanian electoral system. Three earlier attempts at gathering the 250,000 signatures required have failed; this is now the fourth one.

II. Local Level

A local referendum can be held when there are questions of particular interest to the local community. A local referendum took place recently in some counties of Romania regarding the modification of some local administrative divisions, whose citizens claimed autonomy in their relations with the neighboring villages. The result was the creation of several new local divisions within the county.

Any legislative proposals to modify the boundaries of the administrative divisions must be first subjected to a local referendum of the citizens living in those administrative divisions before being sent to parliament. For other issues, referendums can be organized at all levels of the administrative division.

The mayors or the chairmen of the local councils draw up the referendum proposals on the issues which are to be addressed by the referendum. These have to be announced at least 20 days before the chosen date for the referendum.

A local referendum must be held on a Sunday. The rest of the process is the same as for the national referendum, the only difference being in the level of the Electoral Office involved, which is at the local level. A referendum is carried by a simple majority of 50% +1 of the votes cast.

For both levels, a referendum has to be organized much the same as an election: the citizens vote in the polls with the same security measures; the local, regional and national (in the case of a national referendum) electoral offices oversee the whole process. Citizens have to go to the polls and present their identity card, which is checked against the data available on the electoral lists: identity card number, address, and date of birth. The citizens cast their votes in closed booths and on secret referendum ballots.

The electoral office is composed of a president (a judge, prosecutor, lawyer or, if these are not available, another person of good repute) and a maximum of six representatives of the parliamentary political parties in the case of a national referendum or of the parties represented in the local councils in the case of a local referendum.

The presidents are responsible for the whole process in their sections. Their power extends for a radius of 500 meters around the ballot box, where they must keep order and prevent any attempt to influence the free expression of the popular will. In the event that problems should arise, the president of the electoral office may suspend the process for a maximum of one hour. Any conflicts have to be resolved by the superior electoral offices within 24 hours.

People who are house-bound can vote through a special mobile collecting team arranged by the same president. Each electoral office counts the votes and sends the result to the superior electoral office. The Constitutional Court has to confirm the correctness and the result of the referendum and present a special report to Parliament.

III. Trend

The only two national referendums in Romania in the past 12 years were the referendums to adopt the present constitution. On December 8, 1991, the citizens of Romania were called to express their sovereign will by answering either "yes" or "no" to the following question: "Do you approve the Constitution of Romania adopted by the Constituent Assembly on November 21, 1991?" In October, 2003, another referendum took place in order to bring the Romanian constitution in line with requirements for EU membership in 2007.

Main author: Horia Paul Terpe

Constitutional Requirements for Legislation

Title VI: Revision of the Constitution

Article 146 (Initiative): (1) Revision of the constitution may be initiated by the President of Romania on a proposal of the Government made by at least one quarter of the total number of Deputies or Senators, or by at least 500,000 citizens with the right to vote. (2) The citizens who initiate the revision of the constitution must belong to at least half the counties in the country, and in each of the respective counties, or in the City of Bucharest, at least 20,000 signatures must be recorded in support of this initiative.

Article 147 (Majority, Referendum): (1) The draft or proposed revision must be adopted by the Chamber of Deputies and the Senate by a majority of at least two thirds of the members of each Chamber. (2) If no agreement can be reached by a mediation procedure, the Chamber of Deputies and the Senate shall decide thereupon, in joint session, by the vote of at least three quarters of the number of Deputies and Senators. (3) The revision shall be final after approval by a referendum held within 30 days from the date of passing the draft or proposed revision.

Article 148 (Limits to Amendment): (1) The provisions of this Constitution with regard to the national, independent, unitary, and indivisible character of the Romanian State, the Republican form of government, territorial integrity, independence of the judiciary, political pluralism, and official language shall not be subject to revision. (2) Likewise, no revision shall be made if it results in the suppression of the citizens' fundamental rights and freedoms, or the safeguards thereof. (3) The Constitution shall not be revised during a state of siege or emergency or during war.

Slovenia

Slovenia allows a minority of parliament or of the people to trigger a referendum, but the result of the referendum is valid only if more than 50% of the electorate participates. Regarding the popular initiative, the Slovenians can only make petitions to parliament, but the citizens have exclusive rights in the area of optional referendums.

Referendum experience is not extensive, but the independence referendum was an important event with a turnout of 93.2%, of whom 88.5% voted "yes." The Slovenian I&R system is weak in initiatives and rather strong in respect to the popular veto.

- Population: 1,986,000
- Area: 20,253 km²
- Capital: Ljubljana
- Official languages: Slovenian, and regionally Croatian, Hungarian, Italian
- Religion: Roman Catholic (70.8%)
- Political System: Republic (since 1991)
- Constitution: June 25, 1991 (without referendum)
- Membership: EU and NATO (2004)
- GNP/Capita: $17,130
- Human Development Rank: 29
- I&R practice: eight nationwide referendums, one plebiscite (1990: independence), one popular referendum (1996: electoral system), and two parliamentary referendums (1999: energy; 2001: artificial insemination for unmarried women).

Types of Initiative and Referendum

The constitution of the Republic of Slovenia was formally accepted in December 1991. In the preamble, it is stated that it is based on the charter of independence, on fundamental human rights and freedoms, on the right to national self-determination, and on the fact that during the war for national liberation during WWII, Slovenia had proven its independence and affirmed its statehood.

When the new Slovenian state emerged, a process of centralization began. Local autonomy was limited to municipalities with at least five thousand inhabitants. Following a non-binding referendum, the municipalities and their territories were determined by the National Assembly. Prior to the 1998 elections, there were 192 municipalities in Slovenia, which varied widely in terms of economic power, size and number of inhabitants. Urban municipalities have a special status and must have at least 20,000 inhabitants and fulfill certain additional conditions.

In 1999, a law promoting harmonious regional development was passed. The principal objectives of the law are as follows: to reduce differences in economic development and opportunities among Slovenian regions; to maintain the population over the entire territory of Slovenia, taking into account the polycentric trend of population movement; and to promote an environmentally-friendly economy and the protection of natural resources, cultural heritage and other public values.

I. National Level

The Constitution states that the National Assembly can call a referendum on any issue regulated by law, and the National Assembly will be bound by the outcome of the referendum. The National Assembly must call a referendum to decide on its own legislative initiative if at least one third of its members, the National Council, or a group of forty thousand voters demand it.

The law on referendum and popular initiative regulates the referendum on a constitutional amendment, and the legislative and consultative referendums on issues which fall within the competence of the National Assembly. It also regulates the means of carrying out a popular initiative to amend the constitution or to pass a law.

All citizens who are eligible to vote have the right to participate in referendums. An initiative becomes law if a majority of all voters participating in the referendum vote in its favor.

a. Referendum on a Constitutional Amendment

This allows citizens to decide whether to approve a constitutional amendment which was passed by the National Assembly. The National Assembly must call a referendum if at least 30 members demand it and if the demand is issued before the amendment is proclaimed.

The National Assembly must call a referendum within 7 days after the demand is issued. The amendment is confirmed by the referendum if participation is at least 50% + 1 of the total electorate and if a majority of those who participate vote in favor of the amendment. The National Assembly is bound by the outcome of the referendum.

b. Legislative Referendum

There are two kinds of legislative referendum: prior and subsequent referendums, which are held before and after legislation has been passed. A legislative referendum can be called on any matter governed by law, subject to the decision of the Constitutional Court.

A legislative referendum must be called if one third of parliamentarians, the National Council, or 40,000 voters demand it; in the last case, 200 valid signatures must be gathered to begin the initiative, and 40,000 signatures must be delivered within 35 to 45 days, depending on the nature of the referendum.

Signatures must be put on official forms by citizens in person at the administrative office of their municipality. Signatures are counted and considered valid or invalid by the administrative offices. If the National Assembly decides that enough valid signatures were delivered, a date for a prior referendum is set within 30 days after the demand for a referendum is issued. The National Assembly must call a subsequent referendum within seven days after the demand is issued.

The proposal for which the referendum was called is accepted if a majority of the voters who cast their votes are in its favor. The National Assembly is bound by the outcome of the referendum: it must abide by the decision made in the prior referendum and must not pass a law that would oppose the outcome or hold another referendum on the same question within a year after the referendum is held.

c. Consultative Referendum

The National Assembly can call a consultative referendum on questions that fall within its competence and are of broad interest to the citizens. This referendum may be for the whole area of the state, or for part of the state if the question concerns only the inhabitants of that part. Although the National Assembly may call a consultative referendum before it finally decides on a question, it is not bound by the referendum's outcome.

II. Local Level

The provisions of the law on referendum and popular initiative are also valid for local referendums unless the law provides otherwise. The issues on which local referendums are held include the readjustment of municipal boundaries, the foundation of a new municipality, and the name of a municipality. All municipalities allow popular initiatives.

III. Practical Guide

The act calling for a referendum is published in the official bulletin of the Republic of Slovenia at least 15 days before the referendum is called, and the referendum must be held not less than 30 days or more than 45 days after the referendum is called. Two or more referendums may be held on the same day, which must be a Sunday or other non-working day.

All citizens who are entitled to vote in general elections have the right to vote in a referendum. The procedure is directed by the same authorities which arrange for general elections. In a municipal referendum, the municipal voting bureau selects the polling stations, nominates the voting committees, and announces the result of the vote. The result of a national referendum is announced by the national Electoral Bureau.

IV. Trends

Slovenia, which was a relatively independent political unit in Yugoslavia, implemented its first constitution in January 1947. In December 1990, the Assembly of the Republic of Slovenia organized a national plebiscite at which 88.5% of voters voted for the establishment of an independent Slovenia and only 4% opposed it. The turnout was 93.2% of the total electorate.

In January 1999, one third of the deputies in the National Assembly demanded a referendum on a law financing the construction of Thermoelectric Power Station No. 3 in Trbovlje. 78% of participants voted against the proposed law and, as a consequence, the National Assembly did not pass the legislation.

Perhaps the most dramatic use of the referendum took place in December 1996, when the National Council demanded a referendum on revisions to the electoral system. The original legislative initiative proposed a mixed electoral system similar to that in Germany. A nationwide referendum was called, which also included the option of a majority electoral system; this option was inserted at the request of the Social Democrats of Slovenia and was supported by a petition signed by more than 40,000 voters. In addition to these two possible electoral systems, a third proposal introducing a proportional electoral system was added by 30 members of the National Assembly.

None of the proposals won an absolute majority of the votes cast in the December 1996 referendum, so the National Assembly dropped the idea of reforming the electoral system. However, just before the end of the mandate of five of its empanelled justices and by a slim margin of five to four, the Constitutional Court retroactively changed the referendum rule. The new ruling meant that the proposal for a majority electoral system won the referendum with only 44.52% of the vote.

The proportional system had received 26.19% of the vote, and the combined system, 14.38%, while only 37.9% of the voters had participated. Many members of the National Assembly opposed the order of the Constitutional Court by appealing to constitutional provisions in Article 82, which state that members of the National Assembly are not bound by the Court's instructions. In 2000, in order to avoid questions on the legitimacy and legality of future elections, the National Assembly amended the constitution and adopted what is primarily a proportional electoral system. In 2003 four nationwide referendums took place, including the yes decisions on EU and NATO membership.

The government proposes to amend the constitution to make the following requirements for a legislative referendum: a) The exclusion of specific questions that cannot be decided upon in a referendum, such as the budget, fiscal laws, amnesty, the wages of public sector employees, laws passed in cases of natural disaster, and laws about the ratification of certain international treaties. b) The exclusion of the option of the prior referendum, due to problems in interpreting the decision adopted at the referendum and the binding of the National Assembly to the results of the referendum. c) A reduction in the number of agents entitled to initiate a call for a referendum. d) The institution of a quorum, especially for the subsequent referendum.

Main author: Igor Luksic

Procedure for Amending this Constitution

Article 168 (Proposal for the Initiation of Amendment): (1) A proposal to amend this Constitution may be initiated by no less than twenty Deputies of the National Assembly, by the Government, or by no less than thirty thousand voters. (2) Any such proposal shall proceed for determination in the National Assembly only upon the vote of a two-thirds majority of those Deputies of the National Assembly present and voting.

Article 169 (Amendment of This Constitution): The National Assembly may enact legislation to amend this Constitution only upon the vote of a two-thirds majority of all elected Deputies.

Article 170 (Ratification of Constitutional Amendment by Referendum): (1) Any proposal for the amendment of this Constitution before the National Assembly must be presented to the electorate at a referendum if the same is demanded by no less than thirty of its Deputies. (2) An amendment shall be considered accepted in such a referendum if a majority of all voters eligible to vote voted in the referendum, and a majority of those who voted, voted in its favor.

Article 171 (Proclamation of Amendments to this Constitution): An amendment to this Constitution shall take effect upon its proclamation in the National Assembly.

Spain

The procedures for initiative and referendum in Spain are varied. The sovereignty of the people appears clearly only in mandatory referendums for significant constitutional/statutory reforms. The only I&R process that may be launched by citizens is the legislative petition, which is subject to stringent restrictions.

The strongest points of Spain's existing I&R procedures are financial compensation for legislative petition groups (up to 180,000 Euro at the national level; up to 30,000 Euro at the regional level) and the absence of a participation quorum. The weak points are the lack of a popular initiative process and the fact that legislative petitions do not lead to a referendum.

The actual practice of I&R is almost non-existent. Referendums have been held on joining NATO's civil structure but not on joining its military structure or on European integration. However, the question of I&R is now being debated because of the upcoming referendum on the EU constitution.

- Population: 40,200,000
- Area: 504,782 km²
- Capital: Madrid
- Official languages: Spanish, and regionally Catalan, Galician, Basque
- Religion: Roman Catholic (98%)
- Political System: Parliamentary monarchy (since 1978), with autonomous regions (17) and provinces (52)
- Constitution: December 7, 1978 (referendum, 91% yes)
- Membership: EU and NATO
- GNP/Capita: $20,150
- Human Development Rank: 19
- I&R practice: Five nationwide referendums. Two plebiscites organized by Franco (1947, 1966); two reform referendums (1976, 1978); and the NATO vote in 1986 (56% Yes).

Types of Initiative and Referendum

In Spain there are devices for constitutional referendums, consultative referendums and legislative petitions, even though they are rarely used. The new political system was designed in a context dominated by the fear of excessively weak political parties, and this prevented a more generous regulation of the use of I&R.

I. National Level

Citizens have the right to initiate legislation at this level under the following conditions. Most issues are excluded in practice from direct citizen initiative: taxation, general state budgets, economic planning, international affairs, constitutional reform, and the prerogative of pardon, as well as those areas subject to organic laws and thus considered of special national interest (Article 81). Organic laws are those ensuring fundamental rights and public freedoms, approving Statutes of Autonomy (regional states), and regulating the general electoral framework, as well as those set out in the Constitution.

There have been only four national legislative referendums. All except the third (March 1999) were rejected.

1) December 1996: Popular petition to guarantee a minimum budget for education.
2) December 1998: Popular petition to provide schoolbooks free of charge.
3) March 1999: The Law of Horizontal Property, which was the first law to originate in a legislative petition.
4) November 1999: Popular petition to reduce the work week to 35 hours.

Since popular initiatives introduce draft laws (proposiciones de ley), they must be submitted to parliament in the form of drafts (divided into articles, etc.), along with an appropriate rationale and a detailed list of the members of the sponsoring committee. Within 15 days, the Presiding Council of the Congress of Deputies, the lower house of parliament, shall decide on the initial admission of the initiative. It can be rejected because it deals with excluded matters, lacks a single subject, or fails to fill formal requirements; because another initiative with the same or equivalent content has already been presented during the current term; or because it overlaps with an approved motion or a previous draft in an advanced stage of the parliamentary process.

The sponsoring committee can challenge a rejection before the Constitutional Court. If the rejection was due to irregularities in the measure, the sponsoring committee may decide whether to remove the initiative or retain it after making the appropriate adjustments.

After the initiative has been accepted, a six-month period begins in which the sponsoring committee tries to collect a minimum of 500,000 authenticated signatures from Spanish citizens who are registered to vote. The Presiding Council can extend this period for three additional months under exceptional circumstances.

Signatures, specifying full name, ID-card number, and the municipality where the signatory is registered, must be put on forms previously sealed and numbered by the Central Electoral Board and accompanied by a copy of the draft. They must be certified by certain officials, such as notaries, or by persons whom the sponsoring committee can designate for the purpose. Signatures are delivered to the provincial electoral boards, which in turn must send them to the Central Electoral Board within 15 days. Here they are checked and the valid signatures are counted.

When the Central Electoral Board has announced that 500,000 or more signatures have been gathered, the Presiding Council orders the publication of the initiative and it is included in the agenda of the plenary sitting of the Congress of Deputies. The draft then goes through the normal stages of the parliamentary process, just as does an ordinary law. As such, the bill may be partially or fully amended, approved, or rejected. Neither the sponsoring committee nor any other representative of the signatories can participate in that process.

The State must compensate the sponsoring committee up to a maximum of 180,700 Euro for its mailing and signature-collecting expenses if the initiative is accepted to be processed by parliament.

The specification of time frames for gathering signatures and sending them to the Election Board (6 months; 15 days) is a good procedure. However, once the petition is accepted, no time period is specified for the study and amendment of the petition. The first petition, in December 1996, took three (yes, three) years to be rejected.

One important fact is that the legislative petition does not lead to a referendum, so no parliamentary counter-proposal is generated. This is why the expression "legislative petition" is more correct than "legislative initiative," in order to distinguish it from the full initiative practiced in other countries.

Non-mandatory, non-binding referendums can be held at the national level, but only "political decisions of overriding importance" may be submitted to this consultative referendum. The law does not provide further details about what may be submitted, but approved or existing legislation is clearly excluded.

Only the prime minister can propose a consultative referendum, after requesting authorization before the Congress of Deputies; his request must include the exact terms of the referendum. The referendum is authorized by an overall majority of the Congress.

The King calls the referendum by means of a royal decree agreed on by the Council of Ministers. His decree must contain the full text of the decision, the wording of the question or questions, and the date of the referendum. The referendum must take place between 30 and 120 days after the publication of the decree in the Public State Gazette. During the campaign, only parties which are represented in Parliament or have gained at least 3% of the popular vote at the last general elections have the right to express their opinions in the public media.

A referendum cannot be held when a state of emergency or siege is in force or within 90 days after such a state has ended, nor within 90 days before or after national parliamentary or local elections. If a referendum is already scheduled when these circumstances occur, it is automatically cancelled and must be called again. No approval quorum is required.

The outcome of a consultative referendum is not legally binding, though it is hard to imagine a government going against a clear decision of the electorate.

Binding referendums may be held to ratify changes to the Constitution. Once approved by both houses of parliament, proposed amendments must be put to national referendum if demanded by at least one tenth of the members of either house within 15 days after their approval. In the case of a total revision of the Constitution, or of a partial revision that affects the Preliminary Title (guiding principles), Title II (the monarchy) or Chapter II, first section of Title I (basic rights and public liberties), the approval must be followed by general elections. If the newly elected Parliament ratifies the constitutional reform, then it shall be automatically put to a national referendum.

A mandatory referendum for a constitutional amendment is the last step in a sequence which includes, among other requirements, the resignation of parliament and new legislative elections. According to referendum law, the time allowed for campaigning is between 10 and 20 days.

The right of petition is different from the so-called "legislative initiative": it was instituted only in November 2001, 23 years later than the constitution which protects it. Before then, petitioning was still done under the rules for petitioning the dictator, which were enacted in December 1960. It is a well-designed law, which sets out the procedure for asking the institutions to take action. They are given three months to respond, and they are legally bound to do so.

II. Regional Level

All Autonomous Communities have introduced their own laws on the citizens' legislative initiative, which are very similar to those at the national level. They all exclude areas outside their competence and questions of taxation from the citizens' initiative. They differ on other restrictions, but these are mainly of a secondary nature.

The minimum number of signatures is between 6,000 and 75,000, depending on the size of the community, which in most cases means around 1.5% of the total electorate. In Extremadura, the signatures of at least 5% of the electorate are required, while Castile-León requires 25,000 signatures representing at least 1% of the electorate of each constituency.

The periods for collecting and delivering the signatures range from three to six months. Verification is done by the appropriate electoral boards or, in Aragón and the Canary Islands, by a control board constituted for the purpose.

In four communities—Aragón, Balearic Islands, Canary Islands and Galicia—a sponsoring committee can defend its bill before the regional parliament. In Aragón, in addition, the sponsors can remove the initiative if they believe that its original meaning is being distorted in the parliamentary process.

Reform of the basic laws (Estatutos de Autonomía) of the four regions that first gained full autonomy (the Basque Country, Catalonia, Galicia, and Andalusia) must always be put to a binding referendum of the electorates involved.

Spain has one remarkable innovation: initiatives may originate in the municipal councils of at least six communities. Such an initiative must be approved by an overall majority in each of the municipal councils. The support of a certain number of town halls is required, and/or the municipalities concerned must include a specific proportion of the electorate.

III. Local Level

Facultative, non-binding referendums are held in a few municipalities and must follow these requirements: a) Referendums can be held on matters of "municipal competence and local character of special interest to the residents." b) They cannot be held on subjects related to local finance. c) The initiative must be approved by a full majority of the municipal council. The mayor can call the referendum after authorization by the central government, which is always required.

Some Autonomous Communities have further developed this legislation. In Catalonia, for instance, the citizens themselves can request the town hall to hold a referendum. The petition must be signed by a certain proportion of residents, ranging from 5% to 20% depending on the number of inhabitants of the municipality, and it is always subject to the approval of the municipal council and the central government.

IV. Practical Guide

In citizen legislative initiatives at both national and regional levels, the sponsoring committee plays a central role until the bill is accepted in Parliament. No restrictions are set on the nature of these committees, except that they must include a minimum number of members (from 5 to 10) in the Autonomous Communities of Aragón, Castile-La Mancha, Extremadura and Galicia.

In some cases, the Electoral Boards have imposed further requirements in addition to those fixed by law, such as specifying that the home address or date of birth must be included with the signature. Furthermore, a sizeable proportion of delivered signatures (on one occasion estimated at 15%) are often found invalid in the final count.

V. Trend

The construction of the new Spanish political system was strongly influenced by two factors that prevented a more flexible regulation of referendums. First, the Franco regime had used plebiscites to consolidate its power, and this created a suspicion that referendums belonged to an outdated tradition. Second, most political parties feared that they were weak in societal and organizational terms and that the existence of any means of reducing their role in decision-making, such as referendums, would further weaken them in the future.

In fact, during the Constitutional debate only the party of the Franco supporters, AP, was in favor of a larger role for procedures of direct democracy, while the Left tried to avoid giving them any significant role. After 25 years of democracy, the general skepticism of the political elite towards the referendum has not changed, even if some parties have changed their attitudes.

During this period, referendums have been used for different purposes. In the first democratic decade, referendums played a crucial role in helping to legitimize the new democratic institutions: the repeal of laws passed under Franco—which led to the first general election, the new Constitution, and the Constitutions of many of the new regions—was approved through referendums.

Only the last of these regional referendums was controversial, except in the Basque Country, where the referendum on the Spanish Constitution was clearly "heated." The referendum on the Andalusian Estatuto needed a majority of the vote in each of the eight provinces of the region; it achieved it in seven, while in the eighth only 49% of the votes were in favor, which resulted in a negative vote for the entire region.

Surely the most controversial referendum in Spanish history has been the 1986 vote on NATO. The Socialist party promised to hold a consultative referendum on leaving NATO while it was in opposition, but changed its mind once in power. There was first great pressure for the referendum to be held and then a very strong campaign from both sides. The result in favor of remaining in NATO greatly disappointed the peace movement, which had strongly supported the referendum, so that referendums again acquired the image of an easy instrument for the right wing to manipulate.

There was also controversy on whether a referendum should be held to ratify the signing of the Maastricht agreement, but the major parties argued that it was not necessary, since both Parliament and popular polls showed a large majority in favor.

From time to time there is debate on whether a referendum would be a reasonable solution to the conflict in the Basque Country. The debate became stronger than ever in autumn 2001, when the Basque government proposed the holding of two referendums: one to show ETA that the Basque people reject terrorism and another to decide on the future relationship of the Basque Country with Spain. The Spanish government strongly opposes a referendum, arguing that it is unconstitutional and unnecessary.

Some initiatives at the regional level, especially in Catalonia, have had a large social mobilization behind them and have received wide publicity. However, the fact that most of them either have not been approved or have been strongly modified by Parliament has discouraged the potential spread of the process.

In any case, the limited role of referendums in Spanish politics has not been a crucial issue, except at some very specific times. No major movement or organization has mounted any strong and consistent campaign in favor of a wider use. Even if there have been some limited efforts to encourage its use at the local level, they have not been widely accepted.

On the other hand, non-legal referendums with a purely symbolic meaning have been organized by social groups at all political levels. For example, a referendum to abolish the external debt of Third World countries, organized by a citizens' group and held on the same day as the 1996 General Election, was widely publicized and attracted a million voters.

In 1999, the educational administration in Madrid called for a referendum to approve a continuous (single-term) timetable for public schools, requiring an approval quorum of 80%. In 106 schools, parents of 53,000 schoolchildren, a majority of over 80%, voted for a continuous school timetable. However, one person—Gustavo Villapalos, the Regional Director of Education—subsequently decided that the referendum was not binding. This led to huge demonstrations but no change to existing practice.

Main authors: Guillem Rico and Joan Font, with additional remarks by Juan Pablo de Soto

Constitutional Requirements for Legislation

Title X: Constitutional Amendment
Article 166 (Initiative): The right to propose a Constitutional amendment shall be exercised under the terms contained in Article 87 (1) and (2).
Article 167 (Procedure): (1) Bills on Constitutional amendment must be approved by a majority of three fifths of the members of each Chamber. If there is no agreement between the Chambers, an effort to reach it shall be made by setting up a Joint Commission of Deputies and Senators which shall submit a text to be voted on by the House of Representatives and the Senate. (2) If adoption is not obtained by means of the procedure outlined in the foregoing paragraph, and if the text has obtained a favorable vote by an absolute majority of the Senate, the House of Representatives may approve the amendment by a two-thirds vote. (3) Once the amendment has been passed by the Parliament, it shall be submitted to a referendum for its ratification, if so requested by one tenth of the members of either Chamber within fifteen days after its passage.
Article 168 (Revision): (1) When a total revision of the Constitution is proposed, or a partial revision thereof, affecting the Preliminary Title, Chapter II, Section 1 of Title I, or Title II, the principle shall be approved by a two-thirds majority of the members of each Chamber, and the Parliament shall immediately be dissolved. (2) The Chambers elected must ratify the decision and proceed to examine the new Constitutional text, which must be approved by a two-thirds majority of the members of both Chambers. (3) Once the amendment has been passed by the Parliament, it shall be submitted to ratification by referendum.
Article 169 (Restriction): A Constitutional amendment may not be initiated in time of war or when any of the circumstances set out in Article 116 are in operation.

Sweden

Referendums ("folkomröstningar") have been used as a tool by the political majorities, hence mainly as plebiscites. Today, the same forces which previously manipulated ballot decisions are opposed to stronger I&R devices, arguing that the experience of referendums has been negative.

However, the process has been reformed very slowly at all political levels, e.g. by introducing the binding national referendum and the citizens' petition at the local level. Further improvements are currently being debated, such as the nationwide referendum triggered by a minority of the parliament and the citizen-initiated referendum at the local level.

The 1994 EU membership referendum was the first *de facto* binding referendum, setting a new standard. The decision on introducing the Euro followed up this development in late 2003.

- Population: 8,857,000
- Area: 449,964 km²
- Capital: Stockholm
- Official languages: Swedish, and regionally Sami and Finnish.
- Religion: Lutheran (89%)
- Political System: Parliamentary monarchy (1809)
- Constitution: January 1, 1975 (without referendum)
- Membership: EU
- GNP/Capita: $24,180
- Human Development Rank: 3
- I&R practice: seven countrywide referendums since 1910: Alcohol prohibition (1910 and 1922); driving left/right (1955); pension system (1957); nuclear energy (1980); EU membership (November 13, 1994; 52.3% yes; 83% turnout) and Euro referendum (September 14, 2003; 42% yes; 82.6% turnout). More than 100 local referendums since 1977.

Types of Initiative and Referendum

Sweden is a unitary state with limited powers for the provinces but a large degree of local independence for its 289 municipalities, which are ruled by popularly elected local councils.

The Sami in the north of the country (population 25,000) enjoy some degree of autonomy through their own parliament, Sametinget, which however has mainly an advisory status.

Sweden has been a member of the UN and of almost all of its associated organs and branches since 1946. It has been a non-aligned country and a member of the European Union since 1995.

Prime Minister Göran Persson has headed a Social Democrat minority government since 1994. The government has co-operated with the Left Party and the Green Party on budget issues and most other main political issues since 1998. The Conservatives dominate the opposition.

I. National Level

According to the constitution, Sweden has no devices for the popular initiative at the national level, and only a small minority of its parliament has any wish to introduce the popular initiative.

National referendums can be held according to two different provisions, established in the constitution. There are no issues which automatically trigger a referendum.

Since 1979 it has been possible for the Parliament to call an advisory referendum, which is established in the constitution (Regeringsformen 8:4) and in the special law on referendums (SFS 1979:369). A simple majority of the Parliament can call for a popular vote on any issue, including constitutional amendments, and the referendum can be held on any date. The government formulates the alternatives to be presented to the voters, including the alternatives favored by the opposition parties. The electorate is the same as for national elections; however, the Parliament can choose to include people who are normally only allowed to vote at the municipal level.

The constitution also provides for a binding referendum (Regerings-formen 8:15). This can be held only on bills seeking to change the constitution, and is mandatory if at least one tenth (35) of the members of Parliament call for it, with at least one third (117) of the members in favor.

A call for a binding referendum must be made within 15 days after the bill has been approved by Parliament, and the referendum must be held on the day of the national elections. Only those who are eligible to vote at the national level can participate in the referendum. The bill is rejected only if a majority of the electors who vote cast a "no" vote (meaning that all blank votes count as "yes" votes), and only if the "no" votes number more than half of the electors who voted in the national election. If the latter provision is not fulfilled, Parliament will decide on the matter, which is why some scholars call this mechanism semi-binding.

For both the advisory and the binding referendum, Parliament can decide how to put the question to the people and what answers the voters can choose from, with the possibility of having more than two alternatives.

To date, no binding referendum has been held in Sweden; all five national referendums have been held according to the 8:4 advisory clause. These are:

August 27, 1922: "yes" or "no" to prohibition for alcoholic beverages; 50.9% no; 55.1% voter turnout. There was a clear "yes" majority among women, and higher male turnout was a decisive factor for the result.

October 16, 1955: Driving on left/right side; 82.9% voted for continued left-side driving, 15% for changing to the right side (1.6% blank votes); 53% voter turnout. Right-side driving was introduced in 1967.

October 13, 1957: General supplementary pensions (ATP). Three alternatives: 1) Compulsory supplementary pensions, 45.8%; 2) Voluntary supplementary pensions, through the normal insurance companies, 15%; 3) The same as 2, but with the possibility of agreements between employers and trade unions, 35.3%. The voter turnout was 72.4%, with 3.9% casting blank votes. The result was unclear, since compulsory pensions won a majority, but *some kind of* voluntary pension won an absolute majority of the votes. The referendum led to the dissolution of the parliament, and the introduction in 1959 of compulsory supplementary pensions.

March 23, 1980: Nuclear Power. Three alternatives: 1) Discontinuing the use of nuclear power at a pace set by the industry's needs, 18.9%; 2) Identical, but with the nuclear power being owned by the state and municipalities, 39.1%; 3) A total discontinuation of the use of nuclear power within ten years, 38.7%. The voter turnout was 75.6%, with 3.3% blank votes. In this election, by a special provision, those who normally cannot vote in national elections were also eligible to vote. Only 15% of the electors declared themselves satisfied with this referendum, and the result is still under discussion today.

November, 13, 1994: Swedish membership in the European Union; "yes" or "no" to membership according to the agreement reached by the EU and Sweden. 52.3% voted "yes"; 46.8% voted "no"; and 0.9% cast a blank vote. The voter turnout was 83.3%. On January 1, 1995, Sweden joined the European Union.

As we have seen, in several referendums more than two alternatives have been proposed to the electorate, which, when none of them gained an absolute majority, led to much discussion about which action to take.

A large part of the population feels that national referendums have been manipulated, in the sense that they were designed so that the political decision-makers could act according to their own wishes regardless of the result of the referendum. All in all, the Swedish referendum is an instrument in the hands of the politicians, not of the voters.

II. Regional Levels

Regional referendums can be held according to the rules for local referendums (*see below*). However, no referendum has been held at the regional level, although some proposals for this have been made.

III. Local Level

At the municipal level, a simple majority of the Local Council (kommunfullmäktige) suffices to call for a non-binding referendum, with no limits on which issues can be decided and no restrictions on when the referendum should be held. There are no limits on the number and frequency of ballot measures, and the local political authority decides who is eligible to vote. This was introduced in the municipality law of 1977 and remained unchanged in the renewed municipality law of 1991.

In addition to the authority-initiated referendum, a local initiative right was introduced on July 1, 1994. If 5% of those eligible to vote at the local level demand a referendum in writing, the Local Council must decide whether or not to hold such a referendum. However, they are free to decide, using any argument, that a referendum should not be held. If a referendum is to be held, the Local Council decides how to formulate the question(s) and when the voting is to be done. The signatures, printed names, and addresses of the initiators must all be verified by the municipal electoral council.

About 80 local referendums have been held since 1977, all initiated by politicians. A large part of these were held within a year of the national referendums. About half of them have concerned whether or not to change municipal boundaries, which normally creates a new, separate municipality. The most common other subject has been infrastructure such as roads and bridges.

More than 90% of all proposals for referendums raised in the local councils have been turned down, most often with arguments that the issue had already been decided, that the issue was not yet ready for a decision, that the issue was too complicated, or that it was so simple that it did not warrant the complicated and expensive procedure of a referendum.

Of the 80 initiatives called for by the people, many of them signed by more than 10% of the electorate, only five have resulted in referendums. Most of the initiatives concerned the same types of issues that have been the subject of referendums initiated by politicians in the local councils.

IV. Trends

The referendum was first discussed in the Swedish Parliament in 1897, and first introduced into the constitution in 1922 in the form of the advisory referendum.

In the early 1950s, the Parliament came close to strengthening the instrument with binding referendums and the right of a parliamentary minority to call a referendum. These were mainly proposals from right-wing parties aimed at diminishing the Social Democratic hegemony. In 1974, the Parliament decided to keep the instrument as it was established in 1922, but in 1979, it established the right of a minority of one third of the parliamentarians to call for a binding referendum in constitutional matters.

Sweden has been dominated by the Social Democrat Party during most of the 20th century, and until recently it has been culturally very homogenous, with basically one ethnic group, one religion, and one language. As a small and non-aligned country, Sweden has also felt the need for wide agreement on political issues of great importance, especially concerning foreign policy. These are three historic reasons for the rather restrictive use of referendums in Sweden.

The changing reality of the country since the Cold War, now a member of the European Union, with a more mixed population due to the influx of immigrants and with a less hegemonic position for the Social Democrats, means that the ground is now more fertile for new methods of reaching political decisions. This trend is strengthened by the facts that voter turnout is declining, fewer people are involved in party politics, and the electors are becoming more skeptical towards the elected, all of which suggest the need to reform today's model of Swedish representative democracy. All political parties in the Parliament agreed to hold a national referendum on whether Sweden should join the European Monetary Union. This citizen decision took place in September 2003, with a turnout of 82.6% and a 55.9% "no" vote.

At the municipal level, direct democracy is on the rise. Recent initiatives—such as the municipality of Kalix asking its inhabitants how high local taxes should be and how the money should be spent—have been popular and have attracted international attention, which suggests that more municipalities will follow suit. The initiative will probably be strengthened, since today's system has led only to more frustration when hundreds of thousands of people have asked for a referendum, only to be turned down by the city council.

Opinion polls and surveys suggest that referendums and popular initiatives are vastly more popular with the people than with the political parties and elite. According to a poll by Gallup and Votia Empowerment, 59% of the electorate support adding elements of direct democracy to the political agenda, while only three minor political parties in the Parliament (the Greens, the Post-Communists, and the Rural Center) regularly propose such measures. A majority in the Riksdagen has so far rejected bills proposing binding referendums, popular initiatives, and the right of a political minority to trigger a referendum, but little by little, starting at the municipal level, we can expect to see more and more direct democracy.

Main author: Mattias Goldmann, with additional remarks by Bruno Kaufmann

Constitutional Requirements for Legislation

Chapter 8: Laws and Other Regulations

Article 4: Provisions concerning consultative referendums throughout the whole of the country and concerning the procedure for holding referendums on matters concerning the fundamental laws shall be laid down by an Act of law.

Article 13: (1) In addition to what follows from Articles 7 to 10, the Government may issue by statutory order 1) regulations concerning the enforcement of laws and 2) regulations which under the fundamental laws are not to be issued by the Parliament. (2) The Government may not by virtue of Paragraph (1) issue any regulations which concern the Parliament or its agencies. Nor may the Government by virtue of Paragraph (1.2) issue regulations which concern local taxation. (3) The Government may delegate to a subordinate authority the task of issuing regulations in the relevant matter by means of a statutory order under Paragraph (1).

Article 15: (2) The Parliament may not adopt as a decision in suspense any Bill on a fundamental law which conflicts with any other draft legislation of the same nature which is held in suspense, unless the Parliament at the same time rejects the Bill it first adopted. (3) A referendum shall be held on a decision held in suspense for an amendment of a fundamental law if there is a motion to this effect by no fewer than one tenth of the members of the Parliament, provided that no fewer than one third of the members vote in favor of the motion. Such a motion must be made within fifteen days after the date on which the Parliament adopted the Bill held in suspense. Such a motion shall not go for consideration by any Committee of the Parliament. (4) The referendum shall be held simultaneously with the election for the Parliament referred to in Paragraph (1). All those entitled to vote in the election may declare in the referendum whether or not they accept the Bill on the fundamental law which is pending decision. The Bill shall be deemed to be rejected if the majority of those taking part in the referendum vote against the proposal, and if the number of voters exceeds half the number of those who registered valid votes in the election. In all other cases the Parliament shall take up the Bill for final consideration.

Article 17: No law shall be amended or repealed otherwise than by law. Articles 15 and 16 apply *mutatis mutandis* with respect to any amendment or abrogation of a fundamental law.

Switzerland

The basic fact about I&R in Switzerland is: Switzerland did not create the referendum; the referendum created Switzerland. There is a full range of compulsory and citizen-initiated referendum institutions at all levels of government: the federal level, 26 cantons, and 2,973 municipalities.

The I&R institutions were established step by step: compulsory referendum in 1848; optional referendum in 1874; popular initiative at the federal level in 1891.

Average turnout is approximately 50%; this trend has recently become positive again after a long period of decreasing participation. Younger citizens are participating in I&R decisions more than they are in elections.

Important developments have taken place in recent years. Women's suffrage at the national level was introduced only in 1971, and transparency laws were adopted very recently.

- Population: 7,136,000
- Area: 41,284 km^2
- Capital: Berne (Bern)
- Official languages: German (63%), French (20%), Italian (8%), Romansch
- Religion: Roman Catholic (46%), Protestant (40%)
- Political System: Parliamentary Federation (since 1848)
- Constitution: January I, 2000 (referendum: 59% yes)
- Membership: UN, EU non-active candidate.
- GNP/Capita: $28,100
- Human Development Rank: 10
- I&R practice: more than 500 federation-wide referendums since 1848, many thousands at the cantonal level, hundreds of thousands at the local level. On March 3, 2002, Switzerland became the first country in the world in which the citizens decided to join the United Nations (55% yes).

Types of Initiative and Referendum

The forms of direct democracy in Switzerland derive from various historical sources. As specific institutions, referendum and initiative appeared in the Montagnard Constitution of June 24, 1793 (Article 10 and Article 56-60), during the French Revolution.

Before this, the Swiss had preserved both direct-democratic mechanisms of decision-making, such as the "Volksanfragen" (popular consultations) in the cantons of Zürich, Bern, Solothurn and Neuenburg, and hybrid federal-democratic mechanisms, such as the community referendums or "Zendenreferenden" in Graubünden and the district referendums in Wallis, some of which go back as far as the 15th century. It was because of its own longstanding democratic traditions, including "Landsgemeinde" or community citizens' assemblies, that the idea of I & R fell on such fertile ground during the modernization of democracy in the Swiss cantons after the Restoration in 1830.

In the search for forms of which would preserve the traditions of co-determination while permitting a more modern form of government, initiative and referendum formed an acceptable compromise among the positions of the various political factions.

Historically, the introduction of I&R shows three main trends:

1) The rights of direct democracy are introduced gradually over time. First to be established is the right of veto; then the statutory constitutional referendum; then the legislative referendum; and finally the right of initiative.

2) Citizens' rights are introduced first at lower levels, and move upwards. They were introduced first in the member states (cantons), and introduced later at the federal level.

3) Rights are normally established by a broad coalition of differing interests.

When the federal state was established in 1848, only the statutory constitutional referendum was grounded in the constitution. The legislative referendum became law in 1874. Finally, the right of initiative was established in 1891.

The 20th century saw the gradual extension and refinement of direct democracy. The referendum on international treaties was established in 1921: open-ended and irrevocable treaties were now subject to facultative referendum. Direct-democratic control of foreign policy was extended in 1977, when the scope of the optional referendum was widened to include accession to international organizations and acts involving the multilateral standardization of laws. Accession to organizations for collective security (e.g. UNO) and to supranational communities (e.g. the EU) was also made subject to mandatory referendum. In 1949, the popular referendum on urgent federal resolutions was introduced. So far, other possible extensions, such as the legislative initiative or the referendum on the national budget, have been rejected by the people.

The new federal constitution of 2000 contains the first explicit limitations on the subject matter of initiatives. Mandatory rules of international law, e.g. fundamental human rights such as the principle of "Non-Reversal," cannot be subjected to referendum, and initiatives launched on such matters are declared invalid by parliament (cf. note 1).

Direct-democratic rights have had a lasting influence on Swiss institutions, since it was by means of initiative that the right to proportional voting was secured, which then led to the proportionalisation of the whole of political life. Proportionalisation is reinforced by the power of referendum possessed by the most important social groups.

In Switzerland, it can be said that if the citizens' initiative is the daughter of the referendum, proportional voting for the National Council (parliament) is its granddaughter, and the so-called "magic formula" (proportionally elected government) its great-granddaughter.

I. National Level

The various instruments can best be described by quoting from the relevant articles of the constitution:

a. Popular Initiative

Article 138 (Popular Initiative for Total Revision of the Federal Constitution): (1) 100,000 citizens entitled to vote may propose a total revision of the Federal Constitution. (2) This proposal has to be submitted to the people by referendum.

Article 139 (Popular Initiative for Partial Revision of the Federal Constitution): (1) 100,000 citizens entitled to vote may propose a partial revision of the Federal Constitution. (2) The popular initiative for a partial revision of the Federal Constitution may be in the form of a general suggestion or a formulated draft. (3) If an initiative does not respect the principle of unity of form, the principle of unity of subject matter, or mandatory rules of international law, the Federal Parliament shall declare the initiative invalid in whole or in part. (4) If the Federal Parliament approves an initiative in the form of a general suggestion, it shall prepare a draft of the meaning of the initiative and submit it to the vote of the people and the Cantons. If it rejects the initiative, it shall submit it to the vote of the People; the People shall decide whether the initiative should be followed. If the People approve the initiative, the Federal Parliament shall formulate a corresponding draft. (5) An initiative in the form of a formulated draft shall be submitted to the vote of the People and the Cantons. The Federal Parliament shall recommend its approval or its rejection. If it recommends its rejection, it may submit its own counter-draft. (6) The People and the Cantons shall vote simultaneously on the initiative and the counter-draft. The voters may approve both drafts. They may indicate which draft they prefer, should both be approved; should one of the drafts obtain a majority of the People's votes and the other the majority of the votes of the Cantons, neither of them shall come into force.

The period of time allowed for the collection of signatures begins as soon as the Swiss federal chancellery (Bundeskanzlei) publishes the proposed new constitutional text in the Official Gazette of the Confederation (Bundesblatt). Signatures can be collected anywhere, including public places. The signatures are checked by the local government office (Gemeindekanzlei) and given a certificate of eligibility. The initiative committee then passes them on to the Swiss federal chancellery (Bundeskanzlei).

Once 100,000 signatures have been collected, the initiative is declared to formally exist. It then goes to the Parliament to be checked for validity. Unity of subject matter is required, which means that an initiative must not include several different proposals. The purpose of this is to ensure that the clear will of the people can be expressed: without a single subject, the electorate might accept something with which they do not agree because the overall merit of the proposal outweighs the demerits of one or more parts of the proposed constitutional change.

Unity of subject matter is required only for constitutional change, whether that change is made via Citizens' Initiative or Government proposals. It is not required for international treaties, such as EMU, which are subject to statutory referendums.

The fact that Parliament and not a constitutional court decides on the validity of initiatives is a matter of dispute in Switzerland. The initiative committee can decide to withdraw the initiative: as a rule, a clause to this effect must be included in the initiative's text.

A formally successful initiative—one which has secured the minimum 100,000 signatures—must be put to referendum within 39 months after the date on which the signatures are submitted.

The procedures to be followed when there is a counter-proposal have existed only since 1987. Before this, Parliament routinely used the counter-proposal as a tactic to divide and rule by splitting votes between the initiative and the counter-proposal. Since the introduction of the new procedures, direct counter-proposals have become rare.

b. Compulsory Referendum

Article 140 (Compulsory referendum): (1) The following shall be submitted to the vote of the People and the Cantons: a. Revisions of the Federal Constitution; b. The entry into organizations for collective security or into supranational communities; c. Federal Statutes declared urgent which have no constitutional basis and whose validity exceeds one year; such Federal Statutes must be submitted to the vote within one year after their adoption by the Federal Parliament. (2) The following shall be submitted to the vote of the People: a. Popular initiatives for total revision of the Federal Constitution; b. Popular initiatives for partial revision of the Federal Constitution in the form of a general suggestion which were rejected by the Federal Parliament; c. The question whether a total revision of the Constitution should be carried out if both Chambers disagree.

When an issue is presented to both the people (national level) and the "Stände" (cantons) for decision in a referendum, both an absolute majority of the valid votes cast and a majority of the cantons must be in favor. When a referendum is put only to the people, an absolute majority of the valid votes cast decides the issue; in this case, the cantons do not all carry the same weight. For historical reasons, six out of the total of 26 Swiss cantons (Obwalden, Nidwalden, Basel-Stadt (the city of Basle), Basel-Land (the area surrounding Basle), Appenzell Ausserrhoden and Appenzell Innerrhoden) carry only "half-weight."

c. Optional Referendum

Article 141 (Optional Referendum): (1) The following are submitted to the vote of the People at the request of 50,000 citizens entitled to vote, or of eight Cantons: a. Federal Statutes; b. Federal Statutes declared urgent with a validity exceeding one year; c. Federal decrees to the extent the Constitution or statute foresees this; d. International treaties which: 1. are of unlimited duration and may not be terminated; 2. provide for entry into an international organization; 3. involve a multilateral unification of law. (2) The Federal Parliament may submit further international treaties to optional referendum.

Article 142 (Required Majorities): (1) Proposals submitted to the vote of the People shall be accepted if the majority of those voting approve them. (2) Proposals submitted to the vote of the People and the Cantons shall be accepted if the majority of those voting and the majority of the Cantons approve them. (3) The result of a popular vote in a Canton determines the vote of that Canton. (4) The Cantons of Obwald, Nidwald, Basle-City, Basle-Land, Appenzell Outer Rhodes and Appenzell Inner Rhodes have each one half of a cantonal vote. The 50,000 signatures must be collected, verified as to voter eligibility by the communities, and delivered to the Swiss federal chancellery (Bundeskanzlei) within 100 days of the publication of the text of the law in the Official Gazette of the Confederation (Bundesblatt).

II. Regional and Local Level

Direct democracy in Switzerland originated at the local and cantonal levels. Until 1848, except for a brief period, the national level in Switzerland existed only as a loose confederation of states. There is thus a rich variety of forms of local and regional democracy, to which it is not possible to do justice in such a limited space.

Today, about 2350 communities have a community assembly, in which citizens decide publicly on community issues. In the 500 larger communities which have no community assembly, the assembly is replaced by the referendum and by the local community parliament.

In all cantons except the two that still have citizens' assemblies—Appenzell Innerrhoden and Glarus (Landsgemeindekantone)—there are both mandatory and optional referendums as well as the initiative. Many cantons also have an optional, some even a mandatory, referendum on budget matters.

a. Political and Social Agents

Although in Switzerland the signature quota is not very high in relation to the number of registered voters (2.1%), this does not mean that just anyone can launch an initiative. The current estimated cost per signature is two Swiss francs for printing, secretarial work, advertising, etc., even if no paid signature collectors are employed. Thus, a referendum initiative costs at least 100,000 Swiss francs for signature collection alone, in addition to the cost of the subsequent referendum campaign.

As a result, referendums are usually launched by existing organizations or parties — reflecting, as in any democracy, the existing relationships of power in society. This applies somewhat less in the case of the citizens' initiative, which can be launched even by relatively small groups. In such cases, the initiative, which can take several years from its inception to the eventual referendum, often leads to the formation of new political affiliations, which are then more capable of launching referendums in the future. In fact, the term "capable of launching referendums" (referendumsfähig) has in Switzerland become a synonym for "to be taken seriously politically."

The filtering function of the signature quota should not be judged negatively. A direct democracy without filters would burden citizens with a plethora of proposals, leading to public annoyance and the demise of the very instruments of direct democracy.

b. Outcomes and Experiences

The success or otherwise of direct democracy cannot be measured only by concrete political outcomes. Direct democracy offers the greatest possible participation by the general public in the process of decision making in modern societies which are organized into states. This participation should be seen as a human right, and the recognition of the human right to political co-determination does not depend on whether the results of referendums satisfy one's own personal interests; such a judgment would reflect a fundamentally anti-democratic attitude. The outcomes of direct democracy must be judged against this background.

In these terms, Switzerland does not differ fundamentally from other affluent countries with indirect parliamentary systems. Reforms happen more quickly in some countries than in others, but the resulting legislation is very similar. This is not surprising, since the same kinds of power relationships exist in societies with direct democracy as exist in other affluent industrialized countries which have purely parliamentary systems.

For example, if one compares Switzerland with the predominantly two-party, first-past-the-post systems in Great Britain and France, one can see that the existence of citizens' participatory rights exerted pressure for compromise at an earlier stage, but that it has been increasingly recognized even in bi-polar systems that elections are predominantly won on the centre ground. Even though the mechanisms differ, the trend is towards convergence over the longer term.

There are presumably differences in the attitude towards the state and towards taxation, as well as in the level of political awareness, though no studies have yet been carried out on these issues. It is a greater advantage for a person to be politically aware and informed about events and issues under direct democracy, since he can then play a constructive part in referendums. Tax avoidance and negative attitudes towards taxation are probably less prevalent under direct democracy, since people can share in decisions on public spending and approve any tax increases. There is empirical evidence that this connection exists at the local and regional levels. Although Switzerland is not exempt from political alienation and apathy, it may be assumed that these are less common than in purely representative systems.

III. Trends

The Swiss people hold direct democracy is held in high regard. This probably explains why politicians seldom attack the instruments of direct democracy, even though not all Swiss politicians enjoy the limitations placed on their power by direct democracy, any more than do politicians elsewhere.

In recent years, especially before the referendums on European integration (EEA), the media gave more space to academics critical of direct democracy, primarily from neo-liberal circles (cf. note 3). However, support for direct democracy also came from the same quarter (note 4). It is unlikely that such attacks will result in any reduction of direct democracy in Switzerland.

On the other hand, greater political and economic integration tends to reduce political freedom of movement in individual countries. Decisions about new regulations and standards are increasingly being made at the transnational or international level, whether in the United Nations or in the EU.

On March 3, 2002, a majority of 54.6% voted in a national referendum in favor of entering the UN. Because a majority in the cantons was also required, ultimately one canton swung the vote in favor of accession. Switzerland's full membership of the UN has an especially high level of legitimacy because it is the first country in which the people themselves voted in favor of entry.

The question of possible accession to the EU is a much more difficult issue for Swiss citizens. They fear a severe restriction of their direct democracy, because accession would mean that areas in which the EU has competence would automatically be removed from direct-democratic control (note 5). On the other hand, many people stress the fact that Switzerland has the opportunity to contribute reform proposals to the work of the EU Convention on a possible European constitution. They believe that the growing interest in direct democracy in many EU countries enhances the chance that rights of initiative and referendum will eventually be introduced at the EU level, which could compensate for the loss of citizen influence at the lower level.

A new citizens' right, known as the "General Citizens' Initiative" or "Popular Motion," was approved by Swiss citizens in a referendum on February 9, 2003, although it was strongly criticised in the weeks before the referendum. The most disputed part of this package of constitutional amendments to increase citizens' rights was the so-called "General Initiative," which would make it possible, for the first time, for citizens' initiatives to trigger not only constitutional amendments but also legislative change. But the 100,000 signatures required for the initiative would secure only the right to present a general demand: parliament would be responsible for translating the general proposal into a specific constitutional or legislative text. If parliament were unfaithful to the original intention, the Supreme Court could be asked to intervene.

This combination of citizens' demand, parliamentary decree and a possible referral to the Supreme Court is designed to ensure that initiatives enter the legislative process in the most constructive way—and also that they do not conflict with international commitments.

During much of the referendum campaign, it went unnoticed that this process, which was being proposed as an innovation at the federal level, was already in regular use in seven cantons. Few of those who opposed checked whether their objections were actually borne out in practice at the cantonal level. While those on the right complained that the new citizens' right was too complicated, those on the left claimed that it wouldn't be used because it wasn't attractive enough: it required as many signatures as a detailed constitutional initiative.

Cantonal experience with the general/unitary citizens' initiative has been extremely good: according to Robert Heuss, director of the cantonal chancellor's office in Basle, the only plausible explanation for the frequent use of the unitary initiative lies in its "citizen-friendliness." Its introduction at the federal level was approved by a large majority of 70% of the general vote, and all the cantons also voted in its favour. On the other hand, it was approved by the lowest turnout for a national referendum in 30 years: only 28% of the electorate turned out to vote.

Parliament has already implemented most of the constitutional changes agreed by the citizens' rights reform referendum, but the new General Citizens' Initiative tool will only be available after the detailed legislation has been drafted and approved. The government is expected to present its proposals to parliament during the next year. In a recent report, the relevant parliamentary committee referred to "a number of tricky procedural problems" which might well lead to some "intense debates." The prediction is that the new citizens' initiative will not come into force until 2006.

Main author: Paul Ruppen, with additional remarks by Hans-Urs Wili, Rolf Büchi, Bruno Vanoni, and Bruno Kaufmann

Constitutional Requirements for Legislation

Title 6: Revision of the Federal Constitution and Temporal Provisions
Chapter 1: Revision
Article 192 (Principle): (1) The Federal Constitution may be subjected to a total or a partial revision at any time. (2) Where the Federal Constitution and implementing legislation do not provide otherwise, the revision shall follow the legislative process.

Article 193 (Total Revision): (1) A total revision of the Federal Constitution may be proposed by the People or by one of the Chambers, or may be decreed by the Federal Parliament. (2) If the initiative emanates from the People or if the Chambers disagree, the People shall decide whether a total revision shall be undertaken. (3) Should the People accept a total revision, both Chambers shall be newly elected. (4) The mandatory provisions of international law may not be violated.

Article 194 (Partial Revision): (1) A partial revision of the Federal Constitution may be requested by the People or decreed by the Federal Parliament. (2) A partial revision must respect the principle of the unity of subject matter; it may not violate the mandatory provisions of international law. (3) A popular initiative for partial revision must, moreover, respect the principle of the unity of form.

Article 195 (Entry into Force): The Constitution revised in total or in part shall enter into force as soon as it is accepted by the People and the Cantons.

Chapter Four

The Design of Direct Democracy — A Basis for Assessing Sub-Optimal Procedures of Citizen Lawmaking

By Andreas Gross

It has been realized for some time that in the political debate about direct democracy, the central question should not be *whether* to have direct democracy, but rather *how*: what form should that direct democracy take? (See, for example, Schiller/Gross 1995.)

The experiences of recent years should encourage us to deepen and expand this question. In the ways that elements of direct democracy have been handled over the past five years in the federal states of Germany, in other Western European countries (especially Italy and Portugal), in various American states, and in Switzerland, we can see that *how* direct democracy is designed, *how* direct democratic procedures are shaped, and *how* these are harmonized with and integrated into the parliamentary decision-making processes determine the quality—the "goodness"—of direct democracy.

An understanding of the *"optimal"* design of direct democracy and its core procedures is necessary for identifying and evaluating other, *"sub-optimal,"* procedures. This is the aim of the first part of this report, which will provide a basis for the evaluation of direct democratic procedures and institutions in 31 European countries which forms the second part of the report.[1]

I. Direct Democracy As a Subject of Global Comparison and Exchange

It is nothing new to use international comparisons to gain information that can be used to improve direct-democratic procedures. The history of direct democracy in Europe and in the USA, since its beginnings in the states of New England in the 17th/18th centuries, is the history of a unique trans-Atlantic and intra-European process of exchange and comparison.[2]

In order to optimize the qualities of direct democratic procedures, one must first define them. On the one hand, we can look at the statements of those who are considered the pioneers of modern direct democracy in Switzerland and in the United States. Modern Swiss direct democracy owes a great deal to the French Revolution and to the Girondist Marie Jean Condorcet in general and to the German philosopher Friedrich Albert Lange in particular.[3] But in seeking to discover what added value direct democracy can deliver, we can also learn by examining an exclusively parliamentary democracy which needs to be complemented and extended—and thus in practice "democratized"—by elements of direct democracy.

Lange, in his April 1869 commentary on the adoption of the new constitution in the canton of Zurich, which at the time was the most direct-democratic constitution in the world, named the "extraordinarily deep dissatisfaction with the crass deficiencies of the representative system" as the most significant cause of that "convulsion of the emotions" which had "precipitated the principle of direct democracy, like a crystal from a saturated solution" (Der Landbote, Winterthur, 4/20/1869; subsequent quotes all taken from Gross/Klages 1996).

---

1. This article is based in part on a paper by IRI Research Director Andreas Gross—"The Design of Direct Democracy and its Qualities"—which was published in Autumn 2002 in the collection of essays edited by Theo Schiller and Volker Mittendorf: Direkte Demokratie als Systemergänzung. Forschungsbeiträge und Perspektiven, Westdeutscher Verlag, Wiesbaden and the work of the IRI Europe project group "Design & Rating" consisting of Andreas Gross, Bruno Kaufmann, Heiko Dittmer, Frank Rehmet, Gerhard Schuster, Fredi Krebs and Jürgen Zinnel.
2. On the origins, see Kölz (1996, p. 117); on the significance of Switzerland for direct democracy in the US at the beginning of the 20th century, see especially Gross (1999); on the dual significance of Switzerland for the development of direct democracy in Bavaria in the 1940s and 1990s, see Seipe and Mayer (1997, p. 9 ff).
3. On Condorcet, see Kölz (1992); on F.A.Lange, see Mittendorf (1997), Gross (2000) and especially Zinnel (2001).

II. The Claims/Expectations of Direct Democracy

The following claims and expectations for direct democracy have been expressed by its proponents over the years:

- "The decisive control and use of political power should be transferred from the hands of the few onto the broad shoulders of the many."
- "Republican life depends on the continuous steady balancing of opposing tendencies."
- "The people should acquire wider political knowledge and opinions."
- "The authorities, statesmen, and representatives will try much harder to acquaint ordinary people with their thoughts and convictions."
- "The people will approach them with the clear and genuine expression of their needs and preferences."
- "The moral/spiritual/intellectual life of the people" should be stimulated by "being deeply involved with the great issues of the common public weal" (*Der Landbote*, 2/22/1868, p. 273).
- "We are taking into our own hands the decisions which affect the destiny of our country; in some way or other we wish to have the final word on these matters" (*Der Gruetlianer*, Bern, 7/15/1868, p. 274).
- "The will of the people and the spirit of the times, the understanding of the common man and the great thoughts of the statesman, should be peacefully negotiated and reconciled."
- "(I&R enables) the creation of popular rule in happy union with representation" (*Der Landbote*, 12/17/1868, p. 274).

The spokesmen for what was in effect a democratic revolution which between 1867 and 1869 put a system of direct democracy in place of the former liberal rule in the canton of Zurich identified two fundamental elements of "the heart of the democratic movement." First: "In our view, [the heart of the movement] consists of the people's being able by constitutional means to win respect for their own faculty of judgment, which the elected representatives have arrogantly and bluntly denied them on all too many occasions" (*Der Landbote*, 3/1/1868, p. 279). Second: "We protest against the debasement and belittlement of the people of Zurich, which consists in their being declared incompetent to recognize true progress and to make the necessary sacrifices [to achieve it]. We see in this false evaluation of the people the main seeds of the present movement" (*Der Landbote*, 12/8/1868, p. 279).

What is expressed here as expectations and hopes, along with the demand for direct democracy, can be translated into modern political language as the demand for more public thoughtfulness, more debate, more public meetings, more shared reflection, more opportunities for the public to work on issues, more political accommodation and balance, more power for all and less power for a select few, a better balance and finer distribution of power; in short, more public debate and more deliberation, less high-handedness, and greater legitimacy through the effort to persuade rather than dictate and through respect for people's ability to discern and to reach considered judgments.

When John S. Dryzek wrote that "around 1990" there had been a "deliberative turn" in democratic theory, one might be forgiven for concluding—in view of the debates on direct democracy in Switzerland and the pioneering direct-democratic states of the USA over a hundred years ago—that Dryzek was a whole century off in his reckoning. (Dryzek, 2000).[4]

III. The Qualities and Achievements of Direct Democracy

Against the background of the motives, critique, and aims of the movement which can be considered the pioneer of direct democracy in Switzerland and of the experiences with direct democracy in Switzerland since then, the following characteristics can be distinguished as the products of a well-designed direct democracy:

- Direct democracy makes politics more communicative. The legitimacy of political power has to be created, confirmed or challenged by communication.
- Direct democracy forces the public discussion of points of view and differences of opinion which otherwise tend to be ignored or suppressed.
- Direct democracy gives minorities which have inadequate or no representation in parliament the right to be heard in public in a legitimate way.
- Direct democracy enables a wider distribution of political power and allows no one the privilege of possessing so much power that they are not required to modify their views from time to time.

---

4. 24 All original quotes from the "Landbote" of 1/18/1868, p. 273.

If we distinguish the individual, the societal, and the institutional levels from each other, then in a well-organized direct democracy we can assign the following performance expectations or qualities to each level:[5]

Table 1: The performance expectations of Direct Democracy at the individual, societal and institutional levels.

Individual	Societal	Structural, institutional
Stronger political motivation	More public political debate	(Thematically) more open and accessible politics
Better politically informed	More social learning	Higher legitimacy of decisions
More political communication	More efforts to reach agreement	Smaller divide between citizen and politician
More politically qualified	More community interactions	More transparency of motives for making decisions
More opportunities for participation	Better division of powers	More open politics and more accessible media
Greater political orientation	More social integration	Removal of political monopoly

IV. The Most Important Elements of an Optimal Design of Direct Democracy

In considering the design of direct democracy, the shaping of its procedures, and their integration into the parliamentary decision-making process, we have to take care that in each of the ten stages[6] which can be distinguished, the procedures are arranged to produce the best possible result. For each of these ten stages, we can distinguish *crucial*, *highly important*, *sensible* and *helpful* procedural elements aimed at optimizing the quality of direct democracy. This gives us numerous procedural elements, whose design and individual formulation will enable us to make an overall assessment of the quality of direct democracy and its performance and which can also be used to judge sub-optimal direct-democratic designs.

a. The Crucial or Decisive Elements of Direct Democracy

The five most important procedural elements of direct democracy are:
1. List of exclusions on issues: How many political issues are excluded from the direct-democratic decision-making process?
2. Entry hurdles: How many signatures of electors do I have to collect in order to force a referendum?
3. Time limits: How much time do I have to collect these signatures?
4. Majority requirements/quorums: What special requirements exist for the deciding majority of the voters in referendums (participation quorum, majority approval requirement, qualified majority etc.)?
5. Consistency of the direct-democratic elements: The various direct-democratic elements at the constitutional and legislative levels must have an inner consistency, in order to prevent direct-democratic decisions from being thwarted by the authorities or governments.

b. The *Highly Important* Elements of Direct Democracy

The *highly important* elements of a well-designed direct democracy are:
1. The way signatures are collected: How can I collect the signatures? Is there a free collection of signatures with subsequent official verification, or do citizens have to sign in local authority offices and/or under legal supervision?
2. Reception by Parliament and the right of parliament to make a counterproposal: The direct and indirect forms of democracy need to be connected. For example, parliament should have to debate all popular initiatives, and there should be the right for a majority in parliament—or even for a minority—to present a counterproposal to the popular initiative, so that voters can choose between at least three options.
3. Informing the electorate: A great deal of effort should be made to ensure that voters are properly informed on the issues and that the issues can be adequately debated. As an absolute minimum, a voter pamphlet should be provided; modern electronic means of communication permit additional means of providing information.

---

5. This originates in an earlier and subsequently expanded presentation, the first version of which—under the title: "Die Verfahren schaffen die Qualität der Direkten Demokratie"—was given by Andreas Gross at a conference on direct democracy in Marburg in June 2001.
6. Recently published and very good as an introduction: Neidhart (2000), More on direct democracy in Switzerland: Hangartner & Kley (2000); Tschannen (1995).

c. The Useful and Sensible Elements of Direct Democracy

The following can be seen as *useful and sensible* procedural elements of an optimally designed direct democracy:

1. When a popular initiative has been launched, the government and the administration must have time to listen to all the interested groups and organizations and to arrive at a considered opinion on the initiative—a minimum of six months.

2. Parliament must also have enough time to hold hearings and to discuss the initiative and any possible counterproposal. (In a unicameral parliament there should be at least two readings, for which they should have six months.)

3. There must be enough time between parliament's adoption of a position on the initiative and the date of the referendum (another six months, especially if major holiday periods are included).

4. The process by which public opinion is formed and positions adopted must be fair (equal resources for all sides), transparent (sources of funding, etc., should be disclosed), and correct.

5. Voting must be free and secret: People should vote by casting a ballot at a designated polling station, by mail, or perhaps in the future by e-voting.

6. More differentiated instruments of direct democracy should be used, such as the constructive referendum, the right of petition to parliament, and both facultative and obligatory forms of both.

7. Those who organize popular initiatives and referendums should receive a portion of their campaign costs after the signatures have been handed in and the date set for the referendum.

d. The *Helpful* Procedural Elements

The following procedural elements improve the quality of direct democracy and are therefore *helpful*:

1. The administration should support the work of the initiative group.

2. The community should have a democratic and openly communicative infrastructure (free, central places of assembly; a political infrastructure open to all; free advertising space in newspapers, on radio and television, and in public spaces).

3. Political parties, as the essential vehicles of democracy, should be funded by the state.

V. Preliminary Results of a Comparison of Direct-Democratic Procedures

It is possible to identify the specific qualities of one option only by comparing it with others. Since Switzerland is, at least for the moment, the only country in which there is direct democracy throughout the country,[7] we will compare the use of the five most important procedural elements in Switzerland with their use in those American states which have elements of direct democracy[8] and with the federal states of Germany;[9] to simplify matters, we have amalgamated each of the latter two and abstracted an average qualitative trend. This results in the following picture:

Table 2: Qualitative comparison of the five most important direct democratic procedural elements in Switzerland, the U.S. states and the federal states of Germany (Länder)

	US States	Switzerland	German Länder
Signatures needed to launch initiative	Medium (about 5%)	Low (1%–2%)	High (up to 20%)
Time to collect signatures	Short	Long	Very short
Mode of collecting signatures	Free	Free	Restricted, official scrutiny
Turnout and approval quorums	None	None	High and in part double quorums
Restrictions on issues	None	Few	Extensive

---

7. On direct democracy in the USA see especially: Cronin (1989); Bowler, Donovan & Tolbert (1998); Zimmermann (2001); Sabato, Ernst & Larson (2001), Ellis (2002).

8. On direct democracy in the German Länder see: Klages & Paulus (1995); Weixner (2002) (see also Rehmet's paper in this volume); for a comparison of Germany and the USA see Heussner (1994).

9. See: Jung (1999e) and (2001g). Also see (moderately useful): Abromeit (2002). There have been many similar negative experiences of quorums in Italy: see Capretti (1999 and 2001). In Spring of 2000, the then future head of government Berlusconi "won" a referendum which had been approved by the socialist government by telling his supporters to "stay at home" in order to make the government "go home."

The table shows that the arrangement of the procedures in Switzerland makes it much easier to attain the benefits of direct democracy than in Germany, and somewhat easier than in the USA. This assessment becomes even more plausible if one takes into account the background conditions for direct democracy in the three countries.

Because the purpose of direct democracy is to make politics more communicative and to achieve greater legitimacy both for what exists and for what is new or changed—and to do so through fair, extensive, in-depth and serious debate and discussion—the most important background condition is the quality of a society's public structures. We must remember that the structure of public society is influenced by direct democracy, so that it cannot be seen as entirely independent of it.

Table 3: Comparison of the most important background conditions of direct democracy in Switzerland, the U.S. states and the federal states of Germany, in particular with regard to public politics and integration into the parliamentary decision-making processes.

	US States	Switzerland	German Länder
Structure of TV operation	Private ownership dominates	Publicly owned TV; a few private channels	Both private and public
Media in general	Dominated by privately-owned TV stations and major print media	Extremely varied and important print media	A variety of print and TV media
Tradition of public meetings	Marginal	Intact	Decaying
Political culture	Republican political tradition; direct democracy marginal	Direct democracy a central element of political culture	Historic fear of the people; dominated by elite representative system
Culture of democracy	Disintegrative relationship between direct and indirect democracy	Integration of direct and indirect democracy	Domination of indirect democracy
Constitutional jurisdiction	Very highly regarded	Jurisdiction only at cantonal level	Very highly regarded
Importance and nature of political parties	Parties weak (more like voter lobby groups); powerful interest groups	Weak parties, stronger unions	Politics almost completely dominated by parties, strong unions

VI. Evaluation of the Consequences of the Design of Direct Democracy in the Various Regions

The existing procedures for direct democracy in the three countries, along with their respective political/cultural parameters and institutional forms, create different direct-democratic cultures, which are presented in condensed form in the following table.

Table 4: Comparison of direct democratic cultures in Switzerland, the U.S. states and the federal states of Germany

	US States	Switzerland	German Länder
Social	Disintegrative	Integrative	Not sufficient to comment
Relationship to parliament	Antagonistic	Cooperative	Not enough to comment
Character of direct democracy	Confrontational	Interactive	Marginal
Cost of direct democracy	Very expensive	Relatively modest	Expensive but affordable
Direct democratic culture	Colonial, neo-oligarchic	Relatively accessible; oligarchic tendencies	Authoritarian

VII. Proposals for Reform for the Purpose of Optimizing the Design of Direct Democracy in the Various Regions

The analysis suggests potential avenues for the reform of direct democratic procedures, which would allow the various cultures to improve and optimize the quality of their direct democracy. We recommend the following reforms in the three states:

Table 5: The need for reform of direct democracy in Switzerland, the U.S. states and the federal states of Germany

US States	Switzerland	German Länder
Much more time allowed for each phase	Democratization of collective opinion forming	Lowering of entry thresholds
More opportunities for institutions to interact (right of parliamentary counter-proposal)	Greater fairness through reducing imbalances in resources	Massive lowering of participation quorums; abolition of approval quorums
Fairer allocation of resources	Greater transparency in regard to campaign expenses	Longer periods for collecting signatures and considering the issues; more time for all the phases
Issues divided among more referendum dates	State funding of parties and of proponents of initiatives and referendums	Reduction in number of excluded issues

In conclusion, we would like to look more closely at some of these proposals for reform aimed at raising the quality of direct democracy. We earlier identified communication and open debate as the "souls" of direct democracy. This means that direct-democratic procedures should be arranged to encourage communication at all levels and among the widest possible cross-section of citizens.

Participation and approval quorums encourage those who wish to preserve the status quo to refuse to communicate, because it is often easier to prevent those in favor of reform from reaching a quorum by withholding debate and participation then to defeat them in a referendum.[10]

Reflection, discussion, meetings, and interactions take time, as do attempts to reach common ground between the representatives of different interest groups and organizations. If insufficient time is allowed, the procedures favor vested interests, the interests with the greatest resources, and those who simply wish to avoid debate. This is in addition to the fact that without procedures that allow sufficient time, it becomes practically impossible to achieve greater integration. The time allowed for the various parts of the process should be commensurate with the requirements of each part: for example, if only two weeks are allowed for the collection of what are often too many signatures, organizations which are not already established and well organized cannot make successful use of the direct-democratic instrument meant to serve them.

It would be much better if a period of six months to one year were allowed for the collection of signatures. In the report ("Democracy by Initiative") of the official committee to investigate possible reforms of direct democracy in California, a specific recommendation was made that the period of time for collecting signatures be extended (from 150 to 180 days) in order to allow for more public debate, to reduce dependence on funds and paid signature collectors, and to improve the quality of the public debate (California Commission on Campaign Financing: p. 162 ff).

This is also true of the time periods and procedures available to the administration, organized interest groups, political parties, and parliament. In California, every popular initiative bypasses Parliament completely; in Switzerland, once the signatures have been handed in, a very diverse and extensive process of discussion and, in certain circumstances, negotiation begins.[11] If California is to realize the potential for discussing, reaching an understanding, reconciling differing interests, and possibly even finding compromise solutions, it must allow much more time between the submission of signatures and the referendum: six months is not enough.

The institutions themselves need at least a year, if not 18 months. This has nothing to do with stalling or wasting time, but with the attempt to do justice to those who launch initiatives, to take them seriously, and to make the system and the

---

10. In this connection, the Californian Commission has made proposals for reform which would bring parliament back into the initiative process; this would increase their incentive to find a compromise solution and would generate additional public discussion of the initiative, as well as encouraging parliamentarians to act instead of passing the responsibility to the electorate (California Commission on Campaign Financing: p. 330 f).

11. Elisabeth Gerber (1999; p. 145) expressly states that in her view the laws enacted as a result of initiatives have produced more unintended (negative) consequences because the initiative process avoids many of the normal parliamentary negotiating procedures.

procedures more effective and increase the chances of reaching a compromise.[12] Direct democracy is much more than a "public-opinion poll" or "fast food" democracy governed by knee-jerk emotional responses, and it is certainly no "Instant Democracy."[13]

In one respect, Switzerland has something to learn from direct-democratic arrangements in some of the German Länder and from what some people are trying to achieve in California. The German tradition of refunding campaign expenses means that in five of the Länder the initiators of popular demands have received a reasonable contribution to the costs of the referendum campaign and an amount for each signature collected (payable either after the signatures have been handed in or after the referendum—regardless of the result, of course). (See Jung 2000b, p. 83.) Attempts to secure the same provisions failed during the debate on civil rights reform at the national level in Germany and during the current revision of the constitution of Zurich.

In Switzerland, there is still too little awareness of the fact that the quality of the result depends on the quality of the decision-making process: its fairness, transparency and correctness. Transparency of the financial inputs of those involved—the source and the extent of funding—is necessary to appreciate the fact that the public might want a much better balance of financial resources between the "pro" and "con" sides of a reform issue.

There is a chance that some preliminary attempts at reform in Switzerland may succeed in 2004/2005, but the fate of the reforms is still uncertain. In California, for a while, TV companies voluntarily agreed to give the opponents of a campaign 1/10 as much free air time as was paid for by the proponents. There are currently some moves in this direction in Switzerland too, though they have more to so with advertising in daily newspapers and on billboards.

Finally, there is also a need to make sure there is enough time for public debate before a referendum, as well as to ensure that the direct-democratic procedures are consistent. The worst example of the former occurred in Portugal, whose president allowed only three weeks in 1998 for the referendum campaign on the plebiscite for the liberalization of abortion. What took 20 years and numerous popular initiatives and referendums to achieve in the scarcely less Catholic Switzerland, the Portuguese elite wanted to have debated and decided in just a few weeks.

This experience inflicted lasting damage on the credibility of direct democracy in Portugal. More recently, conservative forces in the country have used the experience to frustrate recent attempts at liberalization by suggesting the use of the popular vote, whose legitimacy has been thrown into question.

Lessons may be learned about the consistency of direct-democratic procedures from another negative example, this one in Slovenia. Citizens, as well as a minority in parliament, enjoy the right of legislative referendum but not that of obligatory constitutional referendum. This means that unwelcome referendum decisions on legislation, even though binding, can be overturned by parliament's changing the constitution, which would not only undermine their legitimacy but damage the public's solidarity, motivation and faith in the political process. (xvii)

Improving the performance and optimizing the quality of direct democracy is not an end in itself. Its significance extends far beyond the democratization of local, regional and national democracy, for only highly-motivated and self-assured citizens who have a positive experience of politics in the local, regional and national contexts will have the courage and the self-confidence to demand the introduction of direct-democratic elements where they are most needed: in the European Constitution.

It is not just that Europe needs more democracy; democracy needs to be rooted at the European—transnational—level if its substance is not be eroded to the same extent as the autonomy of the nation state (see Erne, Gross, Kaufmann & Kleger 1995). To prevent such an erosion, a qualitatively optimally designed direct democracy is doubly necessary: both to create the necessary conditions for a European democracy movement to flourish, and to shape the future of a European democracy which realizes that its ultimate expression is not in mere representation and allows itself to be complemented by the most important direct-democratic elements at the transnational level.

---

12. More on this in Gross (1999; p. 97 f); on the consequences of ignoring such considerations: Schrag (1998; p. 188) and Broder (2000).

13. Up-to-date news on this is available on the homepage of the Zurich constitutional council: http://www.verfassungsrat.zh.ch and of the Swiss National Assembly: http://www.parlament.ch.

Chapter Five

Polling

I. Polls among the Population

Germany: 75% in favor. According to a Forsa-poll of September 2000, 75% of all Germans said "yes" to the question: "Are you in favor of decisions directly made by the people [Volksentscheide]?" Moreover, a majority of the voters of all five political parties in parliament are in favor of citizen lawmaking: the SPD voters with 77%, CDU 68%, Greens 69%, FDP 75%, PDS 75%. (*Zeitschrift für Direkte Demokratie* 51 (2001), p. 7.)

An Emnid poll of April 2001 shows that 79% of Germans would like to vote often on laws. Only 19% would prefer to seldom use I&R instruments. 69% think I&R is a good method to restore the trust of voters in their government. 75% think that decisions made by the people through I&R are more democratic than the decisions of elected parliaments. (*Thüringische Landeszeitung*, April 27, 2001)

United Kingdom: 77% in favor. In the 1995 "State of the Nation" poll, 77% of the British said that Britain should adopt a referendum system "whereby certain decisions are put to the people to decide by popular vote" (*Prospect Magazine*, October 1998).

Netherlands: 80% in favor. In a 1998 poll of the Social and Cultural Planning Agency (SCP), 80% of the Dutch said "yes" to the question: "Should the people be able to decide directly on important issues — the so-called referendum?" A majority of the voters of all four large parties are in favor: CDA 70%, PvdA 81%, VVD 83%, D66 86%. Of all the Dutch, only 15% are against the referendum, and 5% are undecided (SCP, *Sociaal Culturele Verkenningen*, Den Haag 1999, p. 37).

An October 1995 NIPO poll, however, showed only 49% of the Dutch in favor of the very restricted government proposal for a rejective referendum with high quorums (which became law on January 1, 2001). When asked whether they would prefer the rejective referendum or the popular initiative, 60% preferred the initiative, 20% preferred the rejective referendum, and 20% were unsure (Bureau O+S, 1992).

Switzerland: 75% in favor. Polls show that three quarters of the Swiss positively appreciate direct democracy. They appreciate direct democracy more than they appreciate other institutions, such as the constitution, the federalist system or the debate between the social partners (J. Verhulst, *Het verdiepen van de democratie*, Brussels 1998, p. 6).

Belgium: 51% in favor. An older poll in Belgium showed 51% of Belgians in favor of I&R (*La Libre Belgique*, April 29, 1992). A poll taken in 1996 showed that 67% of Belgians were in favor of a referendum on the Treaty of Maastricht, which established the European Union (*Le Soir*, March 30, 1996). A 1998 poll showed 58% in favor of a referendum on the introduction of the Euro, 18% against, and 24% unsure (*Het Nieuwsblad*, April 27, 1998).

Denmark: large minority in favor. A GFK poll of May 3, 1992 asked: "In some countries, like Switzerland, Italy and several US states, a proposition is put to the people if a specified number of people have given the required signatures. Do you favor the introduction of such a device in Denmark?" 47% said yes, 36% said no, and 17% were unsure.

In the same poll, the following theses were also put forward. 66% agreed with the thesis: "Representative parliament does not work properly when parliament can pass a law that is approved by only 20% of the electorate," 19% disagreed, and 15% were unsure. 70% agreed with the thesis: "Decisions by parliament on specific issues ought to be in accordance with the views of the electorate — unless superior considerations make it impossible," 15% disagreed, and 15% were unsure. Furthermore, 64% agreed with the thesis: "The citizens of Europe have no say on the important decisions made by the EU," 15% disagreed, and 21% were unsure. (Society for Direct Democracy, Denmark)

II. Polls among Politicians

Belgium: majority against. In 1998 the Institute of Local Socialist Action held a poll among local politicians of the Socialist Party, a major mainstream party in Belgium. Only 16.7% were in favor of the binding referendum. Of the executive politicians (mayors and aldermen), a smaller percentage is in favor than of the legislative politicians (members of the municipal council), whether the latter are in the coalition or in the opposition. (*De Morgen*, January 31, 1998)

Netherlands: majority against. In 1993, political scientist Pieter Tops of the Catholic University of Brabant conducted a poll among members of municipal councils in The Netherlands. Less than a quarter are in favor of introducing the binding referendum. (*NG Magazine*, December 31, 1993)

In a poll by the University of Leiden, it was found that 36% of the members of municipal councils were in favor or the rejective referendum, and 52% opposed it. Of the VVD and CDA members, 70% were against. Of the PvdA, there were around 40% both for and against. Only among members of GroenLinks and D66 were a majority of municipal council members in favor. (*Binnenlands Bestuur*, February 18, 1994)

Denmark: majority against. In a 1998 survey, members of the national Parliament were asked their opinion on the thesis "There ought to be more referendums in Denmark." The overwhelming response was negative: Social Democrats 100% "no"; Left Liberals 100% "no"; Center Democrats 100% "no"; Right Liberals 96% "no"; Conservatives 58% "no"; Socialists 11% "no"; People's Party 0% "no." (*Jyllands Posten*, December 30, 1998)

III. Europeans Want Referendum on Future Constitution

Europeans want a referendum before adopting a new European Union constitution: over 80% of citizens across the 25 European countries support the idea of a referendum on the draft Constitution. However, this opinion is divided into those who believe it is essential and those who believe it is useful but not essential.

In the current EU member states, 41% of citizens think that it is essential that all citizens of the EU give their opinion, by referendum, on the draft Constitution, while 45% believe it is useful but not essential. In the adherent countries, those who believe a referendum is essential represent 40% of the population, compared to 33% who think it is useful but not essential.

In both country groups, very few respondents believe a referendum on this issue is useless: 11% in the EU member states and 15% in the adherent countries. Finally, although the rate of non-responses is low, it is three times as high in the adherent countries (12%) as in the EU member states (4%).

Results by country show that Greece has the highest percentage rate of respondents who believe a referendum is essential (72%): 31 percentage points above the EU average. Cyprus and Sweden follow, with 65% and 62% respectively. Countries in which a majority of respondents believe the referendum is useful but not essential are Portugal (54%), Germany (50%) and Spain (50%).

Slovakia, with 32%, is the country with by far the highest rate of respondents who believe a referendum is useless. This rate is 17 percentage points above the average in the adherent countries. In the current European Union, Finland and Austria have the highest proportion of respondents who hold this opinion (both 23%). The only country in which a considerable number of respondents do not know is Lithuania, with 21% of its population.

Chapter Six

The Future of the European Citizen Initiative

by Victor Cuesta

Introduction

The historical ineffectiveness of the indirect citizen initiative must not prevent us from establishing a regulation in the EU that is friendly to it. The European Convention, attempting to reduce the European Union's deficiency in democracy, has included Article I-46.4 in the draft constitution, which establishes the "citizen initiative," an institutional device of participatory democracy in the future European law-making process. This paper presents some basic deductions from the current and provisional redaction of Article I-46.4, comparing its provisions with several existing national citizens' initiatives. Like the Austrian, Hungarian, Italian, Latvian, Lithuanian, Polish, Portuguese, Slovenian and Spanish popular initiatives, the Europe-wide citizens' initiative will be an indirect institution. However, some recommendations drawn from national experiences could help to design a relatively functional participatory device.

It is a well-known fact that the lack of democratic legitimacy is a substantial problem for the European Union. The democratic deficit has been formally recognized by the Nice Declaration on the Future of the Union, which speaks of "the need to improve and to monitor the democratic legitimacy and transparency of the Union and its institutions, in order to bring them closer to the citizens of the member states." Likewise, the Laeken Declaration on the Future of the European Union declares that one of the necessary challenges in a renewed Union is "to bring citizens, and primarily the young, closer to the European design and the European institutions".

The European Convention, conscious of this democratic gap, has included the principle of participatory democracy in the recently approved draft constitution.[1] Its purpose is to reduce the democratic deficit by acknowledging the citizens' right to express their own views about European matters and by recognizing the voice of representative associations of civil society[2] in the European public debate.

This is excellent news for all of us who support the implementation of participatory democracy. However, the idea of participation needs to be translated into real institutions and to have the appropriate resources if it is to be more than an intangible principle, so the addition of the Europe-wide citizens' initiative (ECI) to Article 46 during the last session of the Convention was even better news. This citizens' initiative is an institutional expression of direct democratic participation in the law-making process of the European Union.

As far as I know, this device will be the very first juridical expression of transnational participatory democracy. The Europe-wide citizens' initiative can be also regarded as a success by those democratic theorists[3] who espouse the ideals of democracy and transnational democratic participation.

---

1. According to De Schutter, participatory democracy is based "on the action of interest groups and citizens' initiatives: people belong to groups that build up expert and grassroots knowledge of the social issues in question. These bodies also participate in public information and communication processes, so helping to create a general perception of the common good." De Schutter, O., "Europe in Search of its Civil Society," *European Law Journal*, 2002, 8, 2, p. 202.

2. Civil Society is defined by the working group "Consultation and Participation of Civil Society" in the White Paper on European Governance, borrowing the definition given by the Economic and Social Committee in its Opinion of 22 September 1999: "Civil society organizations include: the so-called market players; organizations representing social and economic players, which are not social partners in the strict sense of the term; NGOs which bring people together in a common cause, such as environmental organizations, human rights organizations, consumer associations, charitable organizations, educational and training organizations, etc.; CBOs (community-based organizations), e.g. youth organizations, family associations and all organizations through which citizens participate in local and municipal life; religious communities."

3. The introduction of participatory devices at a transnational level is mainly supported by the cosmopolitan theory of democracy that is represented by Held and Archibugi: "What is needed now is the participation of new political subjects. According to the cosmopolitan project, they should be world citizens, provided with the institutional channels to take part and assume duties *vis-à-vis* the global destiny." ARCHIBUGI, D., "Principles of Cosmopolitan Democracy", in Archibugi, Held, Kohler (ed.), *Re-imagining Political Community*, London: Polity Press, 1998, pp. 223–224.

Comparative Law Interpretation

The definitive version of the Constitution still awaits ratification by all the member states; in addition, the participatory device will need legislative development before it can come into force. But despite the interim character of Article 46.4, this is a good time to take a first look at the future institution. In this chapter I will make a few basic deductions from the current version of the article:

> "A significant number of citizens, no less than one million, coming from a significant number of Member States, may invite the Commission to submit any appropriate proposal on matters where citizens consider that a legal act of the Union is required for the purpose of implementing this Constitution. A European law shall determine the provisions for the specific procedures and conditions required for such a citizen' request."

In this chapter I intend to establish a comparison with several existing national citizens' initiatives, better known as popular initiatives,[4] as regulated by the constitutions and the statutes of some European countries. A comparative law interpretation may be useful in imagining the ways in which the Europe-wide citizens' initiative could be legally elaborated. As we know, comparative law is a basic tool used to inform the law-making processes and, as Zweigert and Kötz argue, "legislators all over the world have found that on many matters good laws cannot be produced without the assistance of comparative law."[5]

In comparative constitutional law, a popular initiative can be sent either (1) to a referendum ballot or (2) to the legislature. The former is the direct popular initiative, a classic device of direct democracy that is traditionally represented in Europe by the Swiss *initiative populaire*. Swiss citizens have a strong right of initiative at the cantonal level to submit legislative drafts to popular approval and another at the national/federal level to introduce constitutional amendments subject to the Swiss people's consent. The latter is the indirect popular initiative that goes to Parliament, which may approve, modify or reject the measure. Some indirect initiatives, mainly used in the United States,[6] can be later put to the ballot if Parliament modifies or refuses the popular request.

There is a more geographically extensive kind of indirect initiative in Europe, which is fully subordinated to the representative principle of democracy and in which a legislative rejection will never imply a final popular vote. This very "soft" version of the initiative is recognized in the Austrian, Hungarian, Italian, Latvian, Lithuanian, Polish, Portuguese, Slovenian and Spanish constitutions.[7] This kind of initiative is not well known in political theory and is normally dismissed by the supporters of direct democracy, who do not include the institution in the category of direct democracy and consider it a simple collective petition right.

The Problem with the Commission's Control of the Initiative

Since Article 46.4 of the European Constitutional draft states that European citizens will invite the Commission, it seems safe to assume that the ECI will be an indirect device. In other words, the European participatory device will be

---

4. Many kinds of popular initiatives in force in Europe could be included in this definition: the popular initiative is a device of direct democratic participation which allows a certain number of citizens to propose, either to legislature or to people entitled to vote through referendum, the adoption, approval, reform or abrogation of a legislative or constitutional rule by bearing a petition with a required number of valid signatures. Cuesta, V., *La iniciativa popular en el derecho constitucional europeo comparado;* LLM theses, Florence: European University Institute, 2002.

5. Zweigert and Kötz, *Introduction to comparative law*, Oxford: Clarendon, 1987, p. 15.

6. The indirect initiative is used to submit legislative measures in Alaska, Maine, Massachusetts, Michigan, Nevada, Ohio, Utah, Washington, and Wyoming. The indirect initiative can be used to promote constitutional amendments in Massachusetts and Mississippi.

7. **Austria** (Article 41.2): "Every motion proposed by 100,000 voters or by one-sixth each of the voters in three States shall be submitted by the main electoral board to the House of Representatives for action. The initiative must be put forward in the form of a draft law." **Hungary:** (Article 28-D): "At least 50,000 voting citizens are required for a national popular initiative. A national popular initiative may be for the purpose of forcing the Parliament to place a subject under its jurisdiction on the agenda. The Parliament shall debate the subject defined by the national popular initiative." **Italy** (Article 71): "The people may introduce public initiatives consisting of a bill drafted in articles and supported by at least 50,000 voters." **Latvia** (Article 65): "Draft laws may be submitted to the Parliament by the President, the Government or committees of the Parliament, by not less than five members of the Parliament, or, in accordance with the procedures and in the cases provided for in this Constitution, by one-tenth of the electorate." **Lithuania** (Article 68): "The right of legislative initiative in the Seimas shall belong to the members of the Seimas, the President of the Republic, and the Government. Citizens of the Republic of Lithuania shall also have the right of legislative initiative. A draft law may be presented to the Seimas by 50,000 citizens of the Republic of Lithuania who have the electoral right, and the Seimas must consider such a law." **Poland** (Article 118): "The right to introduce legislation shall also belong to a group of at least 100,000 citizens having the right to vote in elections to the House of Representatives (*Sejm*). The procedure in such matters shall be specified by statute." **Portugal** (Article 167): "The power to initiate laws and to propose referenda lies with Deputies, parliamentary groups and the Government, and further, in accordance with the terms and conditions established by law, with groups of electing citizens; the power to initiate laws with respect to the autonomous regions lies with the appropriate regional legislative assembly." **Slovenia** (Article 88): "Laws may be proposed by the Government or by any deputy. Laws may also be proposed by at least five thousand voters." **Spain** (Article 87.3): "An organic law shall regulate the forms and requirements for the exercise of the popular initiative for the presentation of proposals of law. In any case no fewer than 500,000 valid signatures will be required. This initiative is not applicable to organic laws, taxation, or international affairs, nor to the prerogative of pardon."

an initiative for an initiative. The Europe-wide citizens' initiative will be only a first step in the law-making process which is always launched by the Commission.

Here we have a specific discrepancy between the future European initiative and the national indirect initiatives, which are always sent to the legislature. This discrepancy is a logical consequence of the particular structure of the Union and its institutional balance, which assigns legislative initiative exclusively to the Commission (Article I-25.2: "Union legislative acts can be adopted only on the basis of a Commission proposal"). We should pay special attention to this difference, because in countries such as Spain or Italy the correct submission of the initiative to Parliament automatically initiates the law-making process, and consequently, only the representatives are authorized to decide whether the initiative is or is not politically opportune.

This automatic initiation of the legislative process is the main difference between the indirect popular initiative and the right of petition. However, the ECI will be examined by the Commission before it is submitted to the legislative process. I hope that this preliminary control measure by the Commission will be used only to make sure that the initiative is constitutional and that it satisfies the formal conditions. In my opinion, once the initiative has satisfied these requirements, the Commission should automatically submit the popular request to the lawmaking process. The initiative does not need a prior political judgment from the Commission because that judgment will be made later by the European Council and the European Parliament.

Not for Constitutional Amendments

Another conclusion to be drawn from Article 46.4 is that the Europe-wide citizens' initiative will operate only as a statutory initiative. The popular proposals sent to the Commission must request the adoption of some European legal act. We must suppose, according to Article I-32, that the European citizenry will be able to design both kinds of legal acts: legislative acts (European laws; European framework laws) and non-legislative acts (European regulations; European decisions, recommendations and opinions).

It is obvious from the wording of the article that the ECI will serve to develop the constitutional charter through new statutes, but it also seems clear that the initiative will not be able to promote constitutional amendments (like the Swiss *initiative populaire constitutionelle*), review laws in force (like the Italian *referendum abrogativo*), or demand the popular approval of enacted laws (like the Swiss *referendum facultatif*). In comparative law, institutions like these are always oriented to popular consultation, and, as we have seen above, the ECI does not include referendum initiatives. It must be said, however, that the rejection of a new European legal act proposed by a hypothetical ECI could implicitly weaken a European law already in force.

Another important point to note is that Article I-46.4 does not present a list of issues excluded from the popular request. This is also the situation with the Italian indirect initiative that was not restricted in its fundamental charter; this precedent is particularly important because the initiative was not limited later by its statutory development. On the other hand, we have the Spanish indirect statutory initiative which was substantially limited by the Spanish Constitution and later by legislation; as a consequence, this initiative cannot be used today to promote the adoption of fundamental laws, taxation, or international affairs, nor to the prerogative of pardon.

Fortunately, the European Convention has not followed the restrictive Spanish option. Nevertheless, it seems obvious that our ECI will be automatically dismissed if it conflicts with any constitutional provision and especially if the ECI promotes policies outside the competence of the EU or does not rigorously respect the charter of fundamental rights.

In addition, it must be said that all national indirect initiatives are in one way or another excluded from some legislative procedures which may be proposed only by representatives, such as laws on the national budget. In fact, a second reading of the European constitutional draft shows the difficulties that a popular initiative will have in promoting initiatives that deal with such specific matters as common foreign and security policy, which are excluded from the ordinary legislative process and absolutely dominated by the European Council.

Which Formal Requirements?

It is also significant that the article does not establish any formal requirements regarding the citizen's request. We know that the ECI must be submitted as an appropriate proposal, but there is no further detail. In comparative law, national indirect statutory initiatives must normally satisfy formal requirements on the composition of the legislative draft. Usually, initiatives must consist "of a bill drafted in articles" (Italian initiative) or "must be put forward in the form of a draft law" (Austrian initiative). In contrast, the Hungarian indirect initiative does not need any formal bill from the petitioners, and the Swiss direct constitutional initiative can also be formulated in general terms.

It is relatively easy to draft a general initiative, but it should not be forgotten that such a general proposal would require further intervention by representatives who would draft the final version. Despite the possible difficulties in the design of a legal draft, I venture to suggest that a bill drafted in formal articles would be a more accurate and definitive statement of the citizen's demands.

We should compare the "no less than one million" signatures required for the achievement of ECI with the number of signatures needed to submit the other national indirect statutory initiatives in Europe. In comparative law, the number of required signatures is based either on an absolute number of national citizens or on a proportion of the voting population. The European Convention has chosen a fixed number of signatures: one million. In principle, the number could be increased by a future European law on ECI, but this possibility seems rather unlikely: if we analyze previous constitutional experience, once a constitution has established a minimum number of required signatures, legislative developments have never increased it.

In the table below, we can see how the European Convention has chosen a fairly low number of signatures which represent just 0.2% of the citizens of the future enlarged EU (25 members—around 480 million inhabitants). Only the number of signatures required in Italy represents a lower percentage than the European one.

Indirect statutory initiative from...	Population (millions)	Signatures required	Percentage (%)
Latvia	2.3	10% (230,000)	10
Lithuania	3.4	50,000	1.47
Spain	39.4	500,000	1.26
Austria	8.1	100,000	1.23
Portugal	10.8	75,000	0.69
Hungary	10.2	50,000	0.49
Poland	38.6	100,000	0.25
Slovenia	1.9	5,000	0.26
European Union	**480**	**1,000,000**	**0.20**
Italy	57.6	50,000	0.08

Let us now look at the geographic distribution of the signatures. The European Convention has specified that support for the ECI must come from several member states. The future territorial distribution could be established following the Massachusetts model, where no more than 25% of the signatures may come from any one county; in other words, the proportion of signatures coming from a member state could be limited (for example, if no more than 25% of one million signatures can come from one state, the ECI must be supported in at least five states). Another way to determine the territorial distribution is by an absolute minimum number of involved countries. If the ECI follows this option, an additional important point to be determined will be the number of signatures required in each country for it to be included in the list of the "significant number of Member States."

This territorial requirement could be perceived as a logical consequence of the transnational dimension of the EU. The territorial distribution will contribute to the creation of a Europe-wide democratic consciousness and will encourage the emerging European civil networks. However, this requirement could also be seen as a potential added obstacle to the success of the initiative; it will be very difficult for any initiative committee to organize the collection of signatures from several different and possibly widely separated member states.

Recommendations for the Design

As we have seen, the future European law on the citizen initiative must specify all the important details that will determine the functionality of our participatory device. The statute will be drafted by the Commission and will be adopted according to the normal legislative procedure (Article III-298 of the Constitution). We have reason to be especially concerned about this future law, because previous national experience has shown that the popular initiative has usually been restricted when the national legislature has come to determine its legal status. In the table below I summarize some basic points which should be taken into account:

Legal provisions regarding...	More functional ECI	Less functional ECI
Time period allowed for collection of signatures	Long period	Short period
Number of countries which must support the initiative	Low number	High number
Minimum number of signatures that must be collected in each country	No minimum	High minimum
Verification of signatures	Presumed valid — random sampling verification	Full certification
Formal requirements of the bill	Legislative draft	Drafted in general terms; single subject
Excluded issues?	No explicit restriction	List of issues explicitly excluded
Legal status of initiative committee	- Right to defend the request during the whole law-making process - Right to withdraw the initiative if essential changes are introduced by representatives - Right to be fully compensated for the costs incurred during the campaign	- No intervention granted - No access to ECI once it is submitted to Commission - No reimbursement or only partial reimbursement
Evaluation by the Commission	Technical evaluation	Political evaluation
Period of time for Commission to evaluate the ECI	Short period	Long period
Judicial review in case of the Commission's rejection	Fast judicial review	No judicial review
Period of time for legislature (Council/Parliament) to act on the ECI	Short period	Long period

Learning from the Lessons in Member States

It is undeniably true that national indirect initiatives have not been an effective way of translating citizens' requests into statutes. In Italy, of approximately 105 popular initiatives submitted to the legislature, only eight have been enacted. In Spain, the rate of success is especially low at the national level: of 32 initiatives, only five have passed all the obstacles and have been debated in the legislative plenary session, and the proposals have normally failed due to cumbersome legal requirements: only one of the five initiatives debated was ultimately adopted.[8]

This historical ineffectiveness must not prevent us from establishing a participation-friendly regulation. The practical influence of the ECI in European politics will depend a great deal on citizens' interest in European politics and the positive attitude of institutions towards their participation. Despite the subordinated nature of the ECI, it must be stressed that the exercise of European participatory devices could, at last, contribute to citizens' involvement in European affairs, thus increasing the level of legitimacy of European democracy.

---

8. The Spanish popular initiative enacted was related to the legal regulation of renting/housing costs. In Italy the popular proposals approved were associated with institutional reforms (parliamentary election system), public health (organs transplant), welfare (retirement funds), housing (renting system), education (general law on education system) and environmental protection (hunting).

Appendix

Section A: World Practice by Country 1970–2003

Rank	Country	Number of citizens' referendums				
		1971–80	1981–90	1991–00	2001–03	Total 1970–03
1	Switzerland	87	76	105	24	292
2	Italy	3	16	35	3	57
3	Liechtenstein	11	19	13	4	47
4	Ecuador	1	1	32	0	34
5	Mexico	0	0	23	0	23
6	Ireland	5	4	9	4	22
7	Lithuania	0	0	18	1	19
8	Australia	10	6	2	0	18
9	Egypt	10	2	0	0	12
10	The Philippines	7	5	0	0	12
11	Azerbaijan	0	0	4	8	12
12	Uruguay	3	2	6	0	11
13	Botswana	0	0	3	8	11
14	Micronesia	1	0	4	5	10
15	New Zealand	0	0	9	0	9
16	Poland	0	2	6	1	9
17	Denmark	3	1	4	0	8
18	Comoros	3	1	2	2	8
19	San Marino	0	1	6	0	7
20	Morocco	3	1	3	0	7
21	Hungary	0	5	1	1	7
22	Ukraine	0	0	6	0	6
23	Syria	3	1	2	0	6
24	Slovenia	0	1	0	5	6
25	Guatemala	0	0	5	0	5
26	Brazil	0	0	5	0	5
27	Russia	0	0	5	0	5
28	Belarus	0	0	5	0	5
29	Madagascar	2	0	3	0	5
30	Algeria	2	1	2	0	5
31	Sweden	0	3	1	1	5
32	Kirghistan	0	0	3	2	5
33	Bahamas	0	0	0	5	5
34	France	1	1	2	0	4
35	Venezuela	0	0	4	0	4
36	Slovakia	0	0	3	1	4
37	Central African Republic	0	2	1	0	3
38	Spain	2	1	0	0	3
39	Iran	2	1	0	0	3
40	Chile	2	1	0	0	3
41	Latvia	0	0	2	1	3
42	Romania	0	1	1	1	3
43	Austria	1	0	1	0	2
44	Andorra	0	1	1	0	2
45	Greece	2	0	0	0	2
46	Norway	1	0	1	0	2
47	Guinea	0	1	0	1	2

Section B: World Practice by Continent 1900–2000

Decade	Switzerland	Rest of Europe	Middle East	Asia	North and South America	Australia and Oceania	Africa	Total excl. Switzerland	Total incl. Switzerland
Before 1900	57	11	0	0	3	0	0	14	71
1901–1910	12	2	0	0	0	4	0	6	18
1911–1920	15	6	0	0	3	5	0	14	29
1921–1930	28	8	1	0	2	6	0	17	45
1931–1940	23	17	0	0	7	6	0	30	53
1941–1950	21	15	1	1	3	11	0	31	52
1951–1960	32	6	8	5	3	5	9	36	68
1961–1970	30	14	18	4	4	7	19	66	96
1971–1980	87	29	36	14	8	14	34	135	222
1981–1990	76	53	24	6	12	7	22	124	200
1991–2000	105	130	4	20	76	15	35	280	385
2001–2003	30	36	5	1	7	15	19	81	111
Total	516	327	97	51	128	95	138	831	1352

Section C: Initiatives & Referendums Around the World 1990–2000

A. The Americas

Country	1990	1991	1992	1993	1994	1995	1996	1997	1998	1999	2000	Subject of referendum by date
Bermuda						R 16.08.						Referendum on independence
Brazil				P 21.04. (2 Ref.)							P 07.09. (3 Pleb.)	• Form of statehood (1993); • Form of government (1993); • Continuance of cooperation with the IMF (2000); • Removal of external debt (2000); • Removal of internal debt (2000)
Canada			R 27.10.									Constitutional reform and conditions for secession
Columbia								R 26.10.				For peace, life and liberty
Costa Rica											K 12.03.	Allowing the President to be re-elected (consultative)
Curaçao				R 20.11.								Referendum on independence
Ecuador					R 28.08. (7 Ref.)	R 26.11. (11 Ref.)		P 25.05. (14 Ref.)				• National Assembly (1994); • General passive voting right (1994); • Parliamentary financial jurisdiction (1994); • Distribution of budget (1994); • Removal of restrictions on allowable term of office (1994); • Parliamentary election system (1994); • Recognition of dual citizenship (1994); • Decentralization of welfare system (1995); • Privatization of welfare provision (1995); • Equalization of finances (1995); • Ban on strikes (1995); • Presidential right to dissolve parliament (1995); • Term of office of local authorities (1995); • Term of office of parliamentary leadership (1995); • Transitional law on constitutional change (1995); • Legal protection for official (1995); • Constitutional court (1995); • Dismissal of the acting President (1997); • Appointment of transitional President (1997); • Appointment of a National Assembly (1997);

Country	1990	1991	1992	1993	1994	1995	1996	1997	1998	1999	2000	Subject of referendum by date
												• Method of electing the National assembly (1997); • Limits to electioneering (1997); • Right of voters to change voting lists (1997); • Procedure for electing the President (1997); • Revision of law on strikes (1997); • Reform of courts (1997); • Electing management of publicly owned companies (1997); • Reform of election to Supreme Court (1997); • Election of subordinate courts (1997); • Dismissal of officials who have broken the law (1997); • Transitional law for implementing reforms (1997)
Guatemala					R 30.01.					R 16.05. (4 Ref.)		• New constitution (1994); • Amendment to constitution (welfare rights) (1999); • Amendment to constitution (Legislative) (1999); • Amendment to constitution (Executive) (1999); • (Amendment to constitution (Judiciary) (1999)
Mexico						P 27.08. (22 Ref.)			P 30.08.			• Democratic national reform (16 proposals) (1995); • Foundation of a "broad front" to implement reform of the state (1995); • Reform of voting rights (1995); • Admission of parties (1995); • Admission of electoral alliances (1995); • Equal rights in public life (1995); • Use of government securities (1998)
Panama									R 30.08.			Amendments to constitution
Peru				P 31.10.								New constitution
Puerto Rico				R 14.11.					R 13.12.			Referendums on independence (1993 and 1998)
Quebec						R 30.10.						Referendum on independence
Saint Kitts and Nevis									R 10.08.			Referendum on independence for Nevis (required 2/3-majority narrowly missed)
Uruguay			R 13.12.		R 18.08. R 27.11.					R 31.10. (2 Ref.)		• Referendum on privatization (1992); • Constitutional amendments (8/18/1994);

Country	1990	1991	1992	1993	1994	1995	1996	1997	1998	1999	2000	Subject of referendum by date
Venezuela					(2 Ref.)					P 25.04. (2 Pleb.) R 15.12.	P 03.12.	• Referendum on education budget 11/21/1994 • Limits to pensions 11/27/1994 • Voting hurdles for parliament (1999); • Financial autonomy for the courts (1999) • Appointment of a National Assembly (4/25/1999); • Approval of presidential decrees on composition of the National Assembly (4/25/1999); • New constitution (12/15/1999); • Restricting the trade unions (2000)

B. Australia and Oceania

Country	1990	1991	1992	1993	1994	1995	1996	1997	1998	1999	2000	Subject of referendum by date
Australia										R 06.11. (2 Ref.)		• Republican form of government with own head of state (rejected) • Preamble to constitution
Faichuk											R 30.11.	Accession to Micronesia (accepted)
Indonesia										R 30.08.		"Local" East Timorese referendum
Virgin Islands				R 11.10.								Referendum on independence (rejected)
Micronesia										R 01.07. (4 Ref.)		• Regional sovereignty over natural resources; • Federal tax rate; • Distribution of commercial profits; • Appointment of a National Assembly
New Zealand	R 27.10.		R 19.09. (2 Ref.)	R 06.11. (2 Ref.)		R 02.12.		R 26.09.		R 27.11. (2 Ref.)		• Extension of term of office of legislature (1990); • Electoral system (1992); • Mixed member proportional representation (1992); • Mixed member proportional representation (1993); • Introduction of a senate (1993); • Fire service quotas (1995); • Obligatory insurance for old-age pensions (1997); • Reduction in number of parliamentary seats from 120 to 99 (1999); • Work camps for those committing acts of violence (1999)
Palau				R 09.11.								Referendum on accession to USA (accepted)
Christmas Islands					R 07.05.							Referendum on independence (rejected)

C. Asia

Country	1990	1991	1992	1993	1994	1995	1996	1997	1998	1999	2000	Subject of referendum by date
Abkhasia										R 03.10. (2 Ref.)		• New constitution; • Electoral term for judges
Armenia						R 05.07.						New constitution
Azerbaijan		R 17.03. R 29.12.		P 29.08.		R 05.11.						• Referendums on independence (3/17/1991 and 12/29/1991); • Presidential plebiscite (1993); • New constitution (1995)
Iraq						P 15.10.						Presidential plebiscite
Yemen		R 15.05.										Unification of North and South Yemen: New constitution
Kazakhstan						P 28.04. R 30.08.						• Extension of presidential term of office (4/29); • New constitution (8/30)
Kirghistan					P 30.01. P 22.10.		P 10.02.		P 17.10.			• Extension of presidential term of office (1/30/1994); • New constitution (10/22/1994); • Revision of constitution (1996); • Revision of constitution (1998)
Maldives				P 01.10.					P 16.10.			Presidential plebiscite (1993 und 1998)
Syria										P 10.02.	P 10.07.	Plebiscite on presidential term of office (1999 and 2000)
Tajikistan					P 06.11.					P 26.09.		• New constitution (1994); • Extension of presidential term of office (1999)
Taiwan					P 27.11.							Plebiscite on ending construction of nuclear power stations
Tatarstan			P 21.03.									Plebiscite on sovereignty (not recognized); Country remains Russian
Turkmenistan					P 15.01.							Extension to presidential term of office
Uzbekistan		R 29.12.				P 26.03.						• Referendum on independence (1991); • Extension of presidential term of office (1995)

D. Africa

Country	1990	1991	1992	1993	1994	1995	1996	1997	1998	1999	2000	Subject of referendum by date
Ivory Coast											R 23.07.	New constitution and reform of voting rights
Eritrea				R 25.04.								Referendum on independence
Gabon						R 23.07.						New constitution
Gambia							R 08.08.					New constitution
Ghana			R 28.04.									New constitution
Guinea	R 23.12.											New constitution
Comoros			R 07.06.				R 20.10.					New constitution (2 x)
Congo-Brazzaville			R 18.03.									New constitution
Madagascar			R 26.08.			P 17.09.			R 15.03.			• New constitution (1992); • Nomination of head of government by the president (1995); • Amendments to constitution (1998)
Malawi				P 14.06.								Multi-party system
Mali			R 11.01.									New constitution
Morocco			R 04.09.			R 15.09.	R 13.09.					• Partial revision of constitution (1992); • Budget timetable (1995); • Partial revision of constitution (1996);
Mauretania	P 12.07.											New constitution
Niger							P 12.05.			P 18.07.		New constitution (1996 and 1999)
Seychelles				R 18.06.								New constitution
Sudan									P 20.05.			New constitution
South Africa			R 17.03.									Abandonment of apartheid
Togo			R 27.09.									New constitution
Chad							P 31.03.					New constitution
Uganda											R 29.06.	Multi-party system (rejected)
Central African Republic					R 28.12.							New constitution
Zimbabwe											R 13.02.	Changes to constitution favoring extended presidential powers (rejected)

Section D: Listing of Referendums across Europe[1]

Albania

Date	Subject	Modus	Turnout	Result
11/6/1994	Constitution	Parliamentary plebiscite, consultative	75.00%	Not accepted (41.70%)
6/29/1997	Form of government	ad hoc, consultative		Not accepted (Monarchy: 33.26%) Republic: 66.74%)
11/22/1998	Constitution	Parliamentary plebiscite, binding	50.57%	Accepted (93.50%)

Andorra

Date	Subject	Modus	Turnout	Result
3/14/1993	Constitution	Obligatory constitutional referendum	75.74%	Accepted (74.20%)

Armenia

Date	Subject	Modus	Turnout	Result
9/21/1991	Independence	Parliamentary plebiscite	95.00%	Accepted (99.20%)
7/5/1995	Constitution	Unknown	55.59%	Accepted (70.31%)

Austria

Date	Subject	Modus	Turnout	Result
6/12/1994	Joining the EU	Obligatory referendum	82.35%	Accepted (66.58%)

Belarus

Date	Subject	Modus	Turnout	Result
5/14/1995	President's authority to dissolve parliament	Presidential plebiscite, consultative	64.88%	Accepted (81.26%)
5/14/1995	Russian as second national language	Presidential plebiscite, binding	64.88%	Accepted (86.62%)
5/14/1995	Closer ties to Russia	Presidential plebiscite, binding	64.88%	Accepted (86.84%)
5/14/1995	New state symbols	Presidential plebiscite, binding	64.88%	Accepted (78.44%)
11/24/1996	Exclusive financing of the State agencies by the budget	Parliamentary plebiscite, binding	84.14%	Not accepted (32.83%)
11/24/1996	Direct elections of local government	Parliamentary plebiscite, binding	84.14%	Not accepted (28.69%)

---

1. **Legend: Turnout** = Percent Turnout of Electorate / **Result** = Percent 'Yes Vote'. Also, please note that the dates used in this section are shown in the European style — Day/Month/Year
   Sources of the figures:
   http://www.c2d.unige.ch/int and http://www.ife.ee.ethz.ch/osh/dd/index.html
   (Site from Beat Müller, Switzerland)
   Source of the information about the 'Modus':
   http://www.ife.ee.ethz.ch/osh/dd/index.html (Site from Beat Müller, Switzerland)

Date	Subject	Modus	Turnout	Result
11/24/1996	Constitutional reforms — parliament's proposals	Parliamentary plebiscite, binding	84.14%	Not accepted (10.02%)
11/24/1996	Abolition of the death penalty	Presidential plebiscite, binding	84.14%	Not accepted (18.23%)
11/24/1996	Unrestricted sale and purchase of land	Presidential plebiscite, binding	84.14%	Not accepted (15.62%)
11/24/1996	Constitutional reforms — president's proposals	Presidential plebiscite, binding	84.14%	Accepted (88.24%)
11/24/1996	Day of republic changed to Independence Day, 3rd of July	Presidential plebiscite, binding	84.14%	Accepted (89.39%)

Bosnia/Herzegovina

Date	Subject	Modus	Turnout	Result
3/1/1992	Constitution	Parliamentary plebiscite	62.45%	Accepted (99.69%)

Croatia

Date	Subject	Modus	Turnout	Result
5/19/1991	Independence	Parliamentary plebiscite	86.15%	Accepted (93.24%)
5/19/1991	Remaining within Yugoslavia	Parliamentary plebiscite	86.15%	Not accepted (5.50%)

Denmark

Date	Subject	Modus	Turnout	Result
6/2/1992	EU-Treaty of Maastricht	Obligatory referendum	82.90%	Not accepted (47.93%)
5/18/1993	Union-Treaty with the European Community	Parliamentary plebiscite	85.50%	Accepted (56.77%)
5/28/1998	EU-Treaty of Amsterdam	Obligatory referendum	76.24%	Accepted (55.10%)
9/28/2000	Accession to the single European currency	Obligatory referendum	87.80%	Not accepted (46.87%)

Estonia

Date	Subject	Modus	Turnout	Result
3/3/1991	Independence	Parliamentary plebiscite	82.66%	Accepted (78.41%)
6/28/1992	Voting rights for those who aren't national citizens	Parliamentary plebiscite, binding	66.73%	Not accepted (43.52%)
6/28/1992	Constitution	Parliamentary plebiscite, binding	66.76%	Accepted (91.86%)
9/20/2003	EU accession	Parliamentary plebiscite, binding	64%	Accepted (66.8%)

Finland

Date	Subject	Modus	Turnout	Result
10/16/1994	Joining the European Union	Consultative referendum	70.40%	Accepted (56.88%)
11/20/1994 Åland-Islands	Joining the EU	Consultative referendum	49.1%	Accepted (73.64%)

France

Date	Subject	Modus	Turnout	Result
9/20/1992	EU Treaty of Maastricht	Presidential plebiscite, binding	69.69%	Accepted (51.05%)
11/8/1998 New Caledonia	Treaty of Noumea	Parliamentary plebiscite, binding	74.24%	Accepted (71.87%)
9/24/2000	Presidential Term from 7 to 5 years	Presidential plebiscite, binding	30.19%	Accepted (73.21%)
7/6/2003 Corsica	Modification of the Status of the Island	Parliamentary plebiscite, binding	60.52%	Not accepted (50.98%)

Georgia

Date	Subject	Modus	Turnout	Result
3/31/1991	Independence	Parliamentary plebiscite	90.57%	Accepted (99.08%)
10/3/1999 (Abchasien)	Constitution	Presidential plebiscite, unofficial	87.6%	Accepted (97.7%)
10/3/1999 (Abchasien)	Five-year terms instead of life terms for judges	Presidential plebiscite, unofficial	87.6%	Accepted (97.7%)

Hungary

Date	Subject	Modus	Turnout	Result
7/29/1990	Direct elections of the President	Popular Initiative	13.91%	Not valid (85.90%)
11/16/1997	NATO membership	Parliamentary plebiscite, binding	49.37%	Accepted (85.33%)
4/12/2003	EU membership	Parliamentary plebiscite, binding	45.65%	Accepted(83.72%)

Ireland

Date	Subject	Modus	Turnout	Result
6/18/1992	Maastricht Treaty	Obligatory referendum	57.31%	Accepted (69.05%)
11/25/1992	The right to information on abortion and contraception abroad	Obligatory referendum	68.13%	Accepted (59.88%)
11/25/1992	The right to an abortion and contraception abroad	Obligatory referendum	68.16%	Not accepted (34.65%)
11/25/1992	Freedom to travel	Obligatory referendum	68.18%	Accepted (62.39%)
11/24/1995	Introducing divorce laws	Obligatory referendum	62.15%	Accepted (50.27%)
11/28/1995	Release on bail rendered more difficult for suspected dangerous criminals	Obligatory referendum	29.23%	Accepted(74.83%)
10/30/1997	Confidentiality of discussions at meetings of government	Obligatory referendum	47.17%	Accepted (52.65%)
5/22/1998	Irish authorities on any part of the island of Ireland	Obligatory referendum	56.26%	Accepted (94.39%)
5/22/1998	EU Treaty of Amsterdam	Obligatory referendum	56.26%	Accepted (61.74%)
5/22/1998 (Northern Ireland — Great Britain)	Autonomy Agreement (Northern-Ireland)	Parliamentary plebiscite, consultative	81%	Accepted (71.12%)
6/11/1999	Recognition of the local authorities	Obligatory referendum	51.08%	Accepted (77.83%)

Date	Subject	Modus	Turnout	Result
6/7/2001	Ratification of the Nice Treaty	Obligatory referendum	34.79%	Not accepted (46.13%)
6/7/2001	Prohibition of the Death Penalty	Obligatory referendum	34.79%	Accepted (62.08%)
6/7/2001	Adhesion to the International Criminal Court	Obligatory referendum	34.78%	Accepted (64.22%)
3/6/2002	Protection of Human life in Pregnancy	Obligatory referendum	42.89%	Not accepted (49.58%)
10/19/2002	Ratification of the Nice Treaty	Obligatory referendum	49.47%	Accepted (62.89%)

Italy

Date	Subject	Modus	Turnout	Result
6/4/1990	Prohibition of pesticides in agriculture	Facultative referendum	43.30%	Not valid (93.40%)
6/4/1990	Revoking the permission to trespass private property while hunting	Facultative referendum	43.30%	Not valid (90.87%)
6/4/1990	Revoking the hunting laws	Facultative referendum	43.30%	Not valid (92.10%)
6/10/1991	Revoking the four preferential votes in parliamentary elections	Facultative referendum	62.45%	Accepted (95.57%)
4/19/1993	Ending the treasury's right to appoint the board of directors of the national savings bank	Facultative referendum	77%	Accepted (89.83%)
4/19/1993	Dismantling the ministry for State investments	Facultative referendum	76.90%	Accepted (90.12%)
4/19/1993	Legalizing the consumption of drugs	Facultative referendum	77.00%	Accepted (55.32%)
4/19/1993	Ending financial support from the government for political parties	Facultative referendum	77.00%	Accepted (90.31%)
4/19/1993	Ending proportionate representation in the Senate	Facultative referendum	77.00%	Accepted (82.73%)
4/19/1993	Dismantling the ministry of agriculture	Facultative referendum	77.00%	Accepted (70.12%)
4/19/1993	Dismantling the ministry for tourism and entertainment	Facultative referendum	77.00%	Accepted (82.17%)
4/19/1993	Ending the municipalities' responsibility for environmental protection	Facultative referendum	76.90%	Accepted (82.47%)
6/11/1995	Limiting the number of TV stations on advertising agency may operate with three	Facultative referendum	57.00%	Not accepted (43.60%)
6/11/1995	Complete reorganization of the administrative assemblies	Facultative referendum	57.00%	Not accepted (49.97%)
6/11/1995	Ending the restriction of State concessions to public TV stations	Facultative referendum	57.00%	Accepted (54.90%)

Date	Subject	Modus	Turnout	Result
6/11/1995	Restricting house arrest for Mafiosi to their proper residence	Facultative referendum	57.00%	Accepted (63.67%)
6/11/1995	Revoking the Prime Minister's powers in matters pertaining to the representation of labour unions	Facultative referendum	57.00%	Accepted (64.73%)
6/11/1995	Partial reorganization of the administrative assemblies	Facultative referendum	57.00%	Accepted (62.08%)
6/11/1995	Ending the direct deduction of contributions to labour unions from salaries and pensions	Facultative referendum	57.00%	Accepted (56.25%)
6/11/1995	Abolition of municipal powers regarding liquor licences	Facultative referendum	57.00%	Not accepted (35.61%)
6/11/1995	Abolition of advertising interrupting TV programs	Facultative referendum	57.00%	Not accepted (44.34%)
6/11/1995	Revoking the law limiting the possession of TV stations to three	Facultative referendum	57.00%	Not accepted (43.00%)
6/11/1995	Abolition of municipal powers regarding shop hours	Facultative referendum	57.00%	Not accepted (37.48%)
6/11/1995	Abolition of elections in two rounds for municipalities of over 15000 inhabitants	Facultative referendum	57.00%	Not accepted (49.32%)
6/15/1997	Ending the right to trespass private property when hunting	Facultative referendum	30.20%	Not valid (80.90%)
6/15/1997	Ending restricted access to Civil Service	Facultative referendum	30.20%	Not valid (71.69%)
6/15/1997	Ending the Treasury's 'Golden Share' in privatized business	Facultative referendum	30.20%	Not valid (74.06%)
6/15/1997	Dismantling the Government Association of Journalists	Facultative referendum	30.20%	Not valid (65.54%)
6/15/1997	Ending the right to automatic promotion for civil servants	Facultative referendum	30.20%	Not valid (83.55%)
6/15/1997	Ending the right to additional, extra-judicial professions for members of the Judiciary	Facultative referendum	30.20%	Not valid (85.58%)
6/15/1997	Dismantling the Ministry of Agriculture	Facultative referendum	30.20%	Not valid (66.85%)
4/18/1999	Abrogation of ¼ of the Parliament seats in the respect of the proportional representatives	Facultative referendum	49.58%	Not valid (91.52%)
5/21/2000	Abrogation of the actual electoral system for the composition of the 'Consiglio Superiore Della Magistratura'	Facultative referendum	31.90%	Not valid (70.57%)

Date	Subject	Modus	Turnout	Result
5/21/2000	Abolition of the proportional method of 25% in the attribution of the seat at the Parliament	Facultative referendum	32.40%	Not valid (82.01%)
5/21/2000	Abolition of the reimbursement of the referendum and electoral campaign cost	Facultative referendum	32.20%	Not valid (71.06%)
5/21/2000	Abolition of the Civil servant to have an second gainful employment	Facultative referendum	32.00%	Not valid (75.21%)
5/21/2000	Abrogation of the norm on the reintegration of the work place	Facultative referendum	32.50%	Not valid (33.36%)
5/21/2000	Abrogation of the career link possibility between Prosecutor and Judge	Facultative referendum	32.00%	Not valid (69.00%)
5/21/2000	Abolition of the wage deduction for trade union and worker association	Facultative referendum	32.20%	Not valid (61.82%)
10/7/2001	Amendment of the Title V, second Part, Constitutions (Deepening of Italian Federalism)	Consultative Referendum	34.00%	Accepted (64.20%)
6/16/2003	Art. 18 on Labour Law	Facultative referendum	25.70%	Not valid
6/16/2003	Right of electricity companies to pass cables or antennae on private property	Facultative referendum	25.70%	Not valid

Latvia

Date	Subject	Modus	Turnout	Result
3/3/1991	Independence	Parliamentary Plebiscite, consultative	87.56%	Accepted (74.90%)
10/3/1998	Ending facilitated naturalization	Facultative popular referendum	67.41%	Not accepted (45.91%)
11/13/1999	Changes to pensions law	Facultative popular referendum	25.08%	Not accepted (94.95%)
9/20/2003	EU membership	Parliamentary Plebiscite, binding	72.53%	Accepted (67.02%)

Liechtenstein

Date	Subject	Modus	Turnout	Result
10/21/1990	Fiscal legislation	Facultative referendum	70.46%	Not accepted (31.65%)
9/22/1991	Noise regulation	Facultative referendum	69.17%	Not accepted (20.34%)
9/22/1991	School on Saturdays	Popular Law Initiative	69.10%	Not accepted (34.71%)
3/15/1992	Referendum on international treaty	Popular constitutional Initiative	64.71%	Accepted (71.42%)
6/28/1992	Eligibility at the age of 18	Parliamentary plebiscite	36.49%	Not accepted (43.70%)
11/8/1992	Anti-discrimination laws	Popular constitutional Initiative	53.50%	Not accepted (24.56%)
11/8/1992	Abolishing the 8% clause for Landtag elections	Popular constitutional Initiative	53.50%	Not accepted (32.34%)

Date	Subject	Modus	Turnout	Result
12/13/1992	Joining the EEA	Parliamentary plebiscite	87.00%	Accepted (55.81%)
3/7/1993	Construction of the edifices housing Landtag and government	Facultative referendum	59.53%	Not accepted (20.39%)
4/9/1995	Joining the EEA	Parliamentary plebiscite	82.05%	Accepted (55.88%)
1/31/1999	Diminution of the 'prime' for health-insurance	Popular Law Initiative	82.10%	Not accepted (33.96%)
2/27/2000	Law on housing construction	Popular constitutional Initiative	56.90%	Not accepted (33.87%)
2/27/2000	Law on citizenship	Parliamentary plebiscite	48.60%	Accepted (50.10%)
9/24/2000	Agreement with Switzerland on the tax for heavy truck link to the pre-station	Facultative referendum	56.70%	Accepted (70.98%)
3/10/2002	Sustainable Transport Policy	Popular constitutional Initiative	64.59%	Not accepted (45.48%)
3/10/2002	Financial contribution to Music festival 'Little Big One'	Facultative referendum	64.59%	Not accepted (34.20%)
3/15/2003	Extension of power of Hans-Adam II	Popular constitutional Initiative	87.70%	Accepted (64.30%)
3/15/2003	Constitutional Peace	Popular constitutional Initiative	87.70%	Not accepted (83,5%)

Lithuania

Date	Subject	Modus	Turnout	Result
2/9/1991	Independence	Parliamentary plebiscite	84.74%	Accepted (93.24%)
5/23/1992	Presidential regime	Popular constitutional Initiative	59.18%	Not valid (73.04%)
6/14/1992	Withdrawal of soviet troops by the end of 1992	Parliamentary plebiscite	76.05%	Accepted (92.27%)
10/25/1992	Constitution	Obligatory referendum	75.26%	Accepted (78.23%)
8/27/1994	Concision and Transparency in Protective legislation	Popular Law Initiative	36.89%	Not accepted (89.33%)
8/27/1994	Restoring the value of devalued assets belonging to the State	Popular Law Initiative	36.89%	Not accepted (88.83%)
8/27/1994	Indexing the value of long-term capital investments	Popular Law Initiative	36.89%	Not accepted (88.88%)
8/27/1994	Reimbursement for devalued accounts	Popular Law Initiative	36.89%	Not accepted (89.09%)
8/27/1994	Undoing the consequences of illegal privatizations and future privatizations of State property	Popular Law Initiative	36.89%	Not accepted (88.74%)
8/27/1994	Law on illegal privatizations, devalued accounts, shares and the failure to respect protective legislation" (1st part)	Popular Law Initiative	36.89%	Not accepted (89.00%)
8/27/1994	Law on illegal privatizations (2nd part)	Popular Law Initiative	36.89%	Not accepted (88.96%)
8/27/1994	Implementing the law on illegal privatizations, devalued accounts, shares and the failure to respect protective legislation"'	Popular Law Initiative	36.89%	Not accepted (89.02%)

Date	Subject	Modus	Turnout	Result
10/20/1996	Reducing the number of seats in parliament from 141 to 111	Obligatory referendum	52.09%	Accepted (78.66%)
10/20/1996	Compensations for lost assets prior to 1990	Popular Law Initiative	52.09%	Not accepted (79.55%)
10/20/1996	At least half the State budget going to citizens' social needs such as health, education, social security	Obligatory referendum	52.09%	Accepted (76.94%)
10/20/1996	Elections of parliament on the second Sunday in April every four years	Obligatory referendum	52.09%	Not accepted (77.28%)
11/10/1996	Purchase of agricultural land by certain legal bodies	Obligatory referendum	39.73%	Not valid (52.01%)
5/11/2003	EU membership	Parliamentary plebiscite, binding	63.3%	Accepted (89.93%)

Macedonia

Date	Subject	Modus	Turnout	Result
9/8/1991	Independence	Parliamentary plebiscite, binding	71.85%	Accepted (95.09%)

Moldavia

Date	Subject	Modus	Turnout	Result
3/6/1994	Independence	Presidential plebiscite	75.10%	Accepted (95.40%)
5/23/1999	More power for the President	Presidential plebiscite, consultative	58.33%	Accepted (64.20%)

Norway

Date	Subject	Modus	Turnout	Result
11/28/1994	Joining the European Union	Parliamentary plebiscite, consultative	89.00%	Not accepted (47.80%)

Poland

Date	Subject	Modus	Turnout	Result
2/18/1996	Privatization Program	Presidential plebiscite	32.04%	Not accepted (96.15%)
2/18/1996	Privatization by means of coupons	Parliamentary plebiscite	32.44%	Not accepted (91.31%)
2/18/1996	Extending the scope of mass privatization (National Investment Funds)	Presidential plebiscite	32.44%	Not accepted (23.15%)
2/18/1996	Financing pensions with the profit generated by privatization	Parliamentary plebiscite	32.44%	Not accepted (95.07%)
2/18/1996	Investing the profit generated by privatization in the public pension fund	Parliamentary plebiscite	32.44%	Not accepted (95.99%)
5/25/1997	Constitution	Parliamentary plebiscite, binding	42.86%	Accepted (53.45%)
6/8/2003	EU membership	Parliamentary plebiscite, binding	58.84%	Accepted (77.51%)

Portugal

Date	Subject	Modus	Turnout	Result
6/8/1998	Legalizing abortion	Parliamentary plebiscite	31.94%	Not accepted (49.08%)
11/8/1998	Regionalization	Presidential plebiscite	48.29%	Not accepted (36.49%)

Romania

Date	Subject	Modus	Turnout	Result
12/8/1991	Constitution	Parliamentary plebiscite	67.25%	Accepted (79.11%)
10/19/2003	Constitution/EU	Obligatory Referendum	55.7%	Accepted (89.7%)

Russian Federation

Date	Subject	Modus	Turnout	Result
4/25/1993	Early presidential elections	Parliamentary plebiscite, binding	64.51%	Not accepted (51.21%)
4/25/1993	Early congressional elections	Parliamentary plebiscite, binding	64.51%	Not accepted (69.06%)
4/25/1993	Confidence in President Yeltsin. Yeltsin' economic- and reform policies	Parliamentary plebiscite, binding	64.51%	Accepted (54.35%)
4/25/1993	Confidence in President Yeltsin	Parliamentary plebiscite, binding	64.51%	Accepted (59.95%)
12/12/1993	Constitution	Presidential plebiscite	54.80%	Accepted (58.43%)

San Marino

Date	Subject	Modus	Turnout	Result
9/22/1996	Electoral procedure for citizens living abroad	Parliamentary plebiscite, binding	64.74%	Accepted (60.94%)
9/22/1996	Ending the reimbursement of travel expenses for citizens living abroad	Popular Law Initiative	64.74%	Accepted (64.98%)
9/22/1996	Reducing the maximum number of votes from 6 to 3	Popular Law Initiative	64.74%	Accepted (62.79%)
9/22/1996	Revoking Article 5 of the Hunting Regulations	Popular Law Initiative	64.78%	Accepted (60.54%)
10/26/1997	Prohibition of real estate firms as shareholding societies	Popular Law Initiative	46.43%	Accepted (88.08%)
9/12/1999	Law on citizenship	Parliamentary plebiscite	56.16%	Not accepted (56.88%)

Slovakia

Date	Subject	Modus	Turnout	Result
10/22/1994	Retrospective disclosure of the financial transactions regarding privatizations	Popular Law Initiative	19.98%	Not accepted (93.64%)
5/24/1997	Creating military bases	Parliamentary plebiscite	9.53%	Not valid
5/24/1997	NATO membership	Parliamentary plebiscite	9.53%	Not valid
5/24/1997	Direct presidential elections	Popular Law Initiative	9.53%	Not valid
5/24/1997	Stationing nuclear weaponry	Parliamentary plebiscite	9.53%	Not valid
9/26/1998	No privatizations of strategically important enterprises	Popular Law Initiative	44.06%	Not accepted (84.30%)
11/11/2000	Early elections	Popular Law Initiative	20.03%	Not valid (95.07%)
5/17/2003	EU membership	Parliamentary plebiscite, binding	52.29%	Accepted (92.41%)

Slovenia

Date	Subject	Modus	Turnout	Result
12/23/1990	Independence	Parliamentary plebiscite	93.31%	Accepted (95.71%)
12/8/1996	Electoral system for parliament	Obligatory referendum and Popular Law Initiative	37.4%	All proposals rejected
6/17/2001	Artificial insemination for unmarried women	Parliamentary plebiscite	35.57%	Not accepted (26.69%)
1/19/2003	Entire restitution of the too much paid telephone fees	Popular Initiative	31.15%	Accepted (77.59%)
1/19/2003	No subdivision of the Railroads	Facultative Referendum	31.14%	Not Accepted (51.86%)
3/23/2003	NATO membership	Parliamentary plebiscite	60.43%	Accepted (66.08%)
3/23/2003	EU membership	Parliamentary plebiscite	60.44%	Accepted (89.64%)

Sweden

Date	Subject	Modus	Turnout	Result
10/13/1994	Joining the European Union	Parliamentary plebiscite, consultative	83.32%	Accepted (52.74%)
9/14/2003	Joining the Euro	Parliamentary plebiscite, consultative	82.65%	Not accepted (55.92%)

Ukraine

Date	Subject	Modus	Turnout	Result
3/17/1991	Sovereign State	Parliamentary plebiscite	83.50%	Accepted (83.50%)
12/1/1991	Independence	Parliamentary plebiscite	84.18%	Accepted (92.26%)
4/16/2000	Formation of second Chamber of the Parliament (bicameral system) representing the Ukrainian regions	Popular Law Initiative	81.07%	Accepted (82.94%)
4/16/2000	Restriction of the parliamentary immunity for people's Deputies of Ukraine	Popular Law Initiative	81.06%	Accepted (90.23%)
4/16/2000	President may dissolve the Parliament when no parliamentary majority are constituted or when the Parliament fails to approve the State budget	Popular Law Initiative	81.07%	Accepted (85.91%)
4/16/2000	Reduction of members of parliament from 450 to 300	Popular Law Initiative	81.07%	Accepted (91.14%)

Yugoslavia

Date	Subject	Modus	Turnout	Result
7/2/1990	A new constitution before the next elections	Presidential plebiscite	76.00%	Accepted (96.80%)
3/1/1992 (Montenegro)	Yugoslav Union Treaty	Parliamentary plebiscite	66.03%	Accepted (96.00%)
10/11/1992	Early parliamentary elections	Parliamentary plebiscite	46.10%	Not valid (95.00%)
4/23/1998 (Serbien)	International Observers for Kosovo	Parliamentary plebiscite	73.05%	Not accepted (3.41%)

Compiled by Hans-Urs Wili (−2001) and Bruno Kaufmann (2002–03).

Section E: Initiatives & Referendums from Switzerland 1848–2003

Year	Date	Subject of referendum	Citizens Yes%	Citizens No%	Cantons Yes	Cantons No	Turnout %	Accepted	Rejected
1848	6-Jun	Total revision of constitution	72.8	27.2				X	
1866	14-Jan	Fixing weights and measures	50.4	49.6					X
		Equal domiciliary rights for Jews and naturalized citizens	53.2	46.8				X	
		Settlers' right to vote on community matters	43.1	56.9					X
		Tax and civil rights in relation to settlers	39.9	60.1					X
		Settlers' right to vote on cantonal matters	48.1	51.9					X
		Freedom of belief and religious practice	49.2	50.8					X
		Exclusion of certain punishable offences	34.2	65.8					X
		Protection of intellectual property rights	43.7	56.3					X
		Ban on lotteries and games of chance	44.0	56.0					X
1872	12-May	Total revision of the Constitution	49.5	50.5					X
1874	19-Apr	Total revision of the Constitution	63.2	36.8				X	
1875	23-May	Federal law regarding determination and recording of civil status and of marriage	51.0	49.0				X	
1876	23-Apr	Federal law on voting rights for Swiss citizens	49.4	50.6					X
		Federal law on issue and cashing of bank notes	38.3	61.7					X
1877	9-Jul	Federal law on tax on exemption from military duty	45.8	54.2					X
	21-Oct	Federal law on factory work	51.5	48.5				X	
		Federal law on tax on exemption from military duty	48.4	51.6				X	
		Federal law on the political rights of settlers and the temporarily resident and the loss of political rights of Swiss citizens	38.2	61.8				X	
1879	19-Jan	Federal law on granting of subsidies for Alpine railways	70.7	29.3					X
	18-May	Federal decision on changing Art. 65 of constitution (death penalty)	52.5	47.5	13 4/2	6 2/2			X
1880	31-Oct	Federal decree regarding the proposal made in the citizens' demand of 3 August 1880 for revision of the constitution	31.8	68.2	4 1/2	15 5/2		X	
1882	30-Jul	Federal decree on protection of inventions	47.5	52.5	7 1/2	12 5/2			X
		Federal law on measures to combat dangerous epidemics	21.1	78.9					X
	26-Nov	Federal decree on enactment of Art.27 of the federal constitution	35.1	64.9					X
1884	11-May	Federal law on organization of federal justice and police departments	41.1	58.9			59%		X
		Federal decree on "Patenttaxen" of commercial travelers	47.9	52.1			60%		X
		Federal law on supplement to federal criminal code of 4 Feb 1853	44.0	56.0			60%		X

Year	Date	Subject of referendum	Citizens Yes %	Citizens No %	Cantons Yes	Cantons No	Turnout %	Accepted	Rejected
1885		Federal decree concerning granting of the sum of 10,000 Franks towards the running costs of the Swiss embassy in Washington	38.5	61.5			60%		X
	25-Oct	Federal decree concerning the partial revision of the national constitution	59.4	40.6	13 4/2	6 2/2		X	
1887	15-May	Federal law on spirits	65.9	34.1				X	
	10-Jul	Federal decree on supplementing Art.64 of constitution of 29 May 1874	77.9	22.1	18 5/2	1 1/2	42%	X	
1889	17-Nov	Federal law on prosecution of debt and bankruptcy	52.9	47.1			70%	X	
1890	26-Oct	Federal decree concerning supplementing 29.05.1874 constitution by adding a clause relating to the right to legislate on accident and health insurance	75.4	24.6	18 5/2	1 1/2	59%	X	
1891	15-Mar	Federal law on federal officials and employees who have become unable to work	20.6	79.4			68%		X
	5-Jul	Federal decree on revision of federal constitution	60.3	39.7	16 4/2	3 2/2	49%	X	
	18-Oct	Federal decree on revision of Art.39 of constitution	59.3	40.7	12 4/2	7 2/2	61%	X	
		Federal law on Swiss customs duty	58.1	41.9			61%	X	
1893	20-Aug	National citizens' initiative: 'Ban on slaughter of animals without prior anaesthetizing'	60.1	39.9	10 3/2	9 3/2	49%	X	
1894	4-Mar	Federal decree of 20.12.1893 on addition to the constitution of a clause relating to the right to legislate on trade/business	46.1	53.9	7 1/2	12 5/2	46%		X
	3-Jun	Citizens' initiative on guaranteeing the right to work	19.8	80.2			57%		X
	4-Nov	Citizens' initiative on handing over a portion of customs income to the cantons	29.3	70.7	7 3/2	12 3/2	71%		X
1895	3-Feb	Federal law on foreign representation for Switzerland	41.2	58.8			46%		X
	29-Sep	Federal decree on addition to constitution of a clause on introduction of a monopoly on matches	43.2	56.8	6 3/2	13 3/2	48%		X
	3-Nov	Federal decree on revision of the constitutional articles relating to the military	42.0	58.0	4 1/2	12 5/2	67%		X
1896	4-Oct	Federal law on guarantees in buying and selling of cattle	45.5	54.5			57%		X
		Federal law on railway company accounts	55.8	44.2			57%	X	
		Federal law on disciplinary code for the Swiss army	19.9	80.1			57%		X
1897	28-Feb	Federal law on setting up the Swiss National Bank	43.3	56.7			64%		X
	11-Jul	Federal decree on revision of Art.24 of the constitution	63.5	36.5	14 4/2	5 2/2	38%	X	
		Federal decree concerning federal legislation on trade of foodstuffs and semi-luxury goods and of commodities which may endanger life or health	65.1	34.9	16 5/2	3 1/2	38%	X	

Year	Date	Subject of referendum	Citizens Yes %	Citizens No %	Cantons Yes	Cantons No	Turnout %	Accepted	Rejected
1898	20-Feb	Federal law on acquisition and operation of railways fuer Rechnung des Bundes and the administrative organization of the Swiss national railways	67.9	32.1			78%	X	
	13-Nov	Federal decree concerning revision of Art.64 of the constitution	72.2	27.8	15 3/2	4 3/2	52%	X	
		Federal decree concerning acceptance of Art.64bis into the constitution	72.4	27.6	15 3/2	4 3/2	52%	X	
1900	4-Nov	Citizens' initiative 'for proportional voting for the National Council'	40.9	59.1	9 3/2	10 3/2	58%		X
		Citizens' initiative 'for popular election of the National Council and increasing the number of its members'	35.0	65.0	7 2/2	12 4/2	58%		X
	20-May	Federal law on health and accident insurance, including military insurance	30.2	69.8			66%		X
1902	23-Nov	Federal decree concerning federal support for public primary schools	76.3	23.7	19 5/2		46%	X	
1903	15-Mar	Federal law on Swiss customs duty	59.6	40.4			73%	X	
	25-Oct	Federal law on supplementing federal criminal law of 4 Feb 1853	30.8	69.2			53%		X
		Citizens' initiative 'for electing the National Council based on the Swiss population'	24.4	75.6	3 2/2	16 4/2	53%		X
		Federal decree concerning alteration to Art.32bis of the federal constitution	40.7	59.3		15 6/2	53%		X
1905	19-Mar	Federal decree on revision of Art.64 of federal constitution (extension of patent rights)	70.4	29.6	19 5/2		40%	X	
1906	10-Jun	Federal law on trading of foodstuffs and commodities	62.6	37.4			51%	X	
1907	3-Nov	Military organization of Swiss Confederation	55.2	44.8			74%	X	
1908	5-Jul	Federal decree on extension to the constitution in respect of the right to legislate on trade	71.5	28.5	19 5/2		48%	X	
		Citizens' initiative 'for a ban on absinthe'	63.5	36.5	17 6/2		49%	X	
	25-Oct	Federal decree on adopting supplementary Art.24bis into the constitution relating to federal legislation on exploiting water power and the transmission and use of electrical energy	84.4	15.6	19 5/2		48%	Initiative withdrawn; counter-proposal accepted	
1910	23-Oct	Citizens' initiative 'for the proportional election of the National Council'	47.5	52.5	10 4/2	9 2/2	62%	Initiative failed to gain majority of popular vote	
1912	4-Feb	Federal law on health and accident insurance	54.4	45.6			64%	X	

Year	Date	Subject of referendum	Citizens Yes %	Citizens No %	Cantons Yes	Cantons No	Turnout %	Accepted	Rejected
1913	4-May	Federal decree concerning revision of Arts.69 and 31 (para.2) of constitution (combating human and animal diseases)	60.3	39.7	14 5/2	4 1/2	36%	X	
1914	25-Oct	Federal decree concerning revision of Art.103 of federal constitution and insertion of an Art.114bis	62.3	37.7	16 4/2	3 2/2	44%	X	
1915	6-Jun	Federal decree concerning enactment of constitutional article relating to raising of a non-recurring war tax	94.3	5.7	19 6/2		56%	X	
1917	13-May	Federal decree concerning insertion of articles 41bis and 42 into the constitution (stamp duty)	53.2	46.8	14 1/2	5 5/2	42%	X	
1918	2-Jun	Citizens' initiative 'for the introduction of direct federal taxes'	45.9	54.1	6 3/2	13 3/2	65%		X
	13-Oct	Citizens' initiative 'for proportional election of the National Council' [cf.1910]	66.8	33.2	17 5/2	2 1/2	49%	X	
1919	4-May	Federal decree concerning adoption of an Art.24ter into the constitution (shipping)	83.6	16.4	19 6/2		53%	X	
		Federal decree concerning enactment of a constitutional provision for the raising of a new extraordinary war tax	65.1	34.9	17 6/2		53%	X	
	10-Aug	Federal decree concerning adoption of transitional rules on Art.73 of the constitution	71.6	28.4	19 5/2	1/2	32%	X	
1920	21-Mar	Federal law on regulating working conditions	49.8	50.2			60%		X
		Citizens' initiative 'for a ban on setting up gaming tables'	55.3	44.7	13 2/2	6 4/2	60%	X	
		Counter-proposal to above initiative	26.2	73.8	1/2	19 5/2			X
	16-May	Federal decree on accession of Switzerland to League of Nations	56.3	43.7	10 3/2	9 3/2	77%	X	
	31-Oct	Federal law concerning working hours on railways and other forms of public transport	57.1	42.9			68%	X	
1921	30-Jan	Citizens' initiative 'for submitting all state treaties, either open-ended or lasting for more than 15 years, to referendum'	71.4	28.6	17 6/2	2	63%	X	
		Citizens' initiative 'for the abolition of military courts'	33.6	66.4	3	16 6/2	63%		X
	22-May	Federal decree concerning adoption of new articles 37bis and 37ter into the constitution (automobile and cycle traffic, aeronautics)	59.8	40.2	14 3/2	5 3/2	38%	X	
		Federal decree concerning adoption of new article 37ter into the constitution (aeronautics)	62.2	37.8	18 5/2	1 1/2	38%	X	
1922	11-Jun	Citizens' initiative 'concerning the acquisition of Swiss civil rights, Part I'	15.9	84.1	0	19 6/2	45%		X
		Citizens' initiative 'concerning the deportation of foreigners, Part II'	38.1	61.9	0	19 6/2	45%		X

Year	Date	Subject of referendum	Citizens Yes %	Citizens No %	Cantons Yes	Cantons No	Turnout %	Accepted	Rejected
		Citizens' initiative 'concerning the electability of federal officials to the National Council'	38.4	61.6	4 2/2	15 4/2	45%		X
	24-Sep	Federal law concerning amendment to federal criminal code of 4 Feb 1853 in respect of breaches of constitutional order and internal security and the introduction of conditional sentencing	44.6	55.4			70%		X
1923	3-Dec	Citizens' initiative 'for a non-recurring property tax'	13.0	87.0	0	19 6/2	86%		X
	18-Feb	Citizens' initiative: 'protective custody'	11.0	89.0	0	19 6/2	53%		X
		Federal decree concerning ratification of treaty signed in Paris on 7 August 1921 between Switzerland and France concerning trade relations and border traffic	18.5	81.5			53%		X
	15-Apr	Citizens' initiative 'to preserve national rights in customs affairs'	26.8	73.2	1/2	19 5/2	65%		X
	3-Jun	Federal decree concerning revision of Art.31 and 32bis (alcoholic beverages) of constitution	42.2	57.8	9 2/2	10 4/2	64%		X
1924	17-Feb	Federal law concerning amendment to Art.41 of factory law of 18 June 1914/27 June 1919	42.4	57.6			76%		X
1925	24-May	Citizens' initiative 'for invalidity, old-age and widows/widowers insurance'	42.0	58.0	5 2/2	14 4/2	68%		X
	25-Oct	Federal decree concerning temporary and permanent residence of foreigners	62.2	37.8	16 5/2	3 1/2	67%	X	
	6-Dec	Federal decree on old-age, widows & widowers and invalid insurance	65.4	34.6	15 3/2	4 3/2	63%	X	
1926	5-Dec	Federal decree on adopting a new Art.23bis into the constitution relating to national provision of grain	49.6	50.4	9	10 6/2	72%		X
1927	15-May	Federal decree concerning amendment to Art.30	62.6	37.4	18 6/2	1	55%	X	
		Federal law on automobile and cycle traffic	40.1	59.9			57%		X
1928	20-May	Federal decree on revision of Art.44 (measures to limit foreign ownership)	70.7	29.3	17 5/2	2 1/2	45%	X	
	2-Dec	Citizens' initiative on casinos	51.9	48.1	13 3/2	6 3/2	55%	X	
1929	3-Mar	Citizens' initiative 'grain supply' — original initiative	2.7	97.3	0	19 6/2	67%		X
		Grain supply' initiative — counter-proposal	67.0	33.0	18 6/2	1	67%	X	
		Federal law on amendment to Art.14 of constitution of 10 Oct.1902 on Swiss customs duty	66.4	33.6			67%	X	
	12-May	Citizens' initiative 'on road traffic legislation'	37.2	62.8	2 2/2	17 4/2	65%		X
		Citizens' initiative 'for a ban on spirits'	32.7	67.3	1/2	19 5/2	66%		X
1930	6-Apr	Federal decree on revision to Art.31 and 32bis of constitution and adoption of a new Art.32quater (alcoholic beverages)	60.6	39.4	16 2/2	3 4/2	75%	X	

Year	Date	Subject of referendum	Citizens Yes %	Citizens No %	Cantons Yes	Cantons No	Turnout %	Accepted	Rejected
1931	8-Feb	Federal decree on citizens' demand for revision of Art.12 of constitution (ban on religious orders) — counter-proposal	70.2	29.8	14 6/2	5	41%	Initiative withdrawn, counter-proposal accepted	
	15-Mar	Federal decree on revision to Art.72 of constitution (election of National Council)	53.9	46.1	11 5/2	8 1/2	53%	X	
		Federal decree on revision to Art.76,96,para.1 and 105, para.2 (period of office of National Council, Federal Council and Federal Chancellor)	53.7	46.3	14 4/2	5 2/2	53%	X	
	6-Dec	Federal law on old people's and widows/widowers' insurance	39.7	60.3			78%		X
1933		Federal law on taxation of tobacco	49.9	50.1			78%		X
	28-May	Federal law on temporary lowering of salaries of federal officials	44.9	55.1			80%		X
1934	11-Mar	Federal law on the defense of public order	46.2	53.8			78%		X
1935	24-Feb	Federal law on amendment to federal law of 12 Apr.1907 on organization of the army (reorganizing training)	54.2	45.8			79%	X	
	5-May	Federal law on regulating the transport of goods and animals in motor vehicles on public roads	32.3	67.7			63%		X
	2-Jun	Citizens' initiative 'on combating the economic crisis'	42.8	57.2	4 2/2	15 4/2	84%		X
	8-Sep	Citizens' initiative 'for a total revision of the constitution'	27.7	72.3	1	18 6/2	60%		X
1937	28-Nov	Citizens' initiative 'for a ban on freemasonry'	31.3	68.7	1	18 6/2	65%		X
1938	20-Feb	Federal decree on revision of Arts.107 & 116 of federal constitution (recognition of Rhaeto-Romanic as a national language)	91.6	8.4	19 6/2	0	54%	X	
		Citizens' initiative "concerning urgent federal decrees and the preservation of democratic civil rights".	15.2	84.8	0	19 6/2	54%		X
		Citizens' initiative "private arms industry"	13.6	86.4	0	19 6/2	54%		X
		Counter proposal	0.0	0.0	19 6/2	0	54%	X	
	3-Jul	Swiss penal code	53.5	46.5			57%	X	
	27-Nov	Federal decree on transitional ordering of the budget	72.3	27.7	18 6/2	1	60%	X	
1939	22-Jan	Citizens' initiative "to preserve the constitutional citizens' rights" (extension of constitutional jurisdiction).	28.9	71.1	0	19 6/2	46%		X
		Federal decree on the citizens' submission to restrict the application of the urgency clause — Counter-proposal.	69.1	30.9	18 6/2	1	46%	Initiative withdrawn counter-proposal accepted	
	4-Jun	Federal decree on addition to the federal constitution for setting up and partial guarantee for credits to increase national defense and counter unemployment	69.1	30.9	16 6/2	3	54%	X	

Year	Date	Subject of referendum	Citizens Yes %	Citizens No %	Cantons Yes	Cantons No	Turnout %	Accepted	Rejected
1940	3-Dec	Federal law on changing conditions of service and insurance of government employees	37.6	62.4			63%		X
	1-Dec	Federal law on amendment to Arts.103 and 104 of federal law of 12/05/1907 on military organization (introduction of compulsory military pre-training)	44.3	55.7			63%		X
1941	9-Mar	Citizens' initiative "to rearrange provisions for alcoholic beverages"	40.2	59.8			61%		X
1942	25-Jan	Citizens' initiative "direct popular election of Federal Council and increase in number of members"	32.4	67.6	0	19 6/2	61%		X
	3-May	Citizens' initiative "for the reorganization of the National Council"	34.9	65.1	1/2	19 5/2	51%		X
1944	29-Oct	Federal law on unfair competition	52.9	47.1			50%	X	
1945	21-Jan	Federal law on Swiss Railways	56.7	43.3			52%	X	
	25-Nov	Federal decree on citizens' submission "for the family" — Counter proposal	76.3	23.7	19 5/2	1/2	55%	Initiative withdrawn, counter-proposal accepted	
1946	10-Feb	Federal decree on citizens' submission concerning regulation of goods traffic	33.7	66.3	1	18 6/2	65%	Initiative withdrawn counter-proposal accepted	
1947	8-Dec	Citizens' initiative "right to work"	19.2	80.8	0	19 6/2	50%		X
	18-May	Citizens' initiative "economic reform and employment rights"	31.2	68.8	0	19 6/2	59%		X
	6-Jul	Federal decree on revision of economic articles of federal constitution	53.0	47.0	11 2/2	8 4/2	79%	X	
1948	14-Mar	Federal decree on insurance for elderly and widow(er)s	80.0	20.0			79%	X	
1949	22-May	Federal decree on regulation of Swiss sugar industry	36.2	63.8			56%		X
		Federal decree on revision of Art. 39 of federal constitution concerning the Swiss National Bank	38.5	61.5	1 1/2	18 5/2	61%		X
		Federal law on supplementing federal law of 13 June 1928 on measures against T.B.	24.8	75.2	0	19 6/2	61%		X
	11-Sep	Citizens' initiative "for a return to direct democracy"	50.7	49.3	11 3/2	8 3/2	42%	X	
	11-Dec	Federal law concerning change to federal law of 30/06/1927 on employment conditions of government employees	55.3	44.7			72%	X	
1950	29-Jan	Federal decree on extending the period of applicability and changes to the decree on measures to promote house building	46.3	53.7			52%		X
	4-Jun	Federal decree on constitutional revision of federal budget	35.5	64.5			55%		X

Year	Date	Subject of referendum	Citizens Yes %	Citizens No %	Cantons Yes	Cantons No	Turnout %	Accepted	Rejected
	1-Oct	Citizens' initiative "to protect land and work by preventing speculation"	27.0	73.0	0	19 6/2	43%		X
	3-Dec	Federal decree on change to Art.72 of federal constitution (election of National Council)	67.3	32.7	17 6/2	2	55%	X	
1951	25-Feb	Federal decree on budget for 1951-1954	69.5	30.5	17 6/2	2	55%	X	
		Federal decree on motorized transport of persons and goods on public roads	44.3	55.7			52%		X
	15-Apr	Citizens' initiative "to secure purchasing power and full employment" (free economy initiative)	12.4	87.6	0	19 6/2	53%		X
		Counter-proposal	0.0	0.0	19 6/2	0	53%	Counter-proposal accepted	
	8-Jul	Citizens' initiative "for public companies to pay a contribution to the cost of national defense"	32.6	67.4			37%		X
1952	2-Mar	Federal decree on extending period of applicability of federal decree on requirement to gain approval to open or extend inns	46.1	53.9			40%		X
	30-Mar	Federal law on promoting agriculture and supporting farmers (agriculture law)	54.0	46.0			64%	X	
	20-Apr	Citizens' initiative "turnover tax on goods"	19.0	81.0	0	19 6/2	49%		X
	18-May	Citizens' initiative "financing arms manufacture and protection of social achievements"	43.7	56.3	3 2/2	16 4/2	53%		X
	6-Jul	Federal decree on covering expenditure on arms	42.0	58.0	3	16 6/2	44%		X
	5-Oct	Federal law on changing rules on taxing tobacco in the federal law on insurance for the elderly and widow(er)s	68.0	32.0			52%	X	
		Federal decree on creation of air-raid shelters in existing houses	15.5	84.5			52%		X
	23-Nov	Federal decree on temporary continuation of limited price control	62.8	37.2	14 2/2	5 4/2	56%	X	
1953	19-Apr	Federal decree on national provision of bread-making grain	75.6	24.4	19 5/2	1/2	56%	X	
		Federal law on revision of federal law on postal services	36.5	63.5			52%		X
	6-Dec	Federal decree on constitutional reorganization of federal budget	42.0	58.0	3	16 6/2	60%		X
		Federal decree on supplementing federal constitution by an Art.24quater concerning protection of water bodies against pollution	81.3	18.7	19 6/2	0	59%	X	
1954	20-Jun	Federal decree on certification for shoemakers, hairdressers, saddlers and coachbuilders	33.1	66.9			40%		X
		Federal decree on special aid for expatriate Swiss injured in the war	44.0	56.0			40%		X

Year	Date	Subject of referendum	Citizens Yes %	Citizens No %	Cantons Yes	Cantons No	Turnout %	Accepted	Rejected
	24-Oct	Federal decree on budget for 1955-1958	70.0	30.0	18 6/2	1	46%	X	
	5-Dec	Citizens' initiative "protection of Rheinau flood plain and bequest"	31.2	68.8	1	18 6/2	51%		X
1955	13-Mar	Citizens' initiative "to protect tenants and consumers" (continuation of price controls)	50.2	48.8	6 2/2	13 4/2	55%		X
		Counter proposal	0.0	0.0	7 3/2	12 3/2	55%		X
1956	4-Mar	Federal decree on temporary continuation of limited price control (extension to supplement to constitution of 26/09/1952)	77.5	22.5	19 6/2	0	49%	X	
	13-May	Citizens' initiative "granting of water rights concessions"	36.9	63.1	2 1/2	17 5/2	52%		X
		Federal decree on measures to strengthen the economy of the Graubünden canton by means of a grant to the local timber processing factory	42.5	57.5			52%		X
	30-Sep	Federal decree on revision of national cereals supply laws	38.7	61.3	4 3/2	15 3/2	43%		X
		Federal decree on popular initiative on expenses for National Assembly	45.5	54.5	8 2/2	11 4/2	43%		Initiative withdrawn, counter-proposal rejected
1957	3-Mar	Federal decree on supplement to federal constitution of Art. 22bis on civil defense	48.1	51.9	12 4/2	7 2/2	53%		X
		Federal decree on supplement to federal constitution of Art.36bis on radio and TV	42.8	57.2	9 3/2	10 3/2	52%		X
	24-Nov	Federal decree on supplement to federal constitution of Art. quinquies on nuclear power and radiological protection	77.3	22.7	19 6/2	0	45%	X	
		Federal decree on temporary extension to period of validity of transitional ruling on national supply of bread-making cereals	62.7	37.3	19 5/2	1/2	45%	X	
1958	26-Jan	Citizens' initiative "against the abuse of economic power"	25.9	74.1	0	19 6/2	51%		X
	11-May	Federal decree on constitutional reorganization of federal finances	54.6	45.4	15 5/2	4 1/2	53%	X	
	6-Jul	Federal decree on supplement to federal constitution of Art.27ter on cinemas	61.3	38.7	18 5/2	1 1/2	42%	X	
		Federal decree on citizens' appeal for improvement to road network (counter-proposal)	85.0	15.0	18 6/2	1	42%	Initiative withdrawn counter-proposal accepted	
	26-Oct	Citizens' initiative "for the introduction of a 44-hour working week"	35.0	65.0	1/2	19 5/2	61%		X
	7-Dec	Federal decree on change to federal constitution (gambling in spas and casinos)	59.9	40.1	18 5/2	1 1/2	46%	X	

Year	Date	Subject of referendum	Citizens Yes %	Citizens No %	Cantons Yes	Cantons No	Turnout %	Accepted	Rejected
1959	1-Feb	Federal decree on approval of the agreement reached between the Swiss Confederation and Italy on harnessing the energy of the river Spoel	75.2	24.8			46%	X	
		Federal decree on introduction of women's suffrage at national level	33.1	66.9	3	16 6/2	66%		X
	24-May	Federal decree on supplement to federal constitution of Art.22bis on civil defense	62.3	37.7	19 6/2	0	42%	X	
1960	29-May	Federal decree on continuation of temporary price controls	77.5	22.5	19 6/2	0	38%	X	
	4-Dec	Federal decree on alteration to federal decree on additional economic and financial measures in milk production	56.3	43.7			49%	X	
1961	5-Mar	Federal decree on supplement to federal constitutional by an Art.26bis on pipelines for liquid and gaseous fuels	71.4	28.6	19 6/2	0	62%	X	
		Federal decree on increasing fuel duty to finance motorways	46.6	53.4	0		63%		X
	22-Oct	Citizens' initiative "to introduce the legislative initiative at the federal level"	29.4	70.6	0	19 6/2	40%		X
	3-Dec	Federal decree on Swiss watch industry	66.7	33.3			45%	X	
1962	1-Apr	Citizens' initiative "for a ban on nuclear weapons"	34.8	65.2	4	15 6/2	55%		X
	27-May	Federal decree on a supplement to the federal constitution by an Art.24sexies on nature conservation	79.1	20.9	19 6/2	0	38%	X	
		Federal law on amendment to federal law on salaries and travel expenses for members of the National Council and of the Federal Commission	31.7	68.3			38%		X
	4-Nov	Federal decree on amendment to Art.72 of federal constitution (election of National Council)	63.7	36.3	13 6/2	6	36%	X	
1963	26-May	Citizens' initiative "right of the people to decide on arming the Swiss army with nuclear weapons"	37.8	62.2	4 1/2	15 5/2	48%		X
	8-Dec	Federal decree on continuing federal finance arrangements (extension of period of validity of Art.41ter BV and lowering of army tax)	77.6	22.4	19 6/2	0	41%	X	
		Federal decree on supplement to federal constitution by an Art.27quater on grants and other forms of support for further education	78.5	21.5	19 6/2	0	41%	X	
1964	2-Feb	Federal decree on issuing of a general tax amnesty for 1.1.1965	42.0	58.0	3 1/2	16 5/2	44%		X
	24-May	Federal law on professional education	68.6	31.4			37%	X	
	6-Dec	Federal decree on extension of temporary price control measures	79.5	20.5	19 6/2	0	39%	X	
1965	28-Feb	Federal decree on control of inflation through measures affecting the money and capital markets and banking	57.7	42.3	16 5/2	3 1/2	59%	X	

Year	Date	Subject of referendum	Citizens Yes %	Citizens No %	Cantons Yes	Cantons No	Turnout %	Accepted	Rejected
		Federal decree on control of inflation through measures affecting the building sector	55.5	44.5	16 2/2	3 4/2	59%	X	
	16-May	Federal law concerning amendment to a decree of the Federal Assembly on milk, milk products and edible fats	62.0	38.0			37%	X	
1966	16-Oct	Federal decree on a supplement to the federal constitution by an Art.45bis concerning expatriate Swiss	68.1	31.9	19 6/2	0	47%	X	
		Citizens' initiative "to combat alcoholism"	23.4	76.7	1	18 6/2	48%		X
1967	2-Jul	Citizens' initiative "against speculation on real estate"	32.7	67.3			37%		X
1968	18-Feb	Federal decree on issuing a general tax amnesty	61.9	38.1	19 6/2	0	41%	X	
	18-May	Federal law on tobacco tax	48.2	51.8			36%		X
1969	1-Jun	Federal law on federal Technical Universities	34.5	65.5			33%		X
	14-Sep	Federal decree on supplementing the federal constitution by an Art.22ter and 22quater (property laws)	55.9	44.1	17 5/2	2 1/2	32%	X	
1970	1-Feb	Federal decree on home sugar industry	54.2	45.8			43%	X	
	7-Jun	Citizens' initiative "against foreign infiltration"	46.0	54.0	6 2/2	13 4/2	74%		X
	27-Sep	Federal decree on supplement to federal constitution of an Art.27quinquies on support for gymnastics and sport	74.6	25.4	19 6/2	0	43%	X	
		Citizens' initiative "right to housing and strengthening of protection for the family"	48.9	51.1	7 2/2	12 4/2	43%		X
	15-Nov	Federal decree on amendment to federal budget	55.4	44.6	8 2/2	11 4/2	41%	X	
1971	7-Feb	Federal decree on introduction of women's suffrage at federal level	65.7	34.3	14 3/2	5 3/2	57%	X	
	6-Jun	Federal decree on supplement to federal constitution by an Art.24septies on protecting people and the natural environment from harmful or disagreeable impacts	92.7	7.3	19 6/2	0	37%	X	
		Federal decree on extension of federal budget	72.7	27.3	19 6/2	0	37%	X	
1972	5-Mar	Citizens' initiative "support for house building" — original initiative	28.9	67.1	0	19 6/2	35%		X
		Counter-proposal	62.7	37.3	18 6/2	1	35%	X	
		Federal decree on supplement to the federal constitution by an Art.34septies on declaration of general bindingness of leasing contracts and measures to protect tenants	85.4	14.6	19 6/2	0	35%	X	
	4-Jun	Federal decree on measures to stabilize the construction market	83.3	16.7	19 6/2	0	26%	X	
		Federal decree on protection of Swiss currency	87.7	12.3	19 6/2	0	26%	X	
	24-Sep	Citizens' initiative "for increased arms control and a ban on arms exports"	49.7	50.3	6 2/2	13 4/2	33%		X
	3-Dec	Citizens' initiative "to introduce national old-age pension" (original initiative)	15.6	78.6	0	19 6/2	52%		X
		Counter-proposal	76.9	23.1	19 6/2	0	52%	X	

Year	Date	Subject of referendum	Citizens Yes %	Citizens No %	Cantons Yes	Cantons No	Turnout %	Accepted	Rejected
1973	4-Mar	Federal decree on the agreement between the Swiss Confederation and the EEC and the member states of the EC on coal and steel	72.5	27.5	19 6/2	0	52%	X	
		Federal decree on amendment to federal constitution concerning education	52.8	47.2	9 3/2	10 3/2	27%		X
	20-May	Federal decree on supplement to federal constitution on support for scientific research	64.5	35.5	17 4/2	2 2/2	27%	X	
		Federal decree on repeal of constitutional articles 51 & 52 concerning Jesuits and monasteries	54.9	45.1	14 5/2	5 1/2	40%	X	
	2-Dec	Federal decree on measures to monitor prices	59.8	40.2	17 6/2	2	35%	X	
		Federal decree on measures in the banking sector (credit control)	65.1	34.9	16 5/2	3 1/2	34%	X	
		Federal decree on measures to stabilize the construction market	70.4	29.6	17 6/2	2	35%	X	
		Federal decree on limitation to tax depreciation on federal, cantonal and communal income tax	68.0	32.0	17 5/2	2 1/2	34%	X	
		Federal decree on replacement of Art.25 bis of the federal constitution by an article on animal protection	84.0	16.0	19 6/2	0	34%	X	
1974	20-Oct	Citizens' initiative against foreign infiltration and overpopulation	34.2	65.8	0	19 6/2	70%		X
	8-Dec	Federal decree on improvement to the federal economy	44.4	55.6	4	15 6/2	39%		X
		Federal decree on brake on federal expenditure	67.0	33.0	19 6/2	0	39%	X	
		Citizens' initiative "state health insurance" — original initiative	26.7	70.2	0	19 6/2	39%		X
		Counter-proposal	34.2	65.8	0	19 6/2	39%		X
1975	2-Mar	Federal decree on constitutional article on the economy	52.8	47.2	10 2/2	9 4/2	28%		X
	8-Jun	Federal decree on protection of the currency (amendment of 28.06.1974)	85.5	14.5	19 6/2	0	36%	X	
		Federal decree on financing of national highways (amendment of 4.10.1974)	53.5	46.5			36%	X	
		Federal law on change to general customs duty	48.2	51.8			36%	X	
		Federal decree on raising income from taxes from 1976	56.0	44.0	14 6/2	5	36%	X	
		Federal decree on brake on federal expense	75.9	24.1	19 6/2	0	36%	X	
	7-Dec	Federal decree on amendment to federal constitution (freedom of domicile and social assistance)	75.6	24.4	19 6/2	0	30%	X	
		Federal decree on constitutional amendment relating to water resources	77.5	22.5	18 6/2	1	30%	X	
1976	21-Mar	Federal law on import and export of agricultural produce	52.0	48.0			31%	X	
		Citizens' initiative 'worker participation in decision-making' — original proposal	32.4	66.3	0	19 6/2	39%		X
		As above — counter-proposal	30.7	69.1	0	19 6/2	39%		X

Year	Date	Subject of referendum	Citizens Yes %	Citizens No %	Cantons Yes	Cantons No	Turnout %	Accepted	Rejected
		Citizens' initiative 'for tax reform (fairer taxes and abolition of tax privileges)	42.2	57.8			39%		X
	13-Jun	Federal law on town and country planning	48.9	51.1			34%		X
		Federal law relating to an agreement between Switzerland and the International Development Agency on a loan of 200 million francs	43.6	56.4			34%		X
		Federal decree on a revision of unemployment insurance	68.3	31.7	18 6/2	1	34%	X	
	26-Sep	Federal decree on article of constitution concerning radio and TV	43.3	56.7	3 1/2	16 5/2	33%		X
		Citizens' initiative 'for federal third-party insurance for motor vehicles and bicycles'	24.3	75.7	0	19 6/2	33%		X
	5-Dec	Federal decree on monetary and credit policy	70.3	29.7	19 6/2	0	53%	X	
		Federal decree on price monitoring	82.0	18.0	19 6/2	0	45%	X	
		Citizens' initiative 'for the introduction of a 40-hour week'	22.0	78.0	0	19 6/2	45%		X
1977	13-Mar	Citizens' initiative 'Fourth initiative on excessive foreign influence'	29.5	70.5	0	19 6/2	45%		X
		Citizens' initiative 'for a reduction in naturalization of foreigners'	33.8	66.2	0	19 6/2	45%		X
		Citizens' initiative 'on revising the referendum on international treaties' — original proposal	21.9	72.2	0	19 6/2	44%		X
		As above — counter-proposal	59.9	40.1	18 5/2	1 1/2	44%	X	
	12-Jun	Federal decree on revision to VAT and direct federal taxation	40.5	59.5	1	18 6/2	50%		X
		Federal decree on tax harmonization	61.3	38.7	16 3/2	3 3/2	49%	X	
	25-Sep	Citizens' initiative 'for an effective protection of tenants' — original proposal	42.2	55.3	3 1/2	16 5/2	51%		X
		As above — counter-proposal	45.1	54.9	1 2/2	18 2/2	51%		X
		Citizens' initiative 'against air pollution from vehicles' (Albatross initiative)	39.0	61.0	1 1/2	18 5/2	51%		X
		Federal decree on raising the signature threshold for referendums (Arts. 89 and 89bis).	57.8	42.2	15 6/2	4	51%	X	
		Federal decree on raising the signature threshold for the constitutional initiative (Arts.120 and 121)	56.7	43.3	16 6/2	3	52%	X	
		Citizens' initiative 'for free abortion in first 12 weeks'	48.3	51.7	6 2/2	13 4/2	51%		X
	4-Dec	Citizens' initiative 'for a wealth tax'	44.4	55.6	2 1/2	17 5/2	38%		X
		Federal law on political rights	59.4	40.6			38%	X	
		Federal decree on introduction of civil service as alternative to military service	37.6	62.4	0	19 6/2	38%	X	
		Federal law on measures to balance the national budget	62.4	37.6			38%	X	

Year	Date	Subject of referendum	Citizens Yes %	Citizens No %	Cantons Yes	Cantons No	Turnout %	Accepted	Rejected
1978	26-Feb	Citizens' initiative 'for greater involvement of the National Assembly and of the Swiss people in decisions on planning and building of motorways'	38.7	61.3	0	19 6/2	48%		X
		Federal law on old-age pension act (9th revision)	65.6	34.4			48%	X	
		Citizens' initiative 'to lower retirement age'	20.6	79.4	0	19 6/2	48%		X
		Federal decree on federal constitutional article on economic policy	68.4	31.6	19 6/2	0	48%	X	
	28-May	Law on summer time	47.9	52.1			49%		X
		Law on customs duties, amendment of 7.10.1977	54.8	45.2			48%	X	
		Federal law on protection of pregnancy and abortion as a punishable offence	31.2	68.8			48%		X
		Federal law on funding for higher education and research	43.3	56.7			48%		X
	24-Sep	Citizens' initiative 'for 12 vehicle-free Sundays per year'	36.3	63.7	0	19 6/2	49%		X
		Federal decree on creation of the Canton of Jura (Arts.1 and 80 of Fed. Constitution)	82.3	17.7	19 6/2	0	42%	X	
	3-Dec	1977 milk supply decree	68.5	31.5			43%	X	
		Law on protection of animals	81.7	18.3			43%	X	
		Federal law on federal obligation to provide security police	44.0	56.0			43%		X
		Federal law on professional education	56.0	44.0			43%	X	
1979	18-Feb	Federal decree on lowering voting age to 18	49.2	50.8	8 2/2	12 4/2	49%		X
		Federal decree on citizens' initiative 'promotion of footpaths and trails' — Counter proposal	77.6	22.4	19 6/2	1	49%	Initiative withdrawn counter-proposal accepted	
		Citizens' initiative 'against advertising of tobacco and alcohol'	41.0	59.0	1/2	20 5/2	49%		X
		Citizens' initiative "to preserve citizens' rights and ensure safety in the building and running of nuclear power stations"	48.8	51.2	8 2/2	12 4/2	49%		X
	20-May	Federal decree on revision of VAT and direct federal taxes	34.6	65.4	0	20 6/2	37%		X
		Federal decree on atomic energy	68.9	31.1			37%	X	
1980	2-Mar	Citizens' initiative 'concerning the complete separation of church and state'	21.1	78.9	0	20 6/2	34%		X
		Federal decree on revision of arrangements for commodity supplies	86.1	13.9	20 6/2	0	34%	X	
	30-Nov	Federal traffic law, amendment of 21.3.1980 (compulsory seatbelts and helmets)	51.6	48.4			42%	X	
		Federal decree on withdrawing the cantonal share of revenues from banking "stamp duty"	67.3	32.7	17 6/2	3	41%	X	
		Federal decree on redistribution of receipts of the federal alcohol ministry from the duty on spirits	71.0	29.0	18 6/2	2	41%	X	

Year	Date	Subject of referendum	Citizens Yes %	Citizens No %	Cantons Yes	Cantons No	Turnout %	Accepted	Rejected
1981	5-Apr	Federal decree on revision of national regulations on bread-making cereals	63.5	36.5	17 6/2	3	41%	X	
	5-Apr	Citizens' initiative 'Mitenand initiative for a new policy towards foreigners'	16.2	83.8	0	20 6/2	39%		X
	14-Jun	Federal decree on Citizens' initiative 'Equal rights for men and women' — Counter-proposal	60.3	39.7	14 3/2	6 3/2	33%	Initiative withdrawn counter-proposal accepted	
		Federal decree on Citizens' initiative 'securing consumers' rights' — Counter-proposal	65.5	34.5	18 4/2	2 2/2	33%	Initiative withdrawn counter-proposal accepted	
	29-Nov	Federal decree on extension of budget and improvement in federal finances	69.0	31.0	20 6/2	0	30%	X	
1982	6-Jun	Law on foreigners	49.6	50.4			35%		X
		Swiss penal code, amendment of 9.10.1981	63.7	36.3			35%	X	
	28-Nov	Citizens' initiative 'against dishonest prices' — Original proposal	56.1	40.7	16 2/2	4 4/2	32%	X	
		As above — Counter-proposal	24.8	75.2	0	20 6/2	32%		X
1983	27-Feb	Federal decree on revision of fuel duty	52.7	47.3	14 3/2	6 3/2	32%	X	
		Federal decree on energy policy article in the federal constitution	50.9	49.1	11	9 6/2	32%		X
	4-Dec	Federal decree on changes to nationality rules in the constitution	60.8	39.2	18 5/2	2 1/2	35%	X	
1984		Federal decree on easing naturalization in certain cases	44.8	55.2	4 2/2	16 4/2	35%		X
	26-Feb	Federal decree on raising a heavy goods vehicle tax	58.7	41.3	13 5/2	7 1/2	52%	X	
		Federal decree on a motorway toll	53.0	47.0	13 6/2	7	52%	X	
		Citizens' initiative 'for an evidence-based real civil alternative to military service'	36.2	63.8	1 1/2	19 5/2	52%		X
	20-May	Citizens' initiative 'against the misuse of the secrecy and power of banks'	27.0	73.0	0	20 6/2	42%		X
		Citizens' initiative 'against a sell-out of the homeland' (I.e. land to foreigners)	48.9	51.1	7 3/2	13 3/2	42%		X
	23-Sep	Citizens' initiative 'for a future without any more nuclear power stations'	45.0	55.0	5 2/2	15 4/2	41%		X
		Citizens' initiative 'for a safe, frugal and environmentally fair energy policy'	45.8	54.2	5 2/2	15 4/2	41%		X
	2-Dec	Citizens' initiative 'for an effective protection of motherhood'	15.8	84.2	0	20 6/2	37%		X
		Federal decree on broadcasting	68.7	31.3	20 6/2	0	37%	X	

Year	Date	Subject of referendum	Citizens Yes %	Citizens No %	Cantons Yes	Cantons No	Turnout %	Accepted	Rejected
1985	10-Mar	Federal decree on the citizens' initiative 'compensation for victims of crimes of violence' — Counter-proposal	82.1	17.9	20 6/2	0	37%	Initiative withdrawn counter-proposal accepted	
		Federal decree on ending federal primary school subsidies	58.5	41.5	15 6/2	5	34%	X	
		Federal decree on ending federal public health subsidies	53.0	47.0	10 6/2	10	34%	X	
		Federal decree on education subsidies	47.6	52.4	7 3/2	13 3/2	34%		X
		Citizens' initiative 'for increasing the length of paid holidays'	34.8	65.2	2	18 6/2	34%		X
	9-Jun	Citizens' initiative 'right to life'	31.0	69.0	4 3/2	16 3/2	35%		X
		Federal decree on suspending cantonal share of revenues from banking stamp duty	66.5	33.5	19 6/2	1	35%	X	
		Federal decree on redistribution of income from tax on spirits	72.3	27.7	19 6/2	1	35%	X	
		Federal decree on withdrawal of subsidies on home cereal production	57.0	43.0	16 5/2	4 1/2	35%	X	
	22-Sep	Federal decree on citizens' initiative 'for a standardization of school year starting date' — Counter-proposal	58.8	41.2	14 4/2	6 2/2	41%	Initiative withdrawn counter-proposal accepted	
		Federal decree on insurance against innovation-related risk for small and medium-sized companies	43.1	56.9			40%		X
		Swiss civil law on marriage, amendment of 5.10.1984	54.7	45.3			41%	X	
	1-Dec	Citizens' initiative 'to abolish vivisection'	29.5	70.5	0	20 6/2	37%		X
1986	16-Mar	Federal decree on accession of Switzerland to the UN	24.3	75.7	0	20 6/2	50%		X
	28-Sep	Citizens' initiative 'cultural initiative' — Original initiative	16.7	75.2	0	20 6/2	34%		X
		Counter-proposal	45.0	55.0	0	20 6/2	34%		X
		Citizens' initiative 'for guaranteed vocational training and retraining'	18.4	81.6	0	20 6/2	34%		X
		Federal decree on home sugar production, amendment of 21.6.1985	38.2	61.8			34%		X
	7-Dec	Federal decree on the citizens' initiative 'for the protection of tenants' — Counter-proposal	64.4	35.6	17 3/2	3 3/2	34%	Initiative withdrawn counter-proposal accepted	
		Citizens' initiative 'for a fair taxation of heavy goods vehicles'	33.9	66.1	0	20 6/2	34%		X
1987	5-Apr	Asylum law, revision of 20.6.1986	67.3	32.7			42%	X	
		Federal law on rights of stay and domicile of foreigners, revision of 20.6.1986	65.7	34.3			42%	X	
		Citizens' initiative 'for right of citizens to have a say on all military expenditure'	40.6	59.4	2 1/2	18 5/2	42%		X

Year	Date	Subject of referendum	Citizens Yes %	Citizens No %	Cantons Yes	Cantons No	Turnout %	Accepted	Rejected
	6-Dec	Federal decree on the referendum procedure for citizens' initiatives where there is a counter-proposal ('double yes')	63.3	36.7	18 6/2	2	42%	X	
		Federal decree on "Rail 2000" project	57.0	43.0			47%	X	
		Citizens' initiative 'protection of moorland' (to ban the Rothenturm military base)	57.8	42.2	17 6/2	3	47%	X	
		Federal law on health insurance, revision of 20.3.1987	28.7	71.3			47%		X
1988	12-Jun	Federal decree on the constitutional basis for a coordinated traffic policy	45.5	54.5	3 2/2	17 4/2	41%		X
	4-Dec	Citizens' initiative 'to lower the age of retirement to 62 years for men and 60 for women'	35.1	64.9	2	18 6/2	42%		X
		Citizens' initiative 'town and country against real estate speculation'	30.8	69.2	0	20 6/2	52%		X
1989	4-Jun	Citizens' initiative to reduce the working week' (to 40 hours)	34.3	65.7	2	18 6/2	52%		X
		Citizens' initiative 'to restrict immigration'	32.7	67.3	0	20 6/2	52%		X
		Citizens' initiative 'for natural farming — against animal factories' (small farmers initiative)	48.9	51.1	7 2/2	13 4/2	35%		X
	26-Nov	Citizens' initiative 'for a Switzerland without an army and for a comprehensive peace policy'	35.6	64.4	2	18 6/2	69%		X
1990	1-Apr	Citizens' initiative 'for a (higher) speed limit of 130kph'	38.0	62.0	6	14 6/2	69%		X
		Citizens' initiative 'no more concrete — for a restriction on road building'	28.5	71.5	0	20 6/2	41%		X
		Citizens' initiative 'no motorway between Murten and Yverdon'	32.7	67.3	0	20 6/2	41%		X
		Citizens' initiative 'no motorway between Wettswil and Kronau'	31.4	68.6	0	20 6/2	41%		X
		Citizens' initiative 'no motorway between Biel and Solothurn'	34.0	66.0	0	20 6/2	41%		X
		Federal decree on wine growing	46.7	53.3			40%		X
		Revision of federal judicial law	47.4	52.6			40%		X
	23-Sep	Citizens' initiative 'for an end to the use of nuclear power'	47.1	52.9	6 2/2	14 4/2	40%		X
		Citizens' initiative '10-year moratorium on nuclear power station building'	54.5	45.5	17 5/2	3 1/2	40%	X	
		Federal decree on the constitutional article on energy policy	71.1	28.9	20 6/2	0	40%	X	
		Federal law on road traffic, revision of 6.10.1989	52.8	47.2			40%	X	
1991	3-Mar	Federal decree on lowering the voting age to 18	72.7	27.3	20 6/2	0	31%	X	
		Citizens' initiative 'for funding of public transport'	37.1	62.9	1 1/2	19 5/2	31%		X
	2-Jun	Federal decree on revision of federal finances (introduction of federal VAT to replace corporate tax)	45.6	54.4	2 1/2	18 5/2	33%		X
		Amendment to military penal code of 5.10.1990 (decriminalizing conscientious objection)	55.7	44.3			33%	X	
1992	16-Feb	Citizens' initiative 'for a financially affordable health insurance'	39.3	60.7	1	19 6/2	44%		X
		Citizens' initiative 'for a drastic, progressive restriction on animal experimentation'	43.6	56.4	3 1/2	17 5/2	44%		X

Year	Date	Subject of referendum	Citizens Yes %	Citizens No %	Cantons Yes	Cantons No	Turnout %	Accepted	Rejected
	17-May	Federal decree on Swiss accession to the Bretton Woods institutions (IMF and World Bank)	55.8	44.2			38%	X	
		Federal law governing Swiss involvement with the Bretton Woods institutions	56.4	43.6			38%	X	
		Federal law on protection of waters (reduction of water in reservoirs to protect the environment)	66.1	33.9			39%	X	
		Federal decree on the citizens' initiative 'against misuses of reproductive and genetic technology in humans' — Counter proposal	73.8	26.2	19 6/2	1	39%	Initiative withdrawn counter-proposal accepted	
		Federal decree on the introduction of civil service for conscientious objectors	82.5	17.5	20 6/2	0	39%	X	
		Revision of Swiss penal code and military penal code of 21.6.1991 (punishable offences against sexual integrity)	73.1	26.9			39%	X	
	27-Sep	Citizens' initiative 'to save our waters'	37.1	62.9	0	20 6/2	39%		X
		Federal decree on building of transalpine railway for car transport	63.6	36.4			45%	X	
		Federal law: revised procedures for consideration, publication and introduction of laws	58.0	42.0			45%	X	
		Federal law on stamp duty, amendment of 4.10.1991	61.5	38.5			45%	X	
		Federal law on farmers' inheritance rules	53.6	46.4			45%	X	
		Federal law on MP's salaries and funding of political parties	27.6	72.4			45%		X
		Federal law on improved funding of infrastructure costs for MPs and political parties	30.6	69.4			45%		X
	6-Dec	Federal decree on European Economic Area membership	49.7	50.3	6 2/2	14 4/2	78%		X
1993	7-Mar	Federal law on raising fuel duty	54.5	45.5			51%	X	
		Federal decree on repealing the ban on casino gambling	72.5	27.5	20 6/2	0	51%	X	
		Citizens' initiative 'to ban experiments on animals'	27.8	72.2	0	20 6/2	51%		X
	6-Jun	Citizens' initiative '40 military bases are enough — the army also needs to care for the environment'	44.7	55.3	6 2/2	14 4/2	55%		X
		Citizens' initiative 'for a Switzerland without new fighter aircraft' (halt purchase of F/A-18 and ban purchase of new fighters until 2000)	42.8	57.2	3 2/2	17 4/2	55%		X
	26-Sep	Federal decree against the misuse of weapons	86.3	13.7	20 6/2	0	39%	X	
		Federal decree on the transfer of the district of Laufen from the canton of Berne to the canton of Basel-Land	75.2	24.8	20 6/2	0	39%	X	
		Citizens' initiative 'for a national holiday on 1st August'	83.8	16.2	20 6/2	0	39%	X	
		Federal decree on temporary measures against rising costs in health insurance	80.5	19.5			39%	X	
		Federal decree on measures for unemployment insurance	70.4	29.6			39%	X	

Year	Date	Subject of referendum	Citizens Yes %	Citizens No %	Cantons Yes	Cantons No	Turnout %	Accepted	Rejected
	28-Nov	Federal decree on financial system	66.7	33.3	19 6/2	1	45%	X	
		Federal decree on increased contribution to federal revenues (VAT rate to 6.5%)	57.7	42.3	15 6/2	5	45%	X	
		Federal decree on measures to preserve social insurance	62.6	37.4	19 6/2	1	45%	X	
		Federal decree on certain consumption taxes (adopt federal VAT on all goods and services)	60.6	39.4	17 6/2	3	45%	X	
		Citizens' initiative 'to reduce the problems of alcohol' (ban on alcohol advertising)	25.3	74.7	0	20 6/2	45%		X
		Citizens' initiative 'to reduce the problems of smoking' (ban on tobacco advertising)	25.5	74.5	0	20 6/2	45%		X
1994	20-Feb	Federal decree on continuation of the motorway tax on fuel	68.5	31.5	18 6/2	2	40%	X	
		Federal decree on continuation of the heavy goods vehicle tax	72.2	27.8	20 6/2	0	40%	X	
		Federal decree on introduction of a heavy goods vehicle tax based on engine size or fuel consumption	67.1	32.9	18 6/2	2	40%	X	
		Citizens' initiative 'to protect the alpine area from transit traffic'	51.9	48.1	13 6/2	7	40%	X	
		Air traffic law, revision of 18.6.1993	61.1	38.9			40%	X	
	12-Jun	Federal decree on Art.27septies of the constitution relating to support for culture	51.0	49.0	10 2/2	10 4/2	46%		X
		Federal decree on revision of the naturalization rules in the constitution (making naturalization easier for young foreigners)	52.8	47.2	9 2/2	11 4/2	46%		X
		Federal law on use of Swiss troops in peace-keeping operations	42.8	57.2			46%		X
	25-Sep	Federal decree on ending subsidy for home cereal production	64.6	35.4	20 6/2	0	45%	X	
		Swiss penal code & military penal code, amendment of 18.6.1993	54.6	45.4			45%	X	
	4-Dec	Federal law on health insurance	51.8	48.2			43%	X	
		Citizens' initiative 'for a healthy health insurance'	23.4	76.6	0	20 6/2	43%		X
		Federal law on compulsory measures in the law relating to foreigners	72.9	27.1			43%	X	
1995	12-Mar	Federal decree on the citizens' initiative 'for an environmentally just and efficient agriculture'	49.1	50.9	8 2/2	12 4/2	37%		Initiative withdrawn counter-proposal rejected
		Amendment of 18.3.1994 to 1988 milk production decree	36.5	63.5			37%		X
		Agriculture law, amendment of 8.10.1993	33.6	66.4			37%		X
		Federal decree: brake on expenditure	83.4	16.6	20 6/2	0	37%	X	
	25-Jun	Federal law on old-age and widow/er's pension, amendment of 7.10.1994	60.7	39.3			40%	X	
		Citizens' initiative 'to extend old-age, widow/er's and disabled insurance'	27.6	72.4	0	20 6/2	40%		X

Year	Date	Subject of referendum	Citizens Yes %	Citizens No %	Cantons Yes	Cantons No	Turnout %	Accepted	Rejected
1996		Federal law on acquisition of real estate by persons living abroad, amendment of 7.10.1994	46.4	53.6			40%		X
	10-Mar	Federal decree on revision of the language article in the federal constitution (Art.116)	76.2	23.8	20 6/2	0	31	X	
		Federal decree on the transfer of the Bernese community of Vellerat to the canton of Jura	91.6	8.4	20 6/2	0	30%	X	
		Federal decree on the withdrawal of cantonal competence in respect of the personal equipment of military personnel	43.7	56.3	2 2/2	18 4/2	31%		X
		Federal decree on remission of the obligation to purchase distilling equipment and accept distilled products	80.8	19.2	20 6/2	0	30%	X	
		Federal decree on cessation of federal funding for station car parks	53.9	46.1	11 6/2	9	30%	X	
	9-Jun	Counter-proposal of National Assembly of 21.12.1995 to the citizens' initiative 'Farmers and consumers — for natural farming'	77.6	22.4	20 6/2	0	31%	Initiative withdrawn counter-proposal accepted	
		Law on government and administration of 6.10.1995	39.4	60.6			31%		X
	1-Dec	Federal decree on the citizens' initiative 'against illegal immigration'	46.3	53.7	10 2/2	10 4/2	46%		X
		Federal decree on labour law in industry, trade and commerce, amendment of 22.3.1996	33.0	67.0			46%		X
1997	8-Jun	Citizens' initiative 'public referendum on the EU accession negotiations'	25.9	74.1	0	20 6/2	35%		X
		Citizens' initiative ' for a ban on arms exports'	22.5	77.5	0	20 6/2	35%		X
		Federal decree on cessation of federal monopoly on the manufacture and sale of gunpowder	82.2	17.8	20 6/2	0	35%	X	
	28-Sep	Federal decree of 13.12.1996 on financing of unemployment insurance (proposed reduction in payments)	49.2	50.8			40%		X
		Federal decree on the citizens' initiative 'youth without drugs'	29.3	70.7	0	20 6/2	40%		X
1998	7-Jun	Federal decree on measures to balance the budget	70.7	29.3	20 6/2	0	40%	X	
		Citizens' initiative "protection of life and environment from genetic engineering"	33.3	66.7	0	20 6/2	41%		X
		Citizens' initiative "S.O.S.— Switzerland without secret police"	24.6	75.4	0	20 6/2	40%		X
	27-Sep	Federal law on engine size related heavy goods vehicle tax	57.2	42.8			51%	X	
		Citizens' initiative "for reasonably priced food and environmentally-friendly farms"	23.0	77.0	0	20 6/2	51%		X
		Citizens' initiative "for the 10th revision of old-age pension with no increase in age of retirement"	41.5	58.5	5	15 6/2	51%		X
	29-Nov	Federal decree on construction and financing of public transport infrastructure plans	63.5	36.5	19 3/2	1 3/2	38%	X	

Year	Date	Subject of referendum	Citizens Yes %	Citizens No %	Cantons Yes	Cantons No	Turnout %	Accepted	Rejected
		Federal decree on a temporary new law on cereals	79.4	20.6	20 6/2	0	38%	X	
		Citizens' initiative "for a sensible policy on drugs"	26.0	74.0	0	20 6/2	38%		X
		Federal law on employment in industry, trade and commerce	63.4	36.6			38%	X	
1999	7-Feb	Federal decree on changing the eligibility conditions for election to Nat. Council	74.7	25.3	18 6/2	2	38%	X	
		Federal decree on constitutional position on medical transplantation	87.8	12.2	20 6/2	0	37%	X	
		Citizens' initiative "house ownership for all"	41.3	58.7	3	17 6/2	38%		X
	18-Apr	Federal law on spatial planning (amendment of 20/03/1998)	55.9	44.1			37%	X	
		Federal decree on a new federal constitution	59.2	40.8	12 2/2	8 4/2	35%	X	
	13-Jun	Asylum law	70.6	29.4			45%	X	
		Federal decree on urgent measures in relation to asylum and foreigners	70.8	29.2			45%	X	
		Federal decree on prescription of heroin by doctors	54.4	45.6			45%	X	
		Federal law on insurance for invalids	30.3	69.7			45%		X
		Federal law on insurance for Motherhood	39.0	61.0			45%		X
		Federal decree on reform of judiciary	86.4	13.6	20 6/2	0	41%	X	
2000	12-Mar	Citizens' initiative "for speeding up direct democracy" (time taken to deal with citizens' initiatives in form of detailed proposal)	30.0	70.0	0	20 6/2	42%		X
		Citizens' initiative "for a fair representation for women in federal authorities (3rd March Initiative)"	18.0	82.0	0	20 6/2	42%		X
		Citizens' initiative "to protect humans from manipulation in reproductive technology"	28.2	71.8	0	20 6/2	42%		X
		Citizens' initiative "to reduce motorized traffic by half to preserve and improve the built environment"	21.3	78.7	0	20 6/2	42%		X
	21-May	Federal decree on approval of sectoral agreements between Switzerland and the EC and/or its member states, or Euratom	67.2	32.8			48%	X	
	24-Sep	Citizens initiative "for a solar penny (Solar Initiative)"	31.3	67.0	0	20 6/2	44%		X
		Counter-proposal (article in constitution on a levy to promote renewable energy)	45.3	51.8	4 1/2	16 5/2	44%		X
		Constitutional article on an environmental energy tax (counter-proposal to the withdrawn "Energy-Environment Initiative")	44.5	55.5	2 1/2	18 5/2	44%		Initiative withdrawn counter-proposal rejected
		Citizens' initiative "to regulate immigration"	36.2	63.8	0	20 6/2	45%		X
		Citizens' initiative "More rights for the people by means of the referendum with counter-proposal (constructive referendum)"	34.1	65.9	0	20 6/2	44%		X

Year	Date	Subject of referendum	Citizens Yes %	Citizens No %	Cantons Yes	Cantons No	Turnout %	Accepted	Rejected
	26-Nov	Citizens' initiative "to make the old-age pension system more flexible — no increase in pensionable age for women"	39.5	60.5	6	14 6/2	41%		X
		Citizens' initiative "for a flexible age of retirement from the age of 62 for women and men"	46.0	54.0	7	13 6/2	41%		X
		Citizens' initiative "reduce expenditure on armed forces and overall defense — for more peace and forward-looking workplaces (redistribution initiative)"	37.6	62.4	4	16 6/2	41%		X
		Citizens' initiative "for lower hospital costs"	17.9	82.1	0	20 6/2	41%		X
		Law on federal employees	66.8	33.2			41%	X	
2001	4-Mar	Citizens' initiative "Yes to Europe"	23.2	76.8	0	20 6/2	55%		X
		Citizens' initiative "lower prices for medicines"	30.9	69.1	0	20 6/2	55%		X
		Citizens' initiative "greater road safety — 30kph in built-up areas, with exceptions (Roads for All)"	20.3	79.7	0	20 6/2	55%		X
	10-Jun	Amendment of 6/10/2000 to federal law on army and military authorities (weapons)	51.0	49.0			42%	X	
		Amendment of 6/10/2000 to federal law on army and military authorities (training)	51.1	48.9			42%	X	
		Federal decree of 15/12/2000 on withdrawal of permission to create new bishoprics	64.2	35.8	20 6/2	0	42%	X	
	2-Dec	Federal decree on reducing debts	84.7	15.3	20 6/2	0	37%	X	
		Citizens' initiative "for a guaranteed old-age pension — tax energy instead of work"	22.9	77.1	0	20 6/2	37%		X
		Citizens' initiative "for a credible security policy and a Switzerland without an army"	21.9	78.1	0	20 6/2	37%		X
		Citizens' initiative "security through solidarity: for voluntary civil peace work" (as an alternative to military service)	23.2	76.8	0	20 6/2	37%		X
		Citizens' initiative "for a capital gains tax"	34.1	65.9	0	20 6/2	37%		X
2002	3-Mar	Citizens' initiative "in favor of Switzerland joining the UN"	54.6	45.4	11 2/2	9 4/2	58%	X	
		Citizens' initiative "for a shorter working week"	25.4	74.6	0	20 6/2	58%		X
	2-Jun	Amendment to Swiss criminal code (termination of pregnancy)	72.2	27.8			41%	X	
		Citizens' initiative "for mother and child"	18.2	81.8	0	20 6/2	41%		X
	22-Sep	Federal decree on the citizens' initiative "Surplus gold reserves into pension funds (Gold initiative)" and the counter-proposal "Gold for pension funds, cantons and foundations" — Original Initiative	46.4	51.1	6	14 6/2	45%		X
		Counter-proposal	48.2	51.8	6 1/2	14 5/2	45%		X
		Law on the electricity market	47.4	52.6			44%		X
	24-Nov	Citizens' initiative "against the misuse of asylum rights"	49.9	50.1	10 5/2	10 1/2	48%		X

Year	Date	Subject of referendum	Citizens Yes %	Citizens No %	Cantons Yes	Cantons No	Turnout %	Accepted	Rejected
2003	9-Feb	Amendment to federal law on compulsory unemployment insurance and compensation for insolvency	56.1	43.9	20 6/2	0	47%	X	
		Federal decree on amendment to citizens' rights	70.4	29.6			28%		
		Federal law on adjusting canton's contributions to hospital costs	77.4	22.6			28%		
	18-May	Amendment to federal law on the army and military administration	76.0	24.0			49%	X	
		Federal law on civil defense	80.6	19.4			49%	X	
		Citizens' initiative: "Yes to fair rents"	32.7	67.3	1	19 6/2	49%		X
		Citizens' initiative: "One traffic-free Sunday per quarter — a four-year trial (Sunday Initiative)"	37.6	62.4	0	20 6/2	49%		X
		Citizens' initiative: "Health has to be affordable (Health Initiative)"	27.1	72.9	0	20 6/2	49%		X
		Citizens' initiative: "Equal rights for the disabled"	37.7	62.3	3	17 6/2	49%		X
		Citizens' initiative: "Nuclear-free energy — for a change in energy policy and the gradual shutting down of nuclear power stations"	33.7	66.3	1/2	20 5/2	49%		X
		Citizens' initiative: "Moratorium Plus — for extending the ban on building new nuclear power stations and limiting the nuclear risk"	41.6	58.4	2/2	20 4/2	49%		X
		Citizens' initiative: "For an adequate provision of vocational training (Apprenticeship Initiative)"	31.6	68.4	0	20 6/2	49%		X

Source: Swiss Federal Chancellery. Translated by Paul Carline.

Index